TECHNOLOGY AND CULTURE,
THE FILM READER

Technology and Culture, the Film Reader brings together key theoretical texts from more than a century of writing on film and technology. It begins by exploring the intertwined technologies of cinematic representation, reproduction, distribution and reception, before locating the technological history of cinema as one component of an increasingly complex technological culture.

The selected articles encompass a range of disciplines, perspectives and methodologies, reflecting the multiplicity of contemporary approaches to technology. They are grouped into four thematic sections, each with an introduction by the editor.

- *Origins and evolution* – examines the lineage of cinema's machines, while challenging the received notion that cinema began with a discrete moment of invention.
- *Definitions and determinism* – redefines technology, moving beyond an isolated description of cinema's physical tools to consider the forces that play a part in shaping their form and function.
- *Projections and aesthetics* – analyzes the exchange between cinematic and other technologies, in terms of cinema's capacity to reflect on and negotiate technologies other than its own.
- *Contexts and consequences* – situates the technologies of cinema within a broader framework, charting their engagement with the spheres of discourse at work within society.

Contributors: André Bazin, Walter Benjamin, Jean-Louis Comolli, Douglas Gomery, Morton Heilig, Henry V. Hopwood, Lev Manovich, Vivian Sobchack, Claudia Springer, Lars von Trier, Dziga Vertov, Thomas Vinterberg, Patricia R. Zimmermann.

Andrew Utterson is Senior Lecturer in the Department of Media, Canterbury Christ Church University College, UK where he is director of the degree in Digital Culture, Arts and Media. He has published on film theory, digital theory and on the intersection of these fields.

In Focus: Routledge Film Readers

Series Editors: Steven Cohan (Syracuse University) and Ina Rae Hark (University of South Carolina)

The In Focus series of readers is a comprehensive resource for students on film and cinema studies courses. The series explores the innovations of film studies while highlighting the vital connection of debates to other academic fields and to studies of other media. The readers bring together key articles on a major topic in film studies, from marketing to Hollywood comedy, identifying the central issues, exploring how and why scholars have approached it in specific ways, and tracing continuities of thought among scholars. Each reader opens with an introductory essay setting the debates in their academic context, explaining the topic's historical and theoretical importance, and surveying and critiquing its development in film studies.

Exhibition, The Film Reader
Edited by Ina Rae Hark

Experimental Cinema, The Film Reader
Edited by Wheeler Winston Dixon
and Gwendolyn Audrey Foster

Hollywood Musicals, The Film Reader
Edited by Steven Cohan

Hollywood Comedians, The Film Reader
Edited by Frank Krutnik

Horror, The Film Reader
Edited by Mark Jancovich

Movie Acting, The Film Reader
Edited by Pamela Robertson Wojcik

Movie Music, The Film Reader
Edited by Kay Dickinson

Stars, The Film Reader
Edited by Marcia Landy and Lucy Fischer

Queer Cinema, The Film Reader
Edited by Harry Benshoff and Sean Griffin

Forthcoming Titles:

Color, The Film Reader
Edited by Angela Dalle Vacche
and Brian Price

Marketing, The Film Reader
Edited by Justin Wyatt

Reception, The Film Reader
Edited by Barbara Klinger

TECHNOLOGY AND CULTURE,
THE FILM READER

Edited by Andrew Utterson

Routledge
Taylor & Francis Group

LONDON AND NEW YORK

First published 2005 by Routledge
2 Park Square, Milton Park, Abingdon, Oxon OX14 4RN

Simultaneously published in the USA and Canada
by Taylor & Francis Inc.
270 Madison Ave, New York, NY 10016

Routledge is an imprint of the Taylor & Francis Group

Selection and editorial material © 2005 Andrew Utterson; individual
chapters © copyright holders

Designed and typeset in Novarese and Scala Sans
by Keystroke, Jacaranda Lodge, Wolverhampton
Printed and bound in Great Britain
by Biddles Ltd, King's Lynn

British Library Cataloguing in Publication Data
A catalogue record for this book is available from the British Library

Library of Congress Cataloging in Publication Data
Has been applied for

ISBN 0–415–31984–6 (hbk)
ISBN 0–415–31985–4 (pbk)

Contents

PART FOUR: CONTEXTS AND CONSEQUENCES 97

Notes on Contributors

Henry V. Hopwood (1866–1919) was a writer concerned with the evolution of photography into cinema. *Living Pictures: Their History, Photo-Production and Practical Working* (1899), written shortly after the date most regularly cited as that of cinema's birth, has become a standard reference text for scholars of early moving image technology.

Morton Heilig (1926–97) was an inventor, filmmaker and visionary. He is often described as the "father of virtual reality" in response to his ideas and prototypes, which prefigure contemporary experiments in telepresence.

Lev Manovich is associate professor in the Department of Visual Arts, University of California, San Diego. He is the author of *The Language of New Media* (2001).

André Bazin (1918–58) co-founded the influential film journal *Cahiers du cinéma*, where he worked with critics and filmmakers including François Truffaut, Eric Rohmer and Jean-Luc Godard. His major writings on film are translated from French into English in *What is Cinema? Vol. 1* (1967) and *What is Cinema? Vol. 2* (1971).

Jean-Louis Comolli is a filmmaker and critic who has directed both documentary and fiction films, acted as editor-in-chief for *Cahiers du cinéma* and teaches at institutions in Paris and Barcelona.

Douglas Gomery is resident scholar at the Library of American Broadcasting, University of Maryland. He has won US national book awards for *Shared Pleasures: A History of Movie Presentation in the United States* (1992) and *Who Owns the Media? Competition and Concentration in the Mass Media Industry* (2001).

Claudia Springer is professor in the Department of English, Rhode Island College. She is the author of *Electronic Eros: Bodies and Desire in the Postindustrial Age* (1996).

Lars von Trier is a film director whose work includes the Dogme 95 experiment, *The Idiots (Dogme 2: Idioterne)* (1998).

Thomas Vinterberg directed the first Dogme 95 film, *The Celebration (Dogme 1: Festen)* (1998).

Patricia R. Zimmermann is professor of cinema and photography in the Roy H. Park School of Communications, Ithaca College and coordinator of Culture and Communication in the Division of Interdisciplinary and International Studies. Her publications include *Reel Families: A Social History of Amateur Film* (1995) and *States of Emergency: Documentaries, Wars, Democracies* (2000).

Dziga Vertov (1896–1954) was one of the leading filmmakers and theorists in Russia at a time when the language and expressions of cinema were being reconfigured according to political ideology. His major writings on film are translated from Russian into English in *Kino-Eye: The Writings of Dziga Vertov* (1984).

Walter Benjamin (1892–1940) was a German critic and philosopher. He was forced into exile in 1933 and lived in France until he took his own life in 1940. Many of his key writings are translated into English in *Illuminations: Essays and Reflections* (1968).

Vivian Sobchack is professor of film and media studies at the University of California, Los Angeles. She is the author of several books on film including *The Address of the Eye: A Phenomenology of Film Experience* (1992) and *Screening Space: The American Science Fiction Film* (1987).

Acknowledgements

The author and publishers would like to thank the following copyright holders for permission to reprint material:

3. Manovich, L., "Cinema and Digital Media" in Schwarz, H. P. and Shaw, J. (eds), *Media Art Perspectives: The Digital Challenge – Museums and Art Sciences Respond* (1996). Reproduced by permission of ZKM/Kahrlsruhe.

4. Bazin, A., "The Myth of Total Cinema" (English translation by Gray, H.) in Gray, H. (ed.), *What is Cinema? Vol. 1* © 1967 by the Regents of the University of California. Reproduced by permission of University of California Press and Les editions du cerf.

5. Comolli, J.-L., "Machines of the Visible" in de Lauretis, T. and Heath, S. (eds), *The Cinematic Apparatus* (*Published papers from a conference held 22–24 February 1978 by the Center for Twentieth Century Studies, University of Wisconsin-Milwaukee*) (1980). Reproduced by permission of Palgrave Macmillan.

6. Gomery, D., "The Coming of Sound: Technological Change in the American Film Industry" in Balio, T. (ed.), *The American Film Industry* © 1985. Reproduced by permission of University of Wisconsin Press.

7. Springer, C., "The Pleasure of the Interface" in *Screen* (1991), 32.3 (Autumn). Reproduced by permission of Oxford University Press.

8. von Trier, L. and Vinterberg, T., "Dogme 95: The Vow of Chastity". Presented at the Odéon Théâtre de L'Europe, Paris (20 March 1995). Reproduced by permission of Zentropa Filmbyen.

9. Zimmermann, P. R., "Pirates of the New World Image Orders" in Zimmermann, P. R., *States of Emergency: Documentaries, Wars, Democracies* (2000). Reproduced by permission of University of Minnesota Press.

10. Vertov, D., "Kinoks: A Revolution" (English translation by O'Brien, K.) in Michelson, A. (ed.), *Kino-Eye: The Writings of Dziga Vertov* © 1984 by the Regents of the University of California. Reproduced by permission of University of California Press.

11. Benjamin, W., "The Work of Art in the Age of Mechanical Reproduction" (English translation by Zohn, H.) in Arendt, H. (ed.), *Illuminations* © 1955 by Suhrkamp Verlag, Frankfurt, translation © 1968 and renewed 1996 by Harcourt, Inc. Reproduced by permission of Harcourt Inc. Published in the UK by Pimlico Press. Reproduced by permission of The Random House Group.

12. Sobchack, V., "The Scene of the Screen: Envisioning Cinematic and Electronic 'Presence'" in Gumbrecht, H. U. and Pfeiffer, K. L. (eds), *Materialities of Communication* © 1994 by the Board of Trustees of the Leland Stanford Junior University. Reproduced by permission of Stanford University Press, www.sup.org.

Every effort has been made to obtain permission to reproduce copyright material. If any proper acknowledgement has not been made, we would invite copyright holders to inform us of the oversight.

Technology and Culture,

The Film Reader

General introduction

Throughout the period the history of cinema spans, the world has witnessed a mass proliferation of technologies. During this sustained period of expansion, technologies have taken on reconfigured meaning with regard to human experience, impacting on the fundamental processes by which we make sense of, and interact with, the world around us. The investments of the military-industrial complex, the emergence of cybernetic systems, the development of a global telecommunications network and the rise to prominence of the personal computer are just some of the factors to have played a part in shaping a society predicated on technological exchange.

The lineage of cinema's own development intersects this evolution in a number of elucidating ways. Most explicitly, in keeping with traditional ideas of what technology consists of, theorists have routinely classified cinema according to its own mechanical underpinnings, a technological ontology (from the multiple moving parts of the camera to the whirrs and wheezes of the projector's mechanical breath) that is arguably more explicit than with other visual arts, such as painting or drawing, though one could nevertheless point to the easel, paintbrush or even the human hand as parallel instances of technology.

In an archetypal or traditional scenario, the machines of cinema connect the processes of representation (the role of the camera in capturing the world around us and the subsequent manipulation, processing and reshaping of this representation through editing and other practices), reproduction (the means of duplication and distribution) and exhibition (the dynamic within the space of the cinema itself, between the spectator and the parade of light emitted by the projector). Theorists have endeavoured to extrapolate and explain the precise nature of these technologies (Part One, "Origins and Evolution"), while accounting for the forces that shape and determine their form and function (Part Two, "Definitions and Determinism").

At the same time, an equally significant aspect of cinema's technological history, and how this history might be theorized, concerns its negotiation of a range of social, cultural, political and other contexts likewise steeped in technology. In an era replete with the ramifications and reverberations that surround the more familiar presence of physical devices, theorists have broadened their scope, shifting their attention from the machines of cinema *per se* to cinema's engagement with technologies other than its own, and with technological contexts beyond the purely cinematic.

Like all arts or cultural practices, cinema does not exist in a vacuum. From its representations, the images we see on screen (Part Three, "Projections and Aesthetics"), to the consequences, both foreseen and unforeseen, of the actual uses of cinema's machines (Part Four, "Contexts and Consequences"), the moving image is elemental to a much broader evolution that has seen the influx and influence of technological process across many aspects of our lives. Crucially, it is only in the relation of cinema to this broader context that we can begin to comprehend the relevance of its own technological lineage.

Origins and evolution

In conceptualizing the relationship between cinema and technology, one of the most fundamental areas of enquiry concerns the origins and evolution of cinema's machines. While specific details are likely to shift from one account to the next, a typical history of cinema recounted according to notions of industrial and scientific progress, might read like this: technologies have advanced from the earliest days of primitive imaging devices; towards cinema's integrated inventions of camera, printer, projector and subsequent additions such as sound, 3-D and widescreen; a linear progression that continues today in the shape of assorted digital practices.

For some, this trajectory is rendered according to a predetermined genesis. Cinema's emergence, writes Terry Ramsaye, "fulfils the strivings of a million million years!" (Ramsaye 1926, lxx). This proclamation epitomizes an approach to cinema's history that locates its origins in the primordial imaginings of all who have ever dreamed of motion. From this perspective, the delay in the eventual emergence of cinema (i.e. the lag between conception and technological possibility) is explained in terms of the limitations of science. "Full success was not possible until a later date", affirms Martin Quigley Jr, "because the necessary materials were not available until near the end of the nineteenth century" (Quigley Jr 1953, 11). In evolutionary accounts of cinema's development, it is science rather than society that determines the pace and direction of technological change.

In establishing a history of "magic shadows", Quigley Jr identifies the process of projection, "the fundamental instrument of all screen shows, then and now" (Quigley Jr 1953, 9), as a site of archaeological continuity, linking the machines of cinema with those of its optical precursors. The camera obscura, as one example, projects an image of the outside world by allowing sunlight to pass through a small hole in a darkened room. The magic lantern, another device, casts an image by passing light through a translucent surface, onto which a design is drawn or painted. What links these antecedents with the machines of cinema, historians argue, is their shared dependence on the screen as a source of images projected to an audience.

For others, the notion of a continuum is overly idealistic. Accounts of evolutionary unfolding, argues C. W. Ceram, stem "from a tendency to see the history of civilized man as a continuously progressive process" (Ceram 1965, 15). By contrast, he contends, what matters "is not whether certain chance discoveries take place, but whether they take effect" (Ceram 1965, 16). In other words, a technological history of cinema should record only those discoveries that produce a discernible impact in shaping the eventual dimensions of cinema's machines.

Charted according to these parameters, Ceram suggests, "the prehistory of cinematography begins at a perfectly specific time, the year 1832" (Ceram 1965, 18). What this date signifies is Joseph Plateau's development of the phenakistoscope. It is this invention, argues Ceram, which sets in motion a tangible chain of discovery, that culminates in the birth of cinema. Like other optical toys developed in subsequent decades, Plateau's device operates by giving the impression of motion when still images are viewed in sequence and rotated at speed. In doing so, it relies on the same optical phenomena – persistence of vision (whereby the brain retains images cast upon the retina for a fraction of a second longer than their actual removal from the field of vision) and the illusion of motion (whereby the brain is tricked into thinking that a series of still images, presented at speed, are continuous) – central to the flickering images of cinematic projection.

While this version of technological history has filtered into popular consciousness, theorists less inclined towards the notion of selection suggest it overly determines the criterion of its own historical significance. That is, a select lineage charts a self-fulfilling taxonomy, as only those inventors and inventions that propel cinema towards its present state of technological complexity are deemed appropriate subjects for analysis. As Douglas Gomery puts it, "history is constructed backwards from the present – tracing the evolutionary chain of events and great individuals that recede from today to the nineteenth century and beyond" (Gomery 1985b, 111). As a result, the technological history that emerges from the process of selection is necessarily linear, constructed according to an inevitable sense of progress.

Where this unwavering trajectory, a pantheon of inventors and inventions, leads next are the contributions of Eadweard Muybridge and Étienne-Jules Marey to cinema's eventual emergence. While optical toys aimed to animate still images, bringing them to life, the chronophotographic practices of Muybridge and Marey sought to arrest movement, breaking it down into a succession of photographs. In Muybridge's version of this process, a series of cameras are triggered to expose one after another at tiny intervals, capturing and dissecting motion across a sequence of still images (most famously, in his 1878 experiment to record the motion of a galloping horse).

Later, refining and exploiting these and other optical practices, Thomas Edison's kinetoscope brought motion pictures to a paying audience. "The idea occurred to me", Edison explains, "that it was possible to devise an instrument which should do for the eye what the phonograph does for the ear" (Dickson and Dickson 1895, 4). Having placed a coin in a slot, a loop of moving images could be viewed by peering into a peephole. While the kinetoscope was popular in its own right, a regressive history of cinema (i.e. one that recedes backwards from year zero) can only ever define this device in negative terms, according to the element of cinema it lacks, namely projection.

For the majority of historians, it is 28 December 1895 that offers cinema's founding moment, with the public screening in Paris of films by Auguste and Louis Lumière and the demonstration of their Cinématographe. In mechanical terms, this date represents the coming together of cinema's fundamental devices – camera, printer and projector – with the presentation of films to an audience. In symbolic or evolutionary terms, meanwhile, it crystallizes the technological birth of an idea conceived several centuries earlier.

While faith in the progress of pioneers implicit to this trajectory is appealing, theorists nevertheless point to a number of vexing issues at the heart of this received history. They question the very legitimacy, for instance, of a history delineated according to a notion of autonomous progress. Why, they ask, looking beyond the usual propositions of scientific progress and evolutionary imaginings, did the machines of cinema rise to prominence at the moment they did? What factors account for the precise form and function of cinema's devices? And for what reasons did cinema embody the mechanical archetypes that endure, in one form or another, to this day? Significantly, such questions move us beyond the purely mechanical, into the discourses and methodologies at work beyond cinema, but in which its machines and representations participate.

Definitions and determinism

Cinema is not alone in having to rethink the contours and embodiment of its technological dimensions. From a diverse range of perspectives – including philosophy, computing, science and engineering – theorists such as Bruno Latour, Martin Heidegger and Donna Haraway have proposed numerous ideas concerning the nature of technology, which can be adopted and applied in rethinking the specific circumstances of the moving image. These perspectives present a semantic and conceptual evolution, reconfiguring what might be termed technology and by extension technological culture. For all of these theorists, technology is recognized to consist of more than tools and devices; to include the social and cultural valences that exist in relation to, and which encompass, the purely mechanical.

In the context of science, to take one example, Latour refers to the illuminating notion of technoscience as a way of acknowledging the debates that surround the established institutions and practices of scientific research. Technoscience, according to Latour, should account for more than just traditional laboratory science; it should include "all the elements tied to the scientific contents no matter how dirty, unexpected or foreign they seem".[1] To apply this model to the moving image, cinema's machines become the material, the tangible, the traditional. An examination of cinema's link to the realms of social and cultural politics necessarily heightened in relation to the reverberations of its own and other technologies, meanwhile, invites an engagement with what to much of theoretical writing concerning cinema remains "dirty, unexpected or foreign".

In general terms, the emphasis is on shifting critical attention from the mechanical to the extra-mechanical, from machines to the relation of machines to the wider world. For Heidegger, a key figure in rethinking technology, "the manufacture and utilization of equipment, tools, and machines, the manufactured and used things themselves, and the needs and ends that they serve, all belong to what technology is".[2] Heidegger's influential reworking, which shifts the emphasis of what we refer to when we speak of technology, encourages us to look beyond technology as the physical manifestation of machines to consider the social demands and uses that shape, direct and even anticipate their growth and application.

In relation to these and other conceptions, the technological status of cinema requires further revision. Traditional accounts of cinema's technological history, for all their insights into the development and uses of particular devices, tend to isolate these machines from their social, political and other contexts. "There are no real determinations" (Neale 1985, 159), argues Steve Neale, referring to the broader field of critical enquiry concerning technological determinism, the degree to which society is shaped by technology and vice versa. "Aesthetic, economic, legal or political facts and factors will from time to time be acknowledged and discussed", he continues, "but they will tend to be accounted for in piecemeal fashion and at a purely local level, thus in effect depriving them of any general, systematic significance" (Neale 1985, 159). Despite the heterogeneous approaches to how we might define technology, traditional accounts neglect the social context with which cinema's machines might engage, and whose characteristics these machines might embody.

Douglas Gomery, responding to this dynamic, critiques what he refers to as the "Great Man" approach, whereby "so long as one holds that the ultimate 'cause' of technological change is that of the genius of a few individuals, then there is not much else in the way of historical explanation that need be said" (Gomery 1985b, 111). To deconstruct this tendency, Gomery and others have identified the interplay of forces that might determine the form and function of cinema's physical devices. "Machines do not invent themselves" (Gomery 1985b, 110), Gomery affirms, pointing instead to the predominance of industrial and economic imperatives in shaping technological change. "As the American cinema took on the characteristics of a mature capitalist industry", he suggests, "technological change became largely a matter of economic decision making" (Gomery 1985b, 114). For Gomery, material factors supplant a more general faith in the relentless, autonomous drive of technological evolution.

Elsewhere, multifarious potential determinants have been proposed in attempting to ascertain what shapes technological change. Brian Winston, as a further example, identifies the audience as the vital cause in determining the precise timing of cinema's rise to prominence. "To understand the development of cinema", he explains, "by all means look to Edison, Lumière and the rest; note economics and social practice; appreciate the importance of cinema to the general concept of modernity" (Winston 1997, 38), but to discover why cinema appeared when it did, he suggests, one also has to consider "the 'invention' (as it might be termed) of the modern audience" (Winston 1997, 26–27). What each of these accounts has in common is the desire to look beyond the supposed genius of individual inventors and their respective inventions, to consider the material and other conditions that impact on the emergence and evolution of these machines.

"How is the world in the object, and the object in the world?"[3] asks Donna Haraway of the ways in which machines become visible markers of their social formation. Inspired by the political models of Louis Althusser and Karl Marx, Jean-Louis Comolli (Comolli 1977, 1980) addresses this complex question in relation to the intersection of cinematic technology (most notably, the camera), cinematic technique (in this volume, depth of field cinematography) and ideology (the imperatives embodied in cinema's machines). The form of cinema's devices, he contends, embodies a number of ideological and other determinants. They are inherently ideological, not merely a neutral channel for ideological content.

Presenting their own variation on Comolli's methodology, David Bordwell and Janet Staiger (Bordwell, Staiger and Thompson 1985) suggest that cinema's aesthetics, mediated through machines, are equally prone to the contrivances of determinism. Changes in style, they argue, are the result of a range of business strategies intrinsic to the mode of production, and by understanding these strategies we can explain the precise cause and timing of stylistic change. In negotiating between cinematic style and economic imperatives, as one example, industrial developers (including camera company Bell & Howell and film stock manufacturer Eastman Kodak) and professional associations (such as the Society of Motion Picture Engineers and the American Society of Cinematographers) play as significant a role as that of any individual in defining the range of technical possibilities open to Hollywood film-making at any given time. Technology, in general, fulfils an industrial role that is carefully managed to augment, but not undermine, the existing paradigm.

Such theories, in proposing a connection between technological shift and aesthetic innovation (i.e. between cinematic technology and cinematic style), locate the representational functions of film as qualities inherent to the mechanics of their production. Innovations such as sound (Belton 1985), depth of field (Ogle 1972), color (Buscombe 1978) and widescreen (Spellerberg

1985) have all been analyzed in terms of the complex relationship that exists between economic and ideological imperatives, technological change and their aesthetic corollaries.

Projections and aesthetics

While aesthetics have always been linked to the technology of the medium, a cinematic practice conversant with technology, and with the conditions of technological culture, might also be defined as such in its relation to technologies other than its own. "Cybernated art is very important", writes Nam June Paik, commenting on the context of visual art, "but art for cybernated life is more important, and the latter need not be cybernated".[4] While much has been written about the mechanical underpinnings of cinema, the moving image might also engage with technology through its mass cultural representations and its formal and stylistic refractions.

From the depiction of malfunctioning Artificial Intelligence in Stanley Kubrick's *2001: A Space Odyssey* (1968) to the dehumanizing assembly line of Charlie Chaplin's *Modern Times* (1936), the history of the moving image is replete with depictions of milieux and narratives steeped in technological themes. Yet it is only in recent years, with the growing influence of cultural studies, that critical attention has shifted from cinema's machines and their determination, towards textual readings of the representations these machines produce. The images we see on screen exist as a source of cultural refraction, symptomatic of mass consciousness regarding the technologies that constitute, and which are shaped by, the world in which we live.

Science fiction, in particular, offers myriad opportunities for this type of engagement (Sobchack 1987; Kuhn 1990, 1999; Telotte 1995, 1999, 2001). The moving images consumed within popular culture are symbolic of the preoccupations, attitudes and anxieties of society towards technology at the time of a film's production, on the one hand, and its reception, on the other. By examining these projections, the representational guise of cinema reveals the underlying desires, fantasies and fears that have fuelled representations of technologies past, present and future.

Fritz Lang's *Metropolis* (1927), a text analyzed from a number of disciplinary perspectives (Huyssen 1981–1982; Springer 1991; Elsaesser 2000), is exemplary in this respect. Lang's film envisions a future city in which society is divided between the autocratic thinkers, who live within the hypermodern sheen of a futuristic cityscape, and those whose lives they control, an oppressed underclass of machine workers who toil underground. As a reflection of the early twentieth-century fascination with technology and attitudes to industrialization at a time of mass expansion in this area, *Metropolis* still has much to say about the modern city, the control of people through technologized labour and the broader correlation between humans and machines. More generally, in the context of a connection between cinema, technology and culture, it represents the compelling potential of the moving image to reflect on contexts and technologies other than its own.

Beyond narrative thematics (and the strictures of conventional or classical narrative orderings to which the majority of films on the subject of technology return), cinema's mediation of the technological and the cultural can also occur on the level of a film's fundamental formal construction. There is a corpus of work – from Dziga Vertov's *Man with a Movie Camera* (*Chevlovek s kinoapparatom*) (1929), which examines the technologies of cinema within the framework of mass industrialization, to David Cronenberg's *eXistenZ* (1999), which mirrors the narrative logic of a video game – that shifts and warps the language and expressions of cinema in the direction of technologies and the ways in which technological systems operate.

Manvith

This is nowhere more apparent than in the relation of cinema to the computer. "How does computerization affect our very concept of the moving image?" (Manovich 2001, 287) asks Lev Manovich, in attempting to ascertain what connects the distinctive modes of communication associated with cinema and computing. "Does it offer new possibilities for film language? Has it led to the development of totally new forms of cinema?" (Manovich 2001, 287) At the heart of these questions is the suggestion that digital media function according to a particular set of aesthetic and communicative principles – including programmability, interactivity, simulation, and so on – which have impacted on the language of cinema.

Gene Youngblood's notion of the "aesthetic machine" (Youngblood 1970) addresses these debates in relation to the coming together of the creative vision of the human author and the machine logic and processing power of the programmable computer. "The digital computer opens vast new realms of possible aesthetic investigation" (Youngblood 1970, 189), he suggests, precisely because "the computer is an *active* participant in the creative process" (Youngblood 1970, 191). In its capacity to implement decisions that have been defined in its programming, the computer links the traditional artistic virtues of creative vision with the ability to harness, manipulate and control the technological design of this expression.

For some, this relationship has led to a fundamental reconfiguration. "We are entering an age of narrative chaos", write Martin Rieser and Andrea Zapp, "where traditional frameworks are being overthrown by emergent experimental and radical attempts to remaster the art of storytelling in developing technologies" (Rieser and Zapp 2002, xxv). New technologies in general, and digital technologies in particular, are framed according to the rhetoric of revolution and rupture, a visionary tradition that seeks to embrace the appeal of the new in pursuit of contemporary forms of expression.

Films have been constructed as "linear strings", explains Ted Nelson, a key figure in the development and philosophy of computing, "for mechanical reasons".[5] With the physical objects of mechanical exhibition (from video tape to film reel), there is little option but to begin at the beginning and end at the end, with little by way of spectator control in between. By contrast, Nelson suggests, liberated by the instant access of digital storage, there is nothing to prevent the "hyperfilm – a browsable or vari-sequenced movie"[6] akin to the structure of hypertext, whereby information sources are connected together in the form of a branching matrix of navigable pathways, in which the spectator or user can choose the links he or she wishes to follow.

For others, the radical possibility of an interactive experience remains at odds with the decidedly linear architecture of the medium. Peter Lunenfeld refers to "the myths of interactive cinema" (Harries 2002), debunking the idea that cinema is capable of allowing the spectator to intervene in their own viewing experience in any meaningful way. It is still some way from the type of engagement associated with computing, a realm in which "interaction between user and machine became the Holy Grail . . . and fuelled a hunger for interactivity as an end in itself, rather than simply a means" (Harries 2002, 147).

In these and other instances, theorists explore the connections between cinema's own and other technologies. For the majority, who propose equivocations, the representations and formal characteristics of cinema's projections and aesthetics are evidence of a transformation of subjectivities. We arrive at a "cinema for technological life", to reconfigure Paik's phrase, articulating the conditions that have been brought about by, or which have brought about, an evolving technological culture.

Contexts and consequences

For many theorists, the most important aspects of the relationship between cinema, technology and culture are the consequences – political, psychological, perceptual, and so on – that emerge from the applications and uses of cinema's machines within society. Specifically, the ramifications of the technological means by which the moving image is distributed and consumed, and the ways in which these conditions tap into, or produce, social systems and ways of being.

In terms of politics, the machines of cinema are part of an enduring rhetorical tradition that seeks to imagine technologies in terms of their revolutionary potential. Such accounts are prone to recur at moments of volatility, rupture and change. After all, one way of dealing with an unsatisfactory present, or a troubling past, is to envision a transformed future. Technologies, real and fantasized, are envisaged as a source of emancipation.

The writings of Dziga Vertov (Vertov 1923; Michelson 1984) and the Italian Futurists (Marinetti et al. 1916), which evidence this tendency, seek not simply to represent society but to change it according to their respective political ideals. The Futurists (an international art movement founded in 1909 by Filippo Marinetti) present a case for cinema's potential as a modern, dynamic, politicized form, a corollary of the restlessness and change of modern life. Rather than fearing or attacking technology, their manifestos expound a love of noise, power and machines. Cinema, in particular, is seen to exemplify the shock of the new. The Futurist cinema, they declare, would become "a school of joy, of speed, of force, of courage, of heroism" (Marinetti et al. 1916, 130), locating its nascent technologies within a concomitant context of cultural shift.

Less than a decade later, in some of the most conceptually compelling writing of the early decades of cinema, Vertov postulates a correlation between the idea of new technologies and the possibility of a revelatory or expanded sense of perception, both literally (with the camera augmenting human vision) and metaphorically (in terms of new ways of seeing, and therefore understanding, Soviet life). In the broader context of mass industrialization in which Vertov was working, this interest in cinema's machines represents an awareness of the role they might play in shaping a society in which technologies of all kinds would assume prioritized status. Irrespective of whether or not the revolutions espoused by Vertov and the Italian Futurists ever occured, the textual remnants they left behind become archaeological residue, a barometer by which we can gauge the future visions projected throughout history.

Indeed the idea that cinema's technologies might play a part in facilitating a new political order remains potent. In a contemporary context, Samira Makhmalbaf (Makhmalbaf 2000) discusses digital technologies in terms of the liberation they might offer from a range of global inequalities. "Cinema", she explains, "has always been at the mercy of political power, particularly in the East, financial capital, particularly in the West, and the concentration of means of production, anywhere in the world" (Makhmalbaf 2000, unpaginated). Responding from a perspective of relative subjugation, Makhmalbaf writes with optimism of the potential role technologies might play in undermining the systems of control that exist outside of cinema, but which inevitably impact on the production and dissemination of the moving image. "With astonishing technological innovations now coming to fruition", she notes, "artists no longer seem to be totally vulnerable to these impediments" (Makhmalbaf 2000, unpaginated). In her polemic, technologies are central to the possibility of a new form of cinema, which is capable of usurping the intertwined forces of political, financial and technological control.

Less tangible, but equally resonant, are psychological responses to cinema's technologies. In this volume, Vivian Sobchack (Sobchack 1994) explores this subject from the perspective of phenomenology, concerned with how the practices that shape our interface with the moving image impinge on our sense of self and perception of presence. Similarly, Barbara Creed (Creed 2000) explores the psychological repercussions of the rise of the virtual actor. "Now it is possible", she writes of the digital avatar, "to create computer-generated objects, things and people that do not have referents in the real world but exist solely in the digital domain of the computer" (Creed 2000, 80). Creed's primary concern is how the presence of the virtual actor might alter the relationship between spectator and image, raising questions concerning the nature of our response, in the uncanny scenario of virtual starring alongside corporeal, to the peculiar recognition of a presence not quite human.

Refocusing this concentration on sociological and behavioral practices, theorists also explore how we use and interact with technologies when we consume the moving image. In the space of the home, most notably, theories of digital reception locate the moving image within a context of convergence, where various technologies – television, computer, games system, and so on – come together in the form of a meta or hypermedia. The hub of domestic consumption becomes a vital technology, as Janet Wasko terms it, "beyond the silver screen" (Wasko 1994) of traditional exhibition and reception.

Specifically, theorists propose the technological means by which the moving image is distributed and consumed, within this context, have resulted in the formation of a new type of spectator, more accurately described as a player or user, as notions of passive viewing give way to a sense of active participation. Technologies are marketed in terms of offering a new experience, turning the spectator's attention from what is being depicted to how it is possible for them to interact with and control the moving image.

In this reconfigured setting, proponents argue, new media technologies facilitate a degree of global connection, with the Internet providing an immediacy of exchange, access and acquisition. Such claims promise added value, and even empowerment, in our ability to access and download material from a vast archive of data, and to share and trade moving images across a global network.

Yet, as Makhmalbaf's account reminds us, the mutual flow implied by the utopian rhetoric of collective networking, and the more general, hyperbolic claims of digital revolution, are at odds with the complex realities that underpin this supposedly global exchange.

By situating the interconnected technologies of cinema within these broader contexts, we can better understand their engagement with the spheres of discourse at work within society. If perspectives on the devices of cinema occupy one end of a conceptual spectrum of technological engagement, at the other lies analysis of the role cinema's technologies might play in shaping the processes by which we live our lives, and the broader contexts in which these processes find meaning.

Cinema in technological times

In certain respects, the technological history of cinema appears to be coming full circle. Just as the early machines of cinema refined the existing technologies and aesthetics of photography and other forms, giving rise to a medium predicated on mechanized movement, cinema is now undergoing an equivalent period of transition, as its technologies and expressions are reconfigured in relation to those of the digital computer. Optimists point to ways in which cinema has appropriated these technologies in its own practices. Pessimists, by contrast, suggest the computer has absorbed cinema as one constituent element within a universal hypermedia. Where theorists once celebrated the birth of cinema, they now point to its potential passing.

In dealing with this evolving technological history, this volume is guided by a desire to acknowledge the diversity of theoretical perspectives concerning cinema's own technologies and to explore the multifarious ways its physical devices, moving images and social formations are elemental to a larger evolution. Its collected essays range back and forth, from cinema's own machines, on the one hand, to the participation of these machines in technologized spheres of cultural meaning and social discourse, on the other. Ultimately, the intention is to reconcile these twin perspectives, eliding the conceptual and methodological distance that has tended to separate them in theoretical writing.

In terms of selection, the essays have been organized not merely to be representative of some larger body of work, namely the texts that constitute the field. If it were, then accounts of cinema's mechanical evolution would risk overwhelming the less common, but equally relevant, perspectives on the technological-cultural resonances of cinema. Rather, the selection of texts is designed to straddle traditional as well as modern conceptions of technology.

Likewise, the thematic headings into which the collected essays are organized are not intended to suggest a definitive taxonomy, but to highlight one of many possible cartographies by which we might chart the diversity of critical approaches to the intersection of cinema, technology and culture.

To identify the conditions and extrapolate the revelations of a cinema conversant with this context, as this volume sets out to, is central to an awareness of cinema's own technological status. By twisting the kaleidoscope of history – bringing together writings past and present and recontextualizing familiar terrain – we can begin to consider with fresh eyes the position cinema occupies within a broader matrix of technological and cultural exchange.

Notes

1   Latour, B. (1987) *Science in Action: How to Follow Scientists and Engineers through Society*, Cambridge, Massachusetts: Harvard University Press, 174.

2   Heidegger, M. (1977) "The Question Concerning Technology" (English translation by Lovitt, W.) in *The Question Concerning Technology and Other Essays*, New York: Harper & Row, 4–5. Originally (1954) "Die Frage nach der Technik" in *Vorträge und Aufsätze*, Pfullingen: Günther Neske, 9–40.

3   Haraway, D. cited in Dumit, J. (1992) "Technoculture: Another, More Material, Name for Postmodern Culture?" in *Postmodern Culture* 2.2 (January): published online.

4   Paik, N. J. (1966) "Cybernated Art" in *Manifestos*, New York: Something Else Press (Great Bear Pamphlets), 24.

5   Nelson, T. H. (1965) "A File Structure for the Complex, the Changing and, the Indeterminate" in Winner, L. (ed.), *Association for Computing Machinery: Proceedings of the 20th National Conference*, Cleveland, Ohio: Association for Computing Machinery, 96.

6   Ibid.

PART ONE

ORIGINS AND EVOLUTION

Introduction

While accounts of the origins and evolution of cinema are plentiful within film theory, some of the most influential of these texts work in opposition to the popularly held narrative that posits a single moment of invention (the cry of "Eureka!" most often associated with the Cinématographe and public screenings of films by Auguste and Louis Lumière) and successive periods of technological change.

As early as 1899, only four years after the date most regularly cited as that of cinema's birth, Henry V. Hopwood offered a prescient intervention into debates still raging over a century later. "There is not," he insists, "there never was, an inventor of the Living Picture." Declining to ascribe this status to any one of the most likely candidates – including Thomas Edison, William Dickson, Émile Reynaud, Eadweard Muybridge, Joseph Plateau, Louis Lumière and Étienne-Jules Marey – Hopwood instead points to a more fluid, collective genesis.

This elucidation is notable in that it loosens, and to a certain extent inverts, the assumption that technological invention is necessarily rooted in a single site, a sole inventor, and a discrete moment of origin. As such, any demarcation designed to separate cinema's archetypes and precursors from an identifiable moment of invention will inevitably provoke claims of alternative origins.

Pioneering what would later be termed Virtual Reality, Morton Heilig's version of evolutionary history points towards an entirely immersive cinematic experience. Heilig's ultimate ambition was to find a method for conveying "in all its variety and vitality the full consciousness of man", through an expanded engagement with all of our senses: touch, taste and smell, as well as the more familiar cinematic sensations of sight and sound. This multi-sensory experience recalls the immersion scientists describe as telepresence, whereby a human operator enters into the illusion of being present in a space remote from his or her own physical location. "Open your eyes," he decrees, "listen, smell, and feel – sense the world in all its magnificent colors, depth, sounds, odors, and textures – this is the cinema of the future!"

Heilig wanted the viewer to feel as if they were actually in a film as opposed to simply watching it. In 1962 he patented the Sensorama, an arcade machine designed to expand cinema in the direction of virtuality. In addition to sound and vision, the Sensorama worked through motion and vibration, wafted smells from a bank of chemicals, tactile feedback and a fan designed to produce artificial breezes. These stimuli would serve to immerse the user in various scenarios, from riding through the streets of Brooklyn to watching a belly dancer perform.

Paralleling the matrix of past, present and future outlined by Hopwood, Lev Manovich extrapolates the connections that exist between the archetypes of cinematic invention and those of the modern computer. Significant aspects of digital culture were born from cinema, he proposes, and in crucial respects the computer and cinema merge into one.

In terms of its machines, Manovich explains, computing has always been linked to the construction and reconstruction of images: from Joseph-Marie Jacquard's primitive loom, which wove designs controlled by punched cards, to Konrad Zuse's early computer, that ran by printing binary code onto the images of discarded 35mm film stock. Conceptually, cinema also paved the way for computers by familiarizing us with digital ideas such as sampling, random access, database and simulation. "Cinema", Manovich argues, "taught us to accept the manipulation of time and space, the arbitrary coding of the visible, the mechanization of vision, and the reduction of reality to a moving image."

The dispute over cinema's emergence and evolution offers a useful case study of invention as a critical concept. Even now, theorists continue to debate the status and meaning of cinema's mechanical devices and physical tools.

Past, Present, and Future

1

HENRY V. HOPWOOD

The enquiry has often been made, "Who was the inventor of the Living Picture?" This question has usually been answered, if answered at all, by dogmatic assertion or the presentation of isolated facts; there has been no attempt towards a logical determination of the problem in its widest sense. In the first place some definition of terms is required; let us determine what a Living Picture is. Where shall the line be drawn? If we consider it merely as a view presenting the illusion of motion, then we must go back to the early years of this dying century and attribute its origin to Plateau's Phenakistoscope. If we restrict our definition to views of photographic origin, Wenham's experiments in 1852 fulfilled our requirements forty-six years ago. Should it be required that the photographic record be a true analysis of motion, then thirty-four years have passed since Du Mont indicated the methods of chronophotography. Finally, if it be suggested that the picture must last a definite and somewhat lengthy period, the images being secured at short intervals and in a very restricted space of time, we are compelled to admit the Living Picture as a phenomenon of recent growth; but it must not be forgotten that many views of one action, procured by photography and repeated for as long a period as required, were prepared far earlier than any date which may be termed recent. And, further, it must not be ignored that the different stages quoted above led insensibly one to the other; each step was founded on the labors of previous workers or at least rested on the same basis. No! emphatically No! There is not, there never was, an inventor of the Living Picture. Say that it grew from an infinitely small germ, as unlike its present form as the butterfly is unlike the egg from which it evolves; say that many minds have each contributed, and still are contributing their mite towards the realization of that perfection yet to be attained; say that the Living Picture is the work of nineteenth-century civilized man – and the statement will be as true as any generalization can be. So far as a single inventor can be named, Plateau must be recognized as the originator of the pictorial method of producing an illusion of motion by means of persistence of vision. This in a double sense; for while the Phenakistoscope was the forerunner of all machines in which a rapidly moving picture was momentarily viewed (and this definition includes machines so late in time as Edison's Kinetoscope), yet Plateau's "Diable soufflant" was the first step toward all those forms of apparatus in which a picture is momentarily viewed while stationary. True the picture was not stationary, but the principle of differential speed between image and shutter was established.

And to whom could this invention be attributed with more satisfaction? There is no name in the history of physiological optics more worthy of honour than that of this philosopher. Born in 1801, Joseph Antoine Ferdinand Plateau devoted himself early in life to the study of optics, especially in their physiological aspect. At the age of twenty-eight, in the course of some experiments respecting the effect of light on the retina, he exposed his eyes for a considerable time to the full blaze of the sun. The result was blindness, from which, however, he temporarily recovered. During this period of recovery he invented the Phenakistoscope, and in 1835 was appointed Professor of Physics at Ghent. Over a period of fourteen years his sight gradually deteriorated, and by the year 1843 he was totally blind. Yet in 1849 he invented his Diable soufflant, he continued his researches by the aid of relatives who carried out his instructions for experiments to confirm his theories, he pursued his investigations into the domain of molecular physics, he retained his professorship, and died in harness, leaving works still unpublished behind him, at the ripe age of eighty-three. There is a magnificence in the idea of this blind man carrying on his work, sowing the seeds of pleasure to thousands in future generations by means of that sense of which he was himself totally deprived; there is developed a feeling of pride in human power when we think of a man from whose eyes the light was eternally shut out nevertheless converting the brief glimmer of passing events into permanent embodiment, and leaving to others an elaboration of that sense which was lost to him for ever.

Yet it must not be forgotten that Plateau's Phenakistoscope took its origin from investigations on Roget's researches, which in themselves had nothing whatever to do with Living Pictures. So also with the application of photography. Many experimented long before the necessary appliances were ready to their hand. Mr Wenham tells us that in 1852 he obtained (by posing) a series of views of a man at work; but he also records that when the views were synthesized into motion, the subject declared "he never worked like that!" Du Mont in 1861 seems to have first suggested chronophotography, and Janssen apparently first practised it in 1874, but neither could work rapidly enough to obtain a series fit for recombination. The reproduction of animated scenes was thus not possible until photographic emulsions of greater rapidity were produced; manifestly photographic chemists and plate-makers must receive acknowledgment of a large share in the invention of the Living Picture. Again, let the most rapid emulsion be spread on glass, it is difficult – almost impossible – to obtain an extended series of views. Bands were suggested for carrying a long series of pictures by Stampfer in 1833 and Desvignes in 1860; the idea was in constant evidence from that time forward, but how could it be applied in the taking of a photographic record? Negative paper, improved as it now is, possesses sufficient grain to render it practically useless as a support for one-inch negatives, destined to great enlargement, it was still less suitable years ago. Evidently, therefore, the inventor of celluloid should receive his meed of praise, yet not he alone; celluloid was not invented for the service of the Living Picture, indeed at first it was not suitable for photographic purposes at all. When rendered fit for use as a photographic support, the Living Picture in no way came into consideration; celluloid was applied at first in the ordinary manner as a substitute for glass plates of ordinary sizes.

Given a celluloid film of indefinite length, the road was opened for the inventors of mechanical appliances which should utilize it. Thus while we find Greene and Evans were the first to publish and produce an effective machine, yet it must not be forgotten that others were working too; in fact, Messrs Donisthorpe and Crofts were not two months behind the previously mentioned inventors. Thus throughout the history of the Living Picture names are associated rather with details than with principles, which in fact seem generally to have been pointed out long before the means existed for carrying them to a practical issue.

In fact, throughout the course of the present century the Living Picture has, in popular parlance, been "in the air"; similar ideas and methods have occurred independently, sometimes simultaneously to separate individuals, and this was almost necessarily so; the facts of the case demanded it. Given a series of connected facts capable of leading in combination to one or two well-defined results; given a number of observers equally interested and of similar capability – it is a practical certainty that several will arrive at the same conclusion, the more so as the field of possibility becomes more restricted. In cases of this kind one observer may reach the obvious conclusion before another; that does not prove his right to a national memorial and entry on the roll of fame; there is credit due to the man who extracts a grain of sand from the machine and so renders it workable; he proves his industry and application, but certainly cannot claim recognition as a genius. In proportion as the elementary facts become more numerous and complicated, so does the discovery fall inevitably to the man of greater capability if the solution be reached by reasoning; if it be arrived at by accident, that is a matter personal to the discoverer – he is not bound to mention it!

To substantiate these views several examples taken from the History of Living Pictures can easily be quoted. Plateau and Stampfer invented the phenakistoscope almost simultaneously. When we consider that the subject of wheel phenomena had been before the world for some years it is not surprising that the popular introduction of the Thaumatrope should have caused the idea of the phenakistoscope to crystallize, so to speak, in the mind of more than one man. To come to later years, a comparison of Acre's English invention of May 1895, with Müller's German patent of August in the same year will show an almost similar method of dealing with the same problem. This is probably due to the fact that the solution was a fairly obvious one. Marey had done the same thing less perfectly in 1890; he clamped the film and allowed it to be drawn onward by a spring when the clamp was taken off, Acres and Müller put a roller on the end of the spring. Certainly one device was effective, the other was not; but still in this, as in many other instances, no great natural secret was brought to light. Take another case, this time an application of the cinematograph. It was early recognised that the zoëtrope afforded a means of varying the apparent rate of movement of an object; photographs of birds in flight secured by Marey's photographic revolver were recombined at a slower speed in this manner, for the purpose of leisurely inspection. Yet the subject appears to have exercised a fascination of a widespread character. M. Guéroult thought it worth while in 1896 to demand the opening of a sealed packet, deposited with the Académie des Sciences in 1889, in order to prove that he first evolved the idea. Mach, Corday, and others have (or purport to have) photographed plants at long intervals and subsequently combined the views rapidly; much ink has been spilled, much more will be expended; for the idea "is in the air", and will remain there – it is of the obvious.

[. . .]

Yes, the practical stage is fully reached, but the perfect is yet to come. It has already been declared that accuracy of workmanship has quite as much, probably more, to do with results than the principle of the machine. Yet, given good mechanical treatment all round, there must be one or two types of existing apparatus which will outdistance the others. Will the shutter remain? How will flicker be overcome? Perhaps by alternate and overlapping projection from two lanterns using one film taken from one point of view. Perhaps also the multiple lens travelling with a continually moving film may prove its superiority. It may be that none of the present types will persist; some new idea may carry the day. The use of a mirror to render a travelling film optically stationary is quite a recent suggestion, and though this single mirror must be returned to its first position as each picture passes, there are more unlikely things than the revival of the praxinoscope type, the mirror-drum, which is in continual rotation in one direction, needing no return and rendering all images optically stationary. So too the suggestion of a continually revolving camera, taking a continuous view of the whole horizon, or such part as is left unshielded, needing no shutter and leaving no period of darkness, having a film in constant motion yet practically stationary, may conceivably be the groundwork upon which a perfect, though somewhat expensive, instrument may be built. But why prophesy? Facts in the past remain facts in the present, but the future may be left to fate. If a long course of actuality has had a somewhat sedative effect, if fiction is needed to restore a somewhat wearied brain, let us leave prophecy, which is so easily falsified by the reality of the future, severely on one side, and glance at a living picture of the weirdest type. In Flammarion's "Lumen", as also in a little work introduced to English readers by the late R. A. Proctor, the idea of persistence of light rather than persistence of vision is elaborated. Light and other vibrations to which our limited perceptions afford no clue, travel from this earth into space at a definite velocity. So a continual record of the earth's history in its slightest details is continually streaming off into the eternal void, and, granted an eye capable of perceiving an object under a minute angle, infinitely sensible also to vibrations, it will be seen that at some point or other in space everything that has happened is yet visible. Grant this eye, or rather sense of vision, a capability of infinite speed of translation, it might retreat at the same speed as light and so keep the same event for ever in view, it might approach the outward travelling events and compress a lifetime into a moment. The whole history, not of this world alone, but of every sphere that is or has been is still in vibrating existence, and one universal perception extending through the infinity would embrace within the tremblings of the boundless ether a consciousness of all that was or is, an eternal and universal living picture of all past events. Having started from persistence of vision due to the sluggish action of our mundane eyes or nerves, having lost ourselves in fancied possibilities of the illimitable, what remains for human thought and pen but the simple word

FINIS?

The Cinema of the Future

2

MORTON HEILIG

Pandemonium reigns supreme in the film industry. Every studio is hastily converting to its own "revolutionary" system – Cinerama, Colorama, Panoramic Screen, Cinemascope, 3-D, and Stereophonic Sound. A dozen marquees in Time Square are luring customers into the realm of a "sensational new experience".

Everywhere we see the "initiated" holding pencils before the winked eyes of the "un-initiated" explaining the mysteries of 3-D. The critics are lining up pro and con, concluding their articles profoundly with "after all, it's the story that counts". Along with other film-goers desiring orientation, I have been reading these articles and have sadly discovered that they reflect this confusion rather than illuminate it. It is apparent that the inability to cope with the problem stems from a refusal to adopt a wider frame of reference, and from a meager understanding of the place art has in life generally.

All living things engage, on a higher or lower level, in a continuous cycle of orientation and action. For example, an animal on a mountain ledge hears a rumbling sound and sees an avalanche of rocks descending on it. It cries with terror and makes a mighty leap to another ledge. Here in small is the essence of a process that in animals and man is so automatic – so rapid – as to seem one indivisible act. By careful introspection, however, men have been able to stop its rapid flow, bring it into the light of consciousness, and divide it into three basic phases. The first, observation (the noise and image of the boulders in our example), is the reception of isolated impressions or facts. The second, integration, is the combining of these isolated facts with the inner needs of the life force into an emotional unity that prompts and controls action (the animal's sensation of danger and terror). The third, action (the leap to safety), is a change in the creature's physical relation to the world.

With the forming of society, different men concentrated on one of these three phases, and by learning to cast the results of their labor into concrete forms (that could be passed from man to man, and generation to generation) they created science, art, and industry. These three have the same methods and aims in the social body as the mind, heart, and muscle do in individual man. Their goals are clear. For science it is to bestow the maximum know-ledge on humanity. For art it is to digest this knowledge into the deeper realms of feeling, generating emotions of beauty and love that will guide the crude energies of mankind to constructive actions. And for industry it is to act on the material world so as to procure more living energy for mankind. The success with which each field can approach its goal depends on its understanding of method. Science has come the closest because it has uncovered the individual's scientific thought processes and codified it into a clear and systematic method of experimentation. Consciously applying this method, it makes more discoveries in one year than previously were made in millenniums. Writing, international mail, and international conferences have long been efficient ways of distributing its findings to humanity.

Industry, within the last one hundred years, has also made great strides toward its goal because production geniuses like Ford have rationalized it to the last degree. They have instigated assembly line, mass production techniques that pour out more food, machines, and fuels in one year than were produced in centuries. The problem of distributing its bulky goods has been solved theoretically and only awaits practical application.

It is the middle field, art, which today is furthest from its goal. The world is woefully barren of peaceful, tolerant, humanitarian feelings and the art that should create them. And this is because, as yet, art has evolved no clear-cut methodology to make it as efficient as science and industry in creating its product. Art is now struggling feverishly to achieve this, and only in the light of this struggle and the laws it seeks to establish will we be able to understand the innovations that prompted this article.

The laws of art, like those of science and industry, lie hidden in the subconscious of man. When a primitive man desired to convey to another man the complete emotional texture of an experience that occurred to him he tried to reproduce, as closely as possible, the elements that generated his own emotions. His art was very simple, being limited to the means provided by his own body. He used his voice to growl like the bear that attacked him, pumped his arms and legs to show how he climbed a tree, and then he blew on his listener's face to make him feel the hot breath of the bear. If he were a good storyteller, he would arrange these effects in more or less the same order they originally happened to him. Of course, his listener would feel everything more intensely if he, and not his friend, were attacked by the bear. But aside from being impossible, this is not advisable, for by listening to his friend's story, he can have all the excitement, learn all the lessons, without paying the price for them.

With time language became more complete. A specific word-sound became associated with the impressions, objects, and feelings in man's experience. Words were useful in conveying the general structure of an event to the mind, but could rarely quicken the listener's pulse the way fresh and direct contact with the original sense elements could – that is unless spoken by a very skilled narrator. And even then not a thousand of his choicest words could convey the sensation of yellow better than one glance at yellow, or high C better than listening for one second to high C. And so side by side with verbal language they evolved more direct forms of communication – painting, sculpture, song and dance. They found they could bore deeper into experience by concentrating all their powers of observation on one of nature's aspects and mastering the limited materials necessary to its expression.

Materials became more complex and techniques more refined as each art form sought to exploit the full range and delicacy of its own domain. The few lines scratched on a rock developed into the full glory of painting. The singing voice evolved into symphonic music and the few words into the rich fabric of poetry. For all the apparent variety of the art forms created, there is one thread uniting all of them. And that is man, with his particular organs of perception and action. For all their ingenuity, a race of blind men could never have evolved painting. Similarly, no matter how much they appreciated movement through their eyes a race of limbless men could never have developed dancing. Thus art is like a bridge connecting what man can do to what he can perceive.

What we commonly refer to as the "pure arts" are those whose materials are so simple, so pliable, that one artist can master them sufficiently to express his inner feelings to perfection. The painter fashions color, the musician notes, the poet words. Each additional impression of their artistic form is like an electric charge driving the spectator higher and higher to peaks of pure and intense feeling that he rarely experiences in his daily life. The simple materials of the pure arts are apprehensible through only one sense, but this sense is not a necessary condition of purity. Precision and subtlety of form achieved through *control* is the decisive factor.

Desiring to convey the full richness of experience in more lifelike form, men have combined the pure arts into forms known as the "combined" or "secondary arts", such as opera, ballet, and theater. Their effects were fuller, more spectacular, but rarely deeper. The essential factor of control was missing. Not only did the artist have to master visual, musical, choreographic, and verbal materials, not only did he have to limit the scope of his imagination to the practical limitations of a theatre and depend on the collaborations of dozens of singers, painters, dancers, musicians, and actors, but even after he had masterminded every detail and rehearsed the cast into perfect form he had absolutely no way of fixing his creation so that it could remain exactly the same whenever and wherever played. This was an impasse the artist could never surmount and never did, until the arrival of a strange newcomer on the scene – the machine. The machine with its genius for tireless repetition and infinite exactitude was an extension of the limbs and will of man. It could be trusted to perform all his purely mechanical operations, freeing his energies for more creative tasks.

In the form of the printing press, lithograph, radio, phonograph, and now television, the machine has rapidly solved the second part of art's age-old problem – distribution. Painting, poetry, music, drama, and ballet can now reach millions of people about the globe as they never could before. But the machine has done more. It has entered, as it has done in industry and science, into the very sphere of artistic creation itself, providing the artist with a much wider palette of *sense* material and enabling him to mold them with precision into an aesthetic unity as he never could before. And it is the invasion of such a relentlessly efficient and logical apparatus as the machine into the humane and heretofore romantic field of art that not only suggests but necessitates a clear, efficient *methodology* of art.

If at this point we scan back over our very brief history of art forms it becomes apparent that the first law of such an artistic methodology must be:

> The nature of man's art is fundamentally rooted in his peculiar psychic apparatus and is limited by the material means at his disposal.

Logically, then a proper science of art should be devoted to the revelation of the laws of his psyche and the invention of better means.

Although very little of it was conscious or intentional, nothing demonstrates this research and invention more dramatically than the cinema. The sense was vision – the material, light. The still camera had been invented but it could do no more than a skilled painter could do with time. But when in 1895 the Lumière Brothers set up a little box before their factory and cranked away at it as a group of workers left, they did something no human being could ever do before. They captured visual movement in a form that could exactly reproduce the moving image as often as desired. Only after countless millenniums of existence had man learned how to do what his visual mechanism can do with no effort at all. With time every part of this new machine, from the lens to the film stock, was improved. Lenses were made faster and given wider angles. The iris became adjustable and the film finer-grained and faster. Always the criteria of invention were to reproduce as closely as possible man's miraculous mechanism of vision. The addition of color was inevitable. Man sees color, so must his mechanical eye. Now we have the so-called "revolutionary" 3-D and Wide Screen. The excitement and confusion are great but they need not be. First, 3-D was invented over fifty years ago and shown at the Paris Exposition. Financial, not technical considerations held it up until 1953. The really exciting thing is that these new devices have clearly and dramatically revealed to everyone what painting, photography, and cinema have been semiconsciously trying to do all along – portray in its full glory the visual world of man as perceived by the human eye.

Side by side with the invention of means to freeze visual movement, machines were developed that could (this also for the first time in human history) freeze sound. But again, the public's deep and natural urge for more complete realism in its art had to wait on the wheel of finance until 1933. It is the addition of sound that represents the really great "revolution" in the history of cinema. For with the addition of sound, cinema stepped irrevocably out of the domain of the "pure arts" into the camp of the "combined arts". Rather than attempting to portray the whole through the part, it now began attempting to portray the whole directly. But with this tremendous difference from all other composite arts – it could do it without losing *control* or *permanence*. With the help of the machine radically different sense materials, light and sound, could be dynamically combined into one work without losing any of the control, subtlety, or concreteness formerly attained only by the pure arts. Cinema was no longer just a visual art (notwithstanding the effort of some directors to keep it such by shooting visual films and pouring the sound track over it like some pleasant, superfluous goo), but had set itself the task of expressing in all its variety and vitality the full consciousness of man.

Instead of continuing to stumble along this road with the system of hit and miss, let us, according to our first law, deliberately turn to life and study the nature of man's consciousness.

Man's nervous system – sensory nerves, brain, and motor nerves – is the seat of his consciousness. The substance or component parts of this consciousness can be determined by the process of elimination. If a man lies still, or, due to some disease or drug, has his motor nerves blocked, his consciousness or wideawakeness is not diminished in any way. If, however, he closes his eyes, it is. If he stops his ears, it is diminished further. If he pinches his nose and does not taste anything and avoids tactile impressions, his awakeness is diminished considerably. And if, as is done in anesthesia, all sensory nerves leading to the brain are blocked, he would lose consciousness completely. (Dreams and internal voices merely being sense impressions of former experiences stored away and served up later by memory.) Thus we can state our second law:

Consciousness is a composite of all the sense impressions conveyed to the brain by the sensory part of the nervous system which can be divided into the great receiving organs – the eyes, ears, nose, mouth, and skin.

By concentrating on one organ at a time, we can list the various elements affecting it. These are, for the eye, peripheral imagery – 180° horizontal × 150° vertical, three dimensionality, color and movement; for the ear, pitch, volume, rhythm, sounds, words, and music; for the nose and mouth, odors and flavors; and for the skin, temperature, texture, and pressure. These divisions – although purely subjective and dependent on vocabulary and techniques of reproduction – are nonetheless useful for analysis.

These elements are the building bricks, which when united create the sensual form of man's consciousness, and the science of art must devote itself to inventing techniques for recording and projecting them in their entirety. Celluloid film is a very crude and primitive means of recording light and is already being replaced by a combination television camera and magnetic tape recorder. Similarly sound recording on film or plastic records is being replaced by tape recording.

Odors will be reduced to basic qualities the way color is into primary colors. The intensity of these will be recorded on magnetic tape, which in turn will control the release from vials into the theaters' air conditioning system. In time all of the above elements will be recorded, mixed, and projected electronically – a reel of the cinema of the future being a roll of magnetic tape with a separate track for each sense material. With these problems solved it is easy to imagine the cinema of the future.

Open your eyes, listen, smell, and feel – sense the world in all its magnificent colors, depth, sounds, odors, and textures – this is the cinema of the future!

The screen will not fill only 5 percent of your visual field as the local movie screen does, or the mere 7.5 percent of Wide Screen, or 18 percent of the "miracle mirror" screen of Cinemascope, or the 25 percent of Cinerama – but 100 percent. The screen will curve past the spectator's ears on both sides and beyond his sphere of vision above and below. In all the praise about the marvels of "peripheral vision", no one paused to state that the human eye has a vertical span of 150 degrees[1] as well as a horizontal one of 180 degrees. The vertical field is difficult, but by no means impossible, to provide. Planetariums have vertical peripheral vision and the cinema of the future will provide it along similar lines. This 180° × 150° oval will be filled with true and not illusory depth. Why? Because as demonstrated above this is another essential element of man's consciousness. Glasses, however, will not be necessary. Electronic and optical means will be devised to create illusory depth without them.

Cinemascope, despite all the raving of its publicity men that it is the "crowning glory" of motion picture development, represents one small step forward, and one big one backward. Its increase of screen image from 5 to 18 percent of man's visual field is a definite improvement although there is still 82 percent to go. It has, however, regressed substantially in clarity. One reason that few critics noticed for Cinerama's excellent illusion of reality is its extraordinary clarity. The human eye is one of the most perfect in the animal kingdom. It is not spotty, out-of-focus, or jumpy the way average movie images are. The image it records is limpid, razor-sharp, and solid as a rock, and Cinerama, by using three film strips instead of one, and specially designed projectors, makes a great advancement towards this perfection. Cinemascope, on the other hand, by still using only one film strip to cover two and one-half the normal screen area, is also magnifying grain, and softening the focus two and one-half times, making clarity much worse than it is on the normal screen.[2] The electrically created image of tomorrow's film will be perfect in focus and stability – the grain and spots vanishing along with the film stock.

Stereophonic sound will be developed so that the spectator will be enclosed within a sphere, the walls of which will be saturated with dozens of speakers. Sounds will come from every direction – the sides, top, back and bottom – as they do in real life.

The large number of speakers will permit a much better identity of image and sound than is achieved now where the sound leaping from one distant speaker to another is either behind or ahead of the image. The air will be filled with odors and up to the point of discretion or aesthetic function we will feel changes of temperature and the texture of things. We will feel physically and mentally transported into a new world.

Yes, the cinema of the future will far surpass the "Feelies" of Aldous Huxley's *Brave New World*. And like many other things in this book that are nightmarish because superficially understood, it will be a great new power, surpassing conventional art forms like a Rocket Ship outspeeds the horse and whose ability to destroy or build men's souls will depend purely on the people behind it.

The mastery of so many sense materials poses another problem – selection. People already complain about the excess of realism in films and say the new inventions shall plunge us from bad to worse. Although the spirit of their complaint is valid, their use of the word "realism" is not. "Realism", or, in aesthetic terms, "experience", is that something which is created by the unity of the outer world with the inner. No matter how extensive the artist's means, he must use them to provoke more of the spectator's participation, not less. For without the active participation of the spectator there can be no transfer of *consciousness, no art*. Thus art is never "too" realistic. When either too much or too little is given, there just isn't any "realism". Poor use of cinema's remarkable new powers is no more of a case against them than daubing with oils is a case against painting.

Every capable artist has been able to draw men into the realm of a new experience by making (either consciously or subconsciously) a profound study of the way their attention shifts. Like a magician he learns to lead man's attention with a line, a color, a gesture, or a sound. Many are the devices to control the spectator's attention at the opera, ballet, and theater. But the inability to eliminate the unessential is what loosens their electrifying grip on the attention of a spectator and causes them to remain secondary arts.

The evolution of the aesthetic form of cinema can, in a way, be described as a continuation of the artist's struggle to master attention. Griffith began using the "close-up" to draw the spectator's attention to a significant visual detail. Lenses with narrow focus fields were devised to throw foreground and background out of focus, riveting the eye only on the sharp part of the image. Pudovkin developed the close-up in time by varying camera speeds to parallel the varying intensity of man's observations. Eisenstein proclaimed "montage" and Griffith discovered "parallel cutting", both magnificent weapons in the director's arsenal of attention. Shots and scenes could now be shifted with the same freedom and rapidity possible in man's natural observation or imagination. Sound arrived with undiminished intensity, but in time it too became refined in content, pitch, and volume, sometimes dominating the scene, sometimes leaving it completely, leading the ear as precisely as the eye. But like the search for an additional number of sense materials, the principles involved in this refinement of attention were mostly stumbled on by accident – rarely searched for deliberately, and never formulated consciously.

Again, the only place to search is in the mind of man. We must try to learn how man shifts his attention normally in any situation.

Suppose we are standing on a hilltop overlooking the countryside. First we are struck by the huge sweep of the view before us. Then we notice the vivid green of the fields and the sunshine. Then the silent expansion and rolling of a cumulus cloud entrances us. We feel a warm gust of wind and our nostrils dilate at the smell of new-mown hay. Suddenly, our ears sharpen as the shriek of a jet plane cuts the air. We cannot see it, but we linger on the way its high-tone lowers in pitch and fades away. Here is an example of how attention shifts from one element (space – color – then movement, in our example) within a single sense (the eye) and from one sense to another (the eye, the skin, the nose, the ear). In each moment it fixes itself, if for only an instant, on one sense element to the partial or complete exclusion of all others.

It is estimated that each sense monopolizes man's attention in the following proportions:

Sight	70%
Hearing	20%
Smell	5%
Touch	4%
Taste	1%

Men can have their attention led for them as a bird will do by flying across an empty sky, or can willfully direct it as everyone does at the dinner table when singling out one voice from the maze of chatter. In each case the criterion is "what is the point of greatest interest and significance to me?" Thousands of sense impressions stimulate the sensory nerves every second of the day, but only one or a few are permitted to enter the *realm of higher consciousness at a time*. The organ that screens them out is the brain. The brain is the storehouse – the memory of the physical and spiritual needs of the individual, and through him of the human race, and it is according to this criteria – "what is beneficial for the development of the individual and racial life force?" that a decision is made. We can now state the third law of our methodology of art:

The brain of man shifts rapidly from element to element within each sense and from sense to sense in the approximate proportion of sight, 70 percent; hearing, 20 percent; smell, 5 percent; touch, 4 percent; and taste, 1 percent, selecting one impression at a time according to the needs of individual and racial development.

These unite into the dynamic stream of sensations we call "consciousness". The cinema of the future will be the first direct, complete and conscious application of this law. Since the conventional movie screen fills only 5 percent of the spectator's field of vision, it automatically represents his point of visual attention and the director needs only to point his camera to control the point of attention. But with the invention of means to fill 100 percent of the spectator's field of vision with sharp imagery, he must solve the problem of visual attention another way or lose his main aesthetic power.

In life, only the object being observed is in focus. The area of focus is not necessarily rectangular, including everything in the same plane, as it is in today's films, but can be circular, triangular, vertical, or horizontal, depending on the shape of the objects of interest. Electrical and optical means will be developed to duplicate this flexibility, retaining the hazy frame of peripheral vision as the human eye does for added realism. Naturally, the great visual oval of the camera field will include, exclude, move closer, and recede as it does in life. This zone of focus will generally be at the center of the visual field, but it will be free to shift up and down, or around to the sides, leading the eye wherever it goes. The direction, quality, and intensity of all other sense elements will be controlled and pin-pointed in the same subtle manner.

Each basic sense will dominate the scene in roughly the same proportion we found them to have in man. That is, sight, 70 percent; sound, 20 percent; smell, 5 percent; touch, 4 percent; and taste, 1 percent. Nature turns them on and off without a whimper but film-makers once in possession of a new power usually cling to it like a drowning man to a life raft. Eye-irritating colors, ear-deafening dialogue, and soul-sickening music are loaded one on top of another just to "make sure the point gets across". The cinema of the future will turn off any and all of it, including the visual part, when the theme calls for it. For, and it cannot be stressed too strongly, the cinema of the future will no longer be a "visual art", but an "art of consciousness".

When a great many sense materials are presented in sharp focus simultaneously the spectator must do his own selecting. He is no longer being led along by a work of art, but must begin with great fatigue to create his own patterns. This situation is so life-like that it gives the spectator the sensation of being *physically* in the scene. For example, in Cinerama's famous roller coaster sequence, the spectator's body, not his soul, is riding the roller coaster. This is a tremendous faculty and will, I am sure, be used to great effect in the cinema of the future, but it must be used with great discretion. For aside from being very tiring, after one too many loops, the spectator may be so thoroughly convinced that he is shooting the chutes as to throw up on the lady in front of him. As stated before, art is a specific technique for living vicariously, of weeping without actually losing a loved one, of thrilling to the hunt without being mangled by a lion, in short of reaping the lessons and spiritual nourishment of experience without any loss. The solution of the problem of focus will invalidate the opinion that the widescreen is no good for "the intimate thing". If man can have intimate moments in life with his peripheral vision, stereophonic hearing, smell, and touch, so can his art.

It would seem from the preceding analysis that my conception of the function of the cinema of the future is faithfully to reproduce man's superficial and immediate perception of the world about him. Nothing could be further from the truth. The history of art demonstrates over and over again that some of the most valid experiences come from the inner and not the outer world. But the history not only of art but any other human endeavor, also proves that the outer precedes the inner. The outer world supplies the raw materials of creation. Man cannot originate. He can only take the forces of nature and rearrange them into shapes more friendly to his own existence. Just as nature had to provide water, iron, fire and the laws of thermodynamics before someone could invent the steam engine so nature must supply man with raw impressions before he can fashion them into an imagery more meaningful and useful to himself. The first task of painting was to copy the world, and only when the camera relieved it of this mirror-like function was it really free to explore the full range of man's fantasy. At first, motion picture cameras and sound recorders could not even capture the simplest aspects of man's perception of the outer world. Now, though still far from matching some of these, they are far superior to others. Slow motion, fast motion, and infrared ray photography are able to "see" things no human eye can.

Supersensitive microphones are now able to "hear" sounds way beyond the range of human ears. Similarly, directors at first had to be content with what the natural scene about them offered. Then, in studios, they began to select and arrange what went before the lens. By building sets, and developing trick photography, they could set the world of history and fantasy before the lens. Then, by perfecting the technique of animation, they could do without bulky sets and intricate models entirely and give free reign to their wildest imagination.

Sound has followed a similar evolution – from the objective to the subjective world. First we recorded only natural sounds, or the sounds created by human voices and musical instruments. Then we invented a whole series of odd new sound-making instruments and set them about the microphone. Now people like Norman McLaren are dispensing with expensive instruments and microphones entirely and are creating sound never before heard by painting directly on the sound track.

These developments bring us to our fourth law:

> In his creative process, man is imposed on by outer impressions. He learns the secrets of their basic principles through imitation and then subjects these to the needs of his own expression. He goes from reception to imitation to creation, i.e. from portraying the outer to portraying the inner world.

This law will inevitably hold true for the cinema of the future. While it still must learn to faithfully reproduce man's outer world as perceived in his consciousness, it will eventually learn to create totally new sense materials for each of the senses – shapes, movements, colors, sounds, smells, and tastes – they have never known before, and to arrange them into forms of consciousness never before experienced by man in his contact with the outer world.

[. . .]

Thus, individually and collectively, by thoroughly applying the methodology of art, the cinema of the future will become the first art form to reveal the new scientific world to man in the full sensual vividness and dynamic vitality of his consciousness.

Notes

1   The naked eye actually has a vertical range of 180 degrees, but this is reduced to approximately 150 degrees by the brow and cheek of the head.
2   Vistavision, by photographing a negative frame twice the original size, before printing a normal size positive, has partially returned the screen image to its usual sharpness.

Cinema and Digital Media

3

LEV MANOVICH

Cinema gives birth to a computer

Let us reverse a well-known wisdom: that a modern digital computer is a typical war-time technology developed for the purposes of calculation and real-time control and that its current use to create moving images is a rather specialized and recent application. Not only were computers used to create moving images within a few years of their "birth" but, in fact, the modern digital computer was born from cinema.

What is cinema? If we believe the word itself ("cinematograph" means "writing movement"), its essence is recording and storing visible data in a material form. A film camera records data on film; a film projector reads it off. This cinematic apparatus is similar to a computer in one key respect: a computer is controlled by a program stored externally on some medium. Therefore, it is not accidental that a diagram of the Universal Turing Machine looks suspiciously like a film projector. In fact, the development of a suitable storage medium and a method for coding data represent important parts of both cinema and computer pre-histories. As we know, the former eventually settled on discrete images recorded on a strip of celluloid; the latter – which needed much greater speed of access as well as the ability to quickly read and write data – on storing it electronically in a binary code.

So why was the digital computer born from cinema?

Jacquard loom

Around 1800 J. M. Jacquard invented a loom which was automatically controlled by punched paper cards. The loom was used to weave intricate figurative images, including Jacquard's portrait. This specialized graphics computer inspired Charles Babbage in his work on the Analytical Engine, a general computer for numerical calculations. As Ada Augusta, the daughter of Lord Byron and the first computer programmer, put it, "the Analytical Engine weaves algebraical patterns just as the Jacquard loom weaves flowers and leaves".[1]

Thus, a programmed machine was already synthesizing images even before it was put to processing numbers.

Zuse's film

Even more interesting is the case of Konrad Zuse. Starting in 1936 and continuing into the Second World War, Zuse had been building a computer in the living room of his parents' apartment in Berlin. Zuse's computer pioneered some of the basic ideas of computing: binary arithmetic, floating decimal point and program control by punched tape. For the tape, he used discarded 35 mm movie film.[2]

One of these surviving pieces of film shows the abstract program codes punched over the original frames of some interior shot. The iconic code of cinema is discarded in favor of the more efficient binary one. In a technological remake of the Oedipus complex, a son murders his father. But the story has a new twist – a happy one. Zuse's film with its strange super-imposition of the binary over iconic anticipates the process which gets underway half a century later: the convergence of all media, including film, to digital code. Cinema and computer – the Jacquard loom and the Analytical Engine – merge into one.

Digital media

This story can be summarized as follows. A modern digital computer is developed to perform calculations on numerical data more efficiently; it takes over from numerous mechanical tabulators and calculators already widely employed by companies and governments since the turn of the century. In parallel, we witness the rise of modern media which allow the storage of images, image sequences, sounds and text in different material forms: a photographic plate, a film stock, a gramophone record, etc.

The synthesis of these two histories? The translation, which is taking place today, of all existing media into numerical data accessible for computers. The result: digital media – graphics, moving images, sounds, shapes, spaces and text which become computable, i.e. simply another set of computer data.

If before a computer would read in a row of numbers outputting a statistical result or a gun trajectory, now it can read in pixel values, blurring the image, adjusting its contrast or checking whether it contains an outline of a gun. The iconic – Barthes's famous "message without a code" – finally became securely codified. (It is interesting that image processing and semiotic analysis of iconic signs both develop at the same time – the second half of the 1950s.) And while the numeric coding of an image did not, of course, fulfill the semiotic desire to divide an image into units of meaning, it did come just at the right time for the enormous economic, ideological and military interests already dependent on the instrumental use of the visible and therefore looking for a more efficient way for it to be recorded, stored, manipulated, reproduced, transmitted and displayed. The society of the Spectacle was destined to embrace digital media.

Cinema prepares digital media

Cinema not only plays a special role in the history of the computer. Since the late nineteenth century, cinema was also preparing us for digital media in a more direct way. It worked to make familiar such "digital" concepts as sampling, random access, or a database – in order to allow us to swallow the digital revolution as painlessly as possible. Gradually, cinema taught us to accept the manipulation of time and space, the arbitrary coding of the visible, the mechanization of vision, and the reduction of reality to a moving image as a given. As a result, today the conceptual shock of the digital revolution is not experienced as a real shock – because we were ready for it for a long time.

Sampling

Any digital representation consists of a limited number of samples, a fact which is usually illustrated by a grid of pixels – a sampling of two-dimensional space. Cinema prepares us for digital media because it is already based on sampling – the sampling of time. Cinema samples time twenty-four times per second. All that remains is to take this already discrete representation and to quantify it. But this is simply a mechanical step; what cinema accomplished is a much more difficult conceptual break from the continuous to the discrete.

Cinema is not the only media technology which, emerging towards the end of the nineteenth century, is dependent on a discrete representation. If cinema samples time, fax transmission of images, starting in 1907, samples two-dimensional space; even earlier, the first television experiments (Carey 1875; Nipkow 1884) already involve the sampling of both.[3] However, reaching mass popularity much earlier than these other technologies, cinema is the first to make public knowledge the principle of a discrete representation.

Random access

Another key quality of digital media is random access. For instance, once a film is digitized and loaded into the computer memory, any frame can be accessed equally fast. Therefore, if film samples time but still preserves its linear ordering (subsequent moments of time become subsequent frames), digital media abandons this "human-centered" representation altogether in order to put time fully under our control. Time is mapped onto two-dimensional space, where it can be managed, analyzed and manipulated more easily.

Such mapping was already widely used in nineteenth-century cinema machines. The Phenakistiscope, the Zootrope, the Zoopraxiscope, the Tachyscope, and Marey's photographic gun were all based on placing a number of slightly different images around the perimeter of a circle. Even more striking is the case of Thomas Edison's first cinema apparatus. In 1887 Edison and his assistant, William Dickson, began experiments to adopt the already proven technology of a phonograph record for recording and displaying of motion pictures. Using a special picture-recording camera, tiny pinpoint-size photographs were placed in spirals on a cylindrical cell similar in size to the phonographic cylinder. A cylinder was to hold 42,000 images, each so small ($\frac{1}{2}$ inch wide) that a viewer would have to look at them through a microscope.[4] The storage capacity of this medium was twenty-eight minutes – twenty-eight minutes of continuous time taken apart, flattened on a surface and mapped into a two-dimensional grid. In short, time was prepared to be recreated, manipulated and reordered.

Simulation

It would not be difficult to show how cinema has been preparing us for other concepts now associated with digital media, but, given the limitations of space, I want to focus on the most important one: simulation.

Digital media makes commonplace the simulation of nonexistent realistic worlds. Examples include military simulators, Virtual Reality, computer games, television ("virtual sets" technology), and, of course, special effects of Hollywood films such as *Terminator 2*, *Jurassic Park* and *Casper*. These films demonstrate that, given enough time and money, almost anything can be simulated. Yet, they also exemplify the triviality of what at first may appear to be an outstanding technical achievement – the ability to fake visual reality. For what is faked, of course, is not reality but photographic reality, reality as seen by the camera lens. In other words, what digital simulation has (almost) achieved is not realism, but only photo-realism – the ability to fake not our perceptual and bodily experience of reality but only its film image. This image exists outside of our bodies, on a screen – a window of limited size which presents a still imprint of a small part of outer reality, filtered through the lens with its limited depth of field, filtered through film's grain and its limited tonal range. It is only this film-based image which digital technology has learned to simulate. And the reason we think that this technology has succeeded in faking reality is that cinema, over the course of the last hundred years, has taught us to accept its particular representational form as reality.

What is faked is only a cinematic image. Once we came to accept a moving photograph as reality, the way to its future simulation was open. Conceptually, simulated worlds already appeared with the first films of the Lumières and Georges Méliès in the 1890s. It is they who invented simulation.

A hundred years ago cinema had reduced reality to flat moving images, the images which we now can easily simulate using computers. And it is becoming clear that it is ultimately more advantageous to simulate the world than to film it directly. A simulated image can represent non-existent reality, it can be endlessly modified, it is more manageable, and so on. Because of this our society will try to use digital simulations whenever possible.

Cinema, which was the key method to represent the world throughout the twentieth century, is destined to be replaced by digital media: the numeric, the computable, the synthetic. The historical role played by cinema was to prepare us to live comfortably in the world of two-dimensional moving illusions. Having played this role well, cinema exits the stage. Enter the computer.

Notes

1   Charles and Ray Eames, A *Computer Perspective: Background to the Computer Age*, Harvard University Press, Cambridge, Mass., 1990, 18.
2   Ibid., 120.
3   Albert Abramson, *Electronic Motion Pictures: A History of the Television Camera*, University of California Press, Berkeley, 1955, 15–24.
4   Charles Musser, *The Emergence of Cinema: The American Screen to 1907*, University of California Press, Berkeley, 1994, 65.

PART TWO

DEFINITIONS AND DETERMINISM

Introduction

Theorists have long been concerned with what motivates the emergence and development of cinema's physical devices and the aesthetic corollaries of these tools. Such debates shift how we might define technology, moving beyond an isolated description of cinema's machines to consider the broader forces that play a part in shaping and determining their form and function.

For André Bazin, the enduring myth of a total cinema, which he describes as "the reconstruction of a perfect illusion of the outside world in sound, color, and relief", transcends economic, ideological and scientific determinants. Cinema's emergence can be accounted for in terms of an underlying momentum, an incessant movement towards the total replication of the physical world. "The cinema owes virtually nothing to the scientific spirit", he contends. More important is how the imaginations of cinema's pioneers have envisaged the pursuit of reality, "a recreation of the world in its own image, an image unburdened by the freedom of interpretation of the artist or the irreversibility of time".

By proposing that technological progress stems from the preconceived ideas of its pioneers, as opposed to the tangible conditions of scientific discovery, Bazin raises the important question of why cinema rose to prominence at the moment it did. In technological terms, he contends, "it is clear that all the definitive stages of the invention of the cinema had been reached before the requisite conditions had been fulfilled". According to Bazin, it is the visualization and projection of an idea that anticipates and in turn shapes scientific and industrial discovery.

For Jean-Louis Comolli, there are always material determinants for the form and function of any given technology. What Comolli describes as the "cinema machine", for instance, suggests more than simply physical tools. "The cinema", he argues, was "born immediately as a social machine . . . from the anticipation and confirmation of its *social profitability*; economic, ideological and symbolic". Physical devices reflect this "social machine", perpetuating the belief systems dominant within society.

The camera, as one example, symbolizes the ideological demands dominant at the time of its emergence and perfection. A reading of its "social profitability" aims to pull it apart, questioning every stage of its historical development. We take for granted, for instance, that the camera's representational system is founded on the rules of perspective, in turn based on the human eye. For Comolli, however, this scenario is neither natural nor inevitable. The camera manifests and perpetuates a distinctly western metaphysical tradition, which equates the visible with the real and prioritizes sight above other forms of perception.

Douglas Gomery explains technological change in terms of industrial and economic impera-tives. The precise model he develops is founded on the assumption that companies will always act in ways designed to enhance profit. Accordingly, for Hollywood corporations and those in related industries, technological change is carefully managed and exploited for commercial gain.

Examining the coming of sound in the late 1920s, Gomery explores technological change in terms of successive processes of invention, innovation and diffusion. "Sound films did not spring Minerva-like onto the movie screens of twenties America", he suggests, they arrived according to a sustained transformation over a period of thirty years. During this time, "the movie studios and their suppliers of sound equipment formulated business decisions with a view toward maximizing long-run profits", an approach to technological change that "propelled the American motion picture industry . . . into a new era of growth and prosperity".

The stages by which a given technology emerges are central to debates and discussions concerning various fields, but take on specific relevance to cinema if we consider it to function, in the first instance, as a technological base. In seeking to identify the factors that have shaped, and continue to shape, the technological development of cinema, perspectives range from the determined to the determinable.

The Myth of Total Cinema

ANDRE BAZIN

Paradoxically enough, the impression left on the reader by Georges Sadoul's admirable book on the origins of the cinema is of a reversal, in spite of the author's Marxist views, of the relations between an economic and technical evolution and the imagination of those carrying on the search. The way things happened seems to call for a reversal of the historical order of causality, which goes from the economic infrastructure to the ideological superstructure, and for us to consider the basic technical discoveries as fortunate accidents but essentially second in importance to the preconceived ideas of the inventors. The cinema is an idealistic phenomenon. The concept men had of it existed so to speak fully armed in their minds, as if in some platonic heaven, and what strikes us most of all is the obstinate resistance of matter to ideas rather than of any help offered by techniques to the imagination of the researchers.

Furthermore, the cinema owes virtually nothing to the scientific spirit. Its begetters are in no sense savants, except for Marey, but it is significant that he was only interested in analyzing movement and not in reconstructing it. Even Edison is basically only a do-it-yourself man of genius, a giant of the *concours Lépine*. Niepce, Muybridge, Leroy, Joly, Demeny, even Louis Lumière himself, are all monomaniacs, men driven by an impulse, do-it-yourself men or at best ingenious industrialists. As for the wonderful, the sublime E. Reynaud, who can deny that his animated drawings are the result of an unremitting pursuit of an *idée fixe*? Any account of the cinema that was drawn merely from the technical inventions that made it possible would be a poor one indeed. On the contrary, an approximate and complicated visualization of an idea invariably precedes the industrial discovery which alone can open the way to its practical use. Thus if it is evident to us today that the cinema even at its most elementary stage needed a transparent, flexible, and resistant base and a dry sensitive emulsion capable of receiving an image instantly – everything else being a matter of setting in order a mechanism far less complicated than an eighteenth-century clock – it is clear that all the definitive stages of the invention of the cinema had been reached before the requisite conditions had been fulfilled. In 1877 and 1880, Muybridge, thanks to the imaginative generosity of a horse-lover, managed to construct a large complex device which enabled him to make from the image of a galloping horse the first series of cinematographic pictures. However, to get this result he had to be satisfied with wet collodion on a glass plate, that is to say, with just one of the three necessary elements – namely instantaneity, dry emulsion, flexible base. After the discovery of gelatino-bromide of silver but before the appearance on the market of the first celluloid reels, Marey had made a genuine camera which used glass plates. Even after the appearance of celluloid strips Lumière tried to use paper film.

Once more let us consider here only the final and complete form of the photographic cinema. The synthesis of simple movements studied scientifically by Plateau had no need to wait upon the industrial and economic developments of the nineteenth century. As Sadoul correctly points out, nothing had stood in the way, from antiquity, of the manufacture of a phenakistoscope or a zootrope. It is true that here the labors of that genuine savant Plateau were at the origin of the many inventions that made the popular use of his discovery possible. But while, with the photographic cinema, we have cause for some astonishment that the discovery somehow precedes the technical conditions necessary to its existence, we must here explain, on the other hand, how it was that the invention took so long to emerge, since all the prerequisites had been assembled and the persistence of the image on the retina had been known for a long time. It might be of some use to point out that although the two were not necessarily connected scientifically, the efforts of Plateau are pretty well contemporary with those of Nicéphore Niepce, as if the attention of researchers had waited to concern itself with synthesizing movement until chemistry quite independently of optics had become concerned, on its part, with the automatic fixing of the image.[1]

I emphasize the fact that this historical coincidence can apparently in no way be explained on grounds of scientific, economic, or industrial evolution. The photographic cinema could just as well have grafted itself onto a phenakistoscope foreseen as long ago as the sixteenth century. The delay in the invention of the latter is as disturbing a phenomenon as the existence of the precursors of the former.

But if we examine their work more closely, the direction of their research is manifest in the instruments themselves, and, even more undeniably, in their writings and commentaries we see that these precursors were indeed more like prophets. Hurrying past the various stopping places, the very first of which materially speaking should have halted them, it was at the very height and summit that most of them were aiming. In their imaginations they saw the cinema as a total and complete representation of reality; they saw in a trice the reconstruction of a perfect illusion of the outside world in sound, color, and relief.

As for the latter, the film historian P. Potoniée has even felt justified in maintaining that it was not the discovery of photography but of stereoscopy, which came onto the market just slightly before the first attempts at animated photography in 1851, that opened the eyes of the researchers. Seeing people immobile in space, the photographers realized that what they needed was movement if their photographs were to become a picture of life and a faithful copy of nature. In any case, there was not a single inventor who did not try to combine sound and relief with animation of the image – whether it be Edison with his kinetoscope made to be attached to a phonograph, or Demeny and his talking portraits, or even Nadar who shortly before producing the first photographic interview, on Chevreul, had written, "My dream is to see the photograph register the bodily movements and the facial expressions of a speaker while the phonograph is recording his speech" (February 1887). If color had not yet appeared it was because the first experiments with the three-color process were slower in coming. But E. Reynaud had been painting his little figurines for some time and the first films of Méliès are colored by stencilling. There are numberless writings, all of them more or less wildly enthusiastic, in which inventors conjure up nothing less than a total cinema that is to provide that complete illusion of life which is still a long way away. Many are familiar with that passage from L'Éve Future in which Villiers de l'Isle-Adam, two years before Edison had begun his researches on animated photography, puts into the inventor's mouth the following description of a fantastic achievement:

> the vision, its transparent flesh miraculously photographed in color and wearing a spangled costume, danced a kind of popular Mexican dance. Her movements had the flow of life itself, thanks to the process of successive photography which can retain six minutes of movement on microscopic glass, which is subsequently reflected by means of a powerful lampascope. Suddenly was heard a flat and unnatural voice, dull-sounding and harsh. The dancer was singing the *alza* and the *olé* that went with her *fandango*.

The guiding myth, then, inspiring the invention of cinema, is the accomplishment of that which dominated in a more or less vague fashion all the techniques of the mechanical reproduction of reality in the nineteenth century, from photography to the phonograph, namely an integral realism, a recreation of the world in its own image, an image unburdened by the freedom of interpretation of the artist or the irreversibility of time. If cinema in its cradle lacked all the attributes of the cinema to come, it was with reluctance and because its fairy guardians were unable to provide them however much they would have liked to.

If the origins of an art reveal something of its nature, then one may legitimately consider the silent and the sound film as stages of a technical development that little by little made a reality out of the original "myth". It is understandable from this point of view that it would be absurd to take the silent film as a state of primal perfection which has gradually been forsaken by the realism of sound and color. The primacy of the image is both historically and technically accidental. The nostalgia that some still feel for the silent screen does not go far enough back into the childhood of the seventh art. The real primitives of the cinema, existing only in the imaginations of a few men of the nineteenth century, are in complete imitation of nature. Every new development added to the cinema must, paradoxically, take it nearer and nearer to its origins. In short, cinema has not yet been invented!

It would be a reversal then of the concrete order of causality, at least psychologically, to place the scientific discoveries or the industrial techniques that have loomed so large in its development at the source of the cinema's invention. Those who had the least confidence in the future of the cinema were precisely the two industrialists Edison and Lumière. Edison was satisfied with just his kinetoscope and if Lumière judiciously refused to sell his patent to Méliès it was undoubtedly because he hoped to make a large profit out of it for himself, but only as a plaything of which the public would soon tire. As for the real savants such as Marey, they were only of indirect assistance to the cinema. They had a specific purpose in mind and were satisfied when they had accomplished it. The fanatics, the madmen, the disinterested pioneers, capable, as was Berard Palissy, of burning their furniture for a few seconds of shaky images, are neither industrialists nor savants, just men obsessed by their own imaginings. The cinema was born from the converging of these various obsessions, that is to say, out of a myth, the myth of total cinema. This likewise adequately explains the delay of Plateau in applying the optical principle of the persistence of the image on the retina, as also the continuous progress of the syntheses of movement as compared with the state of photographic techniques. The fact is that each alike was dominated by the imagination of the century. Undoubtedly there are other examples in the history of techniques and inventions of the convergence of research, but one must distinguish between those which come as a result precisely of scientific evolution and industrial or military requirements and those which quite clearly precede them. Thus, the myth of Icarus had to wait on the internal combustion engine before descending from the platonic heavens. But it had dwelt in the soul of everyman since he first thought about birds. To some extent, one could say the same thing about the myth of cinema, but its forerunners prior to the nineteenth century have only a remote connection with the myth which we share today and which has prompted the appearance of the mechanical arts that characterize today's world.

Note

1   The frescoes or bas-reliefs of Egypt indicate a desire to analyze rather than to synthesize movement. As for the automatons of the eighteenth century their relation to cinema is like the relation of painting to photography. Whatever the truth of the matter and even if the automatons from the time of Descartes and Pascal on foreshadowed the machines of the nineteenth century, it is no different from the way that *trompe-l'oeil* in painting attested to a chronic taste for likeness. But the technique of *trompe-l'oeil* did nothing to advance optics and the chemistry of photography; it confined itself, if I can use the expression, to "playing the monkey" to them by anticipation.

Besides, just as the word indicates, the aesthetic of *trompe-l'oeil* in the eighteenth century resided more in illusion than in realism, that is to say, in a lie rather than the truth. A statue painted on a wall should look as if it were standing on a pedestal in space. To some extent, this is what the early cinema was aiming at, but this operation of cheating quickly gave way to an ontogenetic realism.

Machines of the Visible

5

JEAN-LOUIS COMOLLI

Introduction

One of the hypotheses tried out in some of the fragments here gathered together would be on the one hand that the cinema – the historically constitutable cinematic statements – functions with and in the set of apparatuses of representation at work in a society. There are not only the representations produced by the representative apparatuses as such (painting, theatre, cinema, etc.); there are also, participating in the movement of the whole, the systems of the delegation of power (political representation), the ceaseless working-up of social imaginaries (historical, ideological representations) and a large part, even, of the modes of relational behavior (balances of power, confrontations, maneuvers of seduction, strategies of defence, marking of differences or affiliations). On the other hand, but at the same time, the hypothesis would be that a society is only such in that it is *driven by representation*. If the social machine manufactures representations, it also manufactures *itself* from representations – the latter operative at once as means, matter and condition of sociality.

Thus the historical variation of cinematic techniques, their appearance–disappearance, their phases of convergence, their periods of dominance and decline seem to me to depend not on a rational–linear order of technological perfectibility nor an autonomous instance of scientific "progress", but much rather on the offsettings, adjustments, arrangements carried out by a social configuration in order to represent itself, that is, at once to grasp itself, identify itself and itself produce itself in its representation.

What happened with the invention of cinema? It was not sufficient that it be technically feasible, it was not sufficient that a camera, a projector, a strip of images be technically ready.[1] Moreover, they were already there, more or less ready, more or less invented, a long time already before the formal invention of cinema, fifty years before Edison and the Lumière brothers. It was necessary that something else be constituted, that something else be formed: the *cinema machine*, which is not essentially the camera, the film, the projector, which is not merely a combination of instruments, apparatuses, techniques. Which is a machine: a *dispositif* articulating between one another different sets – technological certainly, but also economic and ideological. A *dispositif* was required which implicates its motivations, which be the arrangement of demands, desires, fantasies, speculations (in the two senses of commerce and the imaginary): an arrangement which gives apparatus and techniques a social status and function.

The cinema is born immediately as a social machine, and thus not from the sole invention of its equipment but rather from the experimental supposition and verification, from the anticipation and confirmation of its *social profitability*; economic, ideological and symbolic. One could just as well propose that it is the spectators who invent cinema: the chain that knots together the waiting queues, the money paid and the spectators' looks filled with admiration.

> Never [say Gilles Deleuze and Claire Parnet] is an arrangement-combination tech-
> nological, indeed it is always the contrary. The tools always presuppose a machine,
> and the machine is always social before it is technical. There is always a social machine
> which selects or assigns the technical elements used. A tool, an instrument, remains
> marginal or little used for as long as the social machine or the collective arrangement-
> combination capable of taking it in its *phylum* does not exist.[2]

The hundreds of little machines in the nineteenth century destined for a more or less clumsy reproduction of the image and the movement of life are picked up in this "phylum" of the great representative machine, in that zone of attraction, lineage, influences that is created by the displacement of the social co-ordinates of analogical representation.

The second half of the nineteenth century lives in a sort of frenzy of the visible. It is, of course, the effect of the social multiplication of images: ever wider distribution of illustrated papers, waves of prints, caricatures, etc. The effect also, however, of something of a geographical extension of the field of the visible and the representable: by journies, explorations, colon-izations, the whole world becomes visible at the same time that it becomes appropriatable. Similarly, there is a visibility of the expansion of industrialism, of the transformations of the landscape, of the production of towns and metropolises. There is, again, the development of the mechanical manufacture of objects which determines by a faultless force of repetition their ever identical reproduction, thus standardizing the idea of the (artisanal) copy into that of the (industrial) series. Thanks to the same principles of mechanical repetition, the movements of men and animals become in some sort more visible than they had been: movement becomes a visible mechanics. The mechanical opens out and multiplies the visible and between them is established a *complicity* all the stronger in that the codes of analogical figuration slip irresistibly from painting to photography and then from the latter to cinematography.

At the very same time that it is thus fascinated and gratified by the multiplicity of scopic instruments which lay a thousand views beneath its gaze, the human eye loses its immemorial privilege; the mechanical eye of the photographic machine now sees *in its place*, and in certain aspects with more sureness. The photograph stands as at once the triumph and the grave of the eye. There is a violent decentring of the place of mastery in which since the Renaissance the look had come to reign; to which testifies, in my opinion, the return, synchronous with the rise of photography, of everything that the legislation of the classic optics – that geo-metrical *ratio* which made of the eye the point of convergence and centring of the perspective rays of the visible – had long repressed and which hardly remained other than in the controlled form of anamorphoses: the massive return to the front of the stage of the optical aberrations, illusions, dissolutions. Light becomes less obvious, sets itself as problem and challenge to sight. A whole host of inventors, lecturers and image showmen experiment and exploit in every way the optical phenomena which appear irrational from the standpoint of the established science (refraction, mirages, spectrum, diffraction, interferences, retinal persistence, etc.). Precisely, a new conception of light is put together, in which the notion of wave replaces that of ray and puts an end to the schema of rectilinear propagation, in which optics thus overturned is now coupled with a chemistry of light.

Decentred, in panic, thrown into confusion by all this new magic of the visible, the human eye finds itself affected with a series of limits and doubts. The mechanical eye, the photographic lens, while it intrigues and fascinates, functions also as a *guarantor* of the identity of the visible with the normality of vision. If the photographic illusion, as later the cinematographic illusion, fully gratifies the spectator's taste for delusion, it also reassures him or her in that the delusion is in conformity with the norm of visual perception. The mechanical magic of the analogical representation of the visible is accomplished and articulated from a doubt as to the fidelity of human vision, and more widely as to the truth of sensory impressions.

I wonder if it is not from this, from this lack to be filled, that could have come the extreme eagerness of the first spectators to *recognize* in the images of the first films – devoid of color, nuance, fluidity – the identical image, the double of life itself. If there is not, in the very principle of representation, a force of disavowal which gives free rein to an analogical illusion that is yet only weakly manifested by the iconic signifiers themselves? If it was not necessary at these first shows to forcefully deny the manifest difference between the filmic image and the retinal image in order to be assured of a new hold on the visible, subject in turn to the law of mechanical reproduction . . .

The camera seen

The camera, then.

For it is here indeed, on this *camera-site*, that a confrontation occurs between two discourses: one which locates cinematic technology in ideology, the other which locates it in science. Note that whether we are told that what is essential in the technical equipment which serves to produce a film has its founding origin in a network of scientific knowledges or whether we are told that that equipment is governed by the ideological representations and demands dominant at the time it was perfected, in both cases – discourse of technicians on the one hand, attempts to elaborate a materialist theory of the cinema on the other – the example given is *always* that which produces the cinematic *image*, and it *alone*, considered from the sole point of view of *optics*.[3]

Thus what is in question is a certain image of the camera: metonymically, it represents the whole of cinema technology, it is the part for the whole. It is brought forward as the *visible part* for the *whole of the technics*. This symptomatic displacement must be examined in the very manner of posing the articulation of the couple Technology/Ideology.

To elect the camera as "delegated" representative of the whole of cinematic equipment is not merely synecdochical (the part for the whole). It is above all an operation of reduction (of the whole to the part), to be questioned in that, *theoretically*, it reproduces and confirms the split which is ceaselessly marked in the technical practice of cinema (not only in the practice of filmmakers and technicians and in the spontaneous ideology of that practice; but also in the "idea", the ideological representation that spectators have of work in cinema: concentration on shooting and studio, occultation of laboratory and editing) between the *visible* part of the technology of cinema (camera, shooting, crew, lighting, screen) and its *"invisible"* part (black between frames, chemical processing, baths and laboratory work, negative film, cuts and joins of editing, sound track, projector, etc.), the latter repressed by the former, generally relegated to the realm of the unthought, the "unconscious" of cinema. It is symptomatic, for example, that Lebel, so concerned to assert the scientific regulation of cinema, thinks to deduce it only from geometrical optics, mentioning only once retinal persistence which nevertheless is what brings into play the specific difference between cinema and photography, the synthesis of movement (and the scientific work which made it possible); at the same time that he quite simply forgets the other patron science of cinema and photography, photochemistry, without which the camera would be no more precisely than a *camera obscura*. As for Pleynet's remarks, they apply indiscriminately to the quattrocento *camera obscura*, the seventeenth-century magic lantern, the various projection apparatus ancestors of the *cinématographe* and the photographic apparatus. Their interest is evidently to indicate the links that relate these diverse perspective mechanisms and the camera, but in so doing they risk not seeing exactly what the camera hides (it does not hide its lens): the film and its feed systems, the emulsion, the frame lines, things which are essential (not just the lens) to cinema, without which there would be no cinema.

Hence it is not certain that what is habitually the case in practice should be reproduced in theory: the reduction of the hidden part of technics to its visible part brings with it the risk of renewing the domination of the visible, that *ideology of the visible* (and what it implies: masking, effacement of work) defined by Serge Daney:

> Cinema postulated that from the "real" to the visual and from the visual to its filmed reproduction a same truth was infinitely reflected, without distortion or loss. In a world where "I see" is readily used for "I understand", one conceives that such a dream had nothing fortuitous about it, the dominant ideology – that which equates the real with the visible – having every interest in encouraging it . . . But why not, going further back still, call into question what both serves and precedes the camera: a truly blind confidence in the visible, the hegemony, gradually acquired, of the eye over the other senses, the taste and need a society has to put itself in spectacle, etc. . . . The cinema is thus bound up with the western metaphysical tradition of seeing and vision whose photological vocation it realizes. What is photology, what could be the discourse of light? Assuredly a teleological discourse if it is true, as Derrida says, that teleology "consists in neutralizing duration and force in favor of the *illusion* of simultaneity and form".[4]

Undeniably, it was this "hegemony of the eye", this specularization, this ideology of the visible linked to western logocentrism that Pleynet was aiming at when stressing the pregnancy of the quattrocento perspective code in the basic apparatus: the image produced by the camera cannot do otherwise than confirm and reduplicate "the code of specular vision such as it is defined by the renaissant humanism", such that the human eye is at the centre of the system of representation, with that centrality at once excluding any other representative system, assuring the eye's domination over any other organ of the senses and putting the eye in a strictly divine place (Humanism's critique of Christianity).

Thus is constituted this situation of *theoretical paradox*: that it is by identifying the domination of the camera (of the visible) over the whole of the technology of cinema which it is supposed to represent, inform and programme (its function as *model*) that the attempt is made to denounce the submission of that camera, in its conception and its construction, to the dominant ideology of the visible.

If the gesture privileging the camera in order to set out from it the ideological chain in which cinema is inscribed is theoretically grounded by everything that is implied in that apparatus, as in any case by the determining and principal role of the camera in the production of the film, it too will nevertheless remain caught in the same chain unless taken further. It is therefore necessary to change perspective, that is, to take into account what the gesture picking out the camera sets aside in its movement, in order to avoid that the stress on the camera – necessary and productive – is not reinscribed in the very ideology to which it points.

It seems to me that a materialist theory of the cinema must at once disengage the ideological "heritage" of the camera (just as much as its "scientific heritage", for the two, contrary to what seems to be stated by Lebel, are in no way exclusive of one another) and the ideological investments in that camera, since neither in the production of films nor in the history of the invention of cinema is the camera alone at issue: if it is the fact that what the camera brings into play of technology, of science and/or ideology is determining, this is so only in relation to other determining elements which may certainly be secondary relative to the camera but the *secondariness* of which must then be questioned: the status and the function of what is covered over by the camera.

To underline again the risk entailed in making cinema function theoretically entirely on the *reduced model* of the camera, it is enough to note the almost total lack of theoretical work on the sound track or on laboratory techniques (as if the sight of light – geometrical optics – had blocked its work: the chemistry of light), a lack which can only be explained by the dominance of the visible at the heart of both cinematic practice and reflection. Is it not time, for example, to bring out the ideological function of two techniques (instruments + processes + knowledges + practice – interdependent, together to realize an *aim*, an objective which henceforth constitutes that technique, founds and authorizes it), both of which are on the side of the hidden, the cinematic unthought (except by very few filmmakers: Godard, Rivette, Straub): *grading* and *mixing*?

Covering over and loss of depth of field

No more than in the case of the "close-up" is it possible to postulate a continuous chain (a filiation) of "depth-of-field shots" running through the "history of cinema". No more than in the case of the "close-up" (or of any other term of cinematic practice and technical metalanguage) is the history of this technical disposition possible without considering determinations that are *not exclusively technical* but economic and ideological: determinations which thus go beyond the simple realm of the cinematic, working it over with series of supplements, grasping it on other scenes, having other scenes inscribe themselves on that of cinema; which shatter the fiction of an autonomous history of cinema (of its "styles and techniques"); which effect the complex articulation of this field and this history with other fields, other histories; which thus allow the taking into account, here for the particular technical procedure of depth of field, of the regulation of the functions it assumes – that is to say, of the *meanings* it assumes – in filmic signifying production through codes that are not necessarily cinematic (in this instance: pictorial, theatrical, photographic), allowing the taking into account of the (economic/ideological) forces which put pressure for or against the inscription of this regulation and these codes.

For historian–aestheticians like Mitry and theoreticians like Bazin to have let themselves fall for a determination of filmic writing and of the evolution of cinematic language by the advances of technology (development and improvement of means), to fall, that is, for the idea of a "treasure house" of techniques into which filmmakers could "freely" dip according to the effects of writing sought, or, again, for an "availability" of technical processes which located them in some region outside of systems of meaning (histories, codes, ideologies) and "ready" to enter into the signifying production, it was necessary that the whole technical apparatus of cinema seem so "natural" to them, so "self-evident", that the question of its utility and its purpose (what it is used for) be totally obscured by that of its utilization (how to use it).

It is indeed of "strength of conviction", "naturalness" – and, as a corollary, of the blindness on the part of the theoreticians – that we must talk. Mitry, for example, who notes the fact that deep focus, almost constantly used in the early years of cinema, disappears from the scene of filmic signifiers for some twenty years (with a few odd exceptions: certain films by Renoir), offers strictly technical reasons as sole explanation for this abandonment, hence establishing technology as the last instance, constituting a closed and autonomous circuit within which technical fluctuations are taken as determined only by other technical fluctuations.

From the very first films, the cinematic image was "naturally" an image in deep focus; the majority of the films of Lumière and his cameramen bear witness to that depth which appears as constituent of these images. It is in fact most often in out-of-doors shooting that depth in the period finds its field. The reason is indisputably of a technical nature: the lenses used before 1915 were, Mitry stresses, "solely f35 and f50", "medium" focal lengths which had to be stopped down in order to produce an image in depth, thus necessitating a great deal of light, something to be found more easily and cheaply outside than in the studio.

One must then ask why, precisely, these "medium" focal lengths only were in use during the first twenty years of cinema. I can see no more pertinent reason than the fact that they restore the spatial proportions corresponding to "normal vision" and that they thereby play their role in the production of the impression of reality to which the *cinématographe* owed its success. These lenses themselves are thus dictated by the codes of analogy and realism (other codes corresponding to other social demands would have produced other types of lenses). The depth of field that they permit is thus also that which permits them, that which lays the ground for their utilization and their existence. The deep focus in question is not a supplementary "effect" which might just as well have been done without; on the contrary, it is what *had* to be obtained and what it was necessary to strive to produce. Set up to put its money on, and putting its money wholeheartedly on, the identification – the desire to identify, to duplicate, to recognize specularly – of the cinematic image with "life itself" (consider the fantastic efforts expended over decades by hundreds of inventors in search of "total cinema", of complete illusion, the reproduction of life with sound and color and relief included), the ideological apparatus cinema could not, in default of realizing in practice the technical patent for relief, neglect the production of effects of relief, of effects of depth. Effects which are due on the one hand to the inscription within the image of a vanishing perspective and on the other to the movements of people or other mobile elements (the La Ciotat train) along vanishing lines (something which a photograph cannot provide, nor *a fortiori* a painting; which is why the most perfect *trompe-l'oeil* minutely constructed in conformity with the laws of perspective is powerless to trick the eye). The two are linked: in order that people can move about "perpendicularly" on the screen, the light must be able to go and take them there, it requires a depth, planes spaced out, in short the code of artificial perspective. Moreover in studio filming, where space was relatively tight and lighting not always adequate, the backgrounds were often precisely painted *trompe-l'oeil* canvases which, while unable to inscribe the movement in depth of the characters, at least inscribed its perspective.

We know what perspective brings with it and thus what deep focus brings into the cinematic image as its *constitutive codes*: the codes of classic western representation, pictorial and theatrical. Méliès, specialist in "illusion" and interior shooting, said as early as 1897 of his Montreuil "studio": "in brief, it is the coming together of a gigantic photographic workshop and a theatrical stage." No more exact indication could be given of the double background on which the cinematic image is raised, and not fortuitously but explicitly, deliberately. Not only is deep focus in the early cinematic image the mark of its submission to these codes of representation and to the histories and ideologies which necessarily determine and operate them, but more generally it signals that the ideological apparatus cinema is itself produced by these codes and by these systems of representation, as at once their complement, their perfectionment and the surpassing of them. There is nothing accidental, therefore, or specifically technical in the cinematic image immediately claiming depth, since it is just this depth which governs and informs it; the various optical instruments are regulated according to the possibility of restoring depth. Contrary to what the technicians seem to believe, the restoration of movement and depth are not effects of the camera; it is the camera which is the effect, the solution to the problem of that restoration.

Deep focus was not "in fashion" in 1896, it was one of the factors of credibility in the cinematic image (like, even if not quite with the same grounds, the faithful reproduction of movement and figurative analogy). And it is by the transformation of the conditions of this credibility, by the displacement of the codes of cinematic verisimilitude from the plane of the impression of reality alone to the more complex planes of fictional logic (narrative codes), of psychological verisimilitude, of the impression of homogeneity and continuity (the coherent space–time of classical drama) that one can account for the effacement of depth. It will not then be a question merely of technical "delays": such "delays" are themselves caught up in and effects of the displacement, of this replacement of codes.

It seems surprising indeed (at least if one remains at the level of "technical causes") that a process which "naturally" dominated a large proportion of the films made between 1895 and 1925 could disappear or drop into oblivion for so long without – leaving aside a few exceptions, Renoir being one – filmmakers showing the slightest concern (so it seems).

Everything, Mitry assures us, stems from "the generalization of panchromatic stock round about 1925". Agreed. But to say that – offered with the weight of the obvious – and to pass on quickly to the unsuitability of the lighting systems to the spectrum of this emulsion is exactly *not to say* what necessity attaches to this "generalization", what (new) function the new film comes to fulfil that the old was unable to serve. It is to avoid the question as to what demands the replacement of an emulsion in universal use and which (if we follow Mitry) did not seem so mediocre by another which (still according to Mitry) was far from its immediate equal. As far as we know, it is not exactly within the logic of technology, nor within that of the economics of the film industry (in the mid-twenties already highly structured and well-equipped) to adopt (or impose) a new product which in an initial moment poses more problems than the old and hence incurs the expense of adaptation (modification of lighting systems, lenses, etc.) *without somewhere finding something to its advantage and profit.*

In fact, it is a matter not simply of a gain in the sensitivity of the film but also of a gain in *faithfulness* "to natural colors", a *gain in realism.* The cinematic image becomes more refined, perfects its "rendering", competes once again with the quality of the photographic image which had long been using the panchromatic emulsion. The reason for this "technical progress" is not merely technical, it is ideological: it is not so much the greater sensitivity to light which counts as "being more true". The hard, contrasty image of the early cinema no longer satisfied the codes of photographic realism developed and sharpened by the spread of photography. In my view, depth (perspective) loses its importance in the production of "reality effects" in favour of shade, range, color. But this is not all.

A further advantage, that is, that the film industry could find "round about 1925" in imposing on itself – despite the practical difficulties and the cost of the operation – the replacement of orthochromatic by panchromatic stock depends again on the greater sensitivity of the latter. Not only did the gain in sensitivity permit the realignment of the "realism" of the cinematic image with that of the photographic image,[5] it also compensated for the loss of light due to the change from a shutter speed of sixteen or eighteen frames per second to the speed of twenty-four frames per second necessitated by sound. This "better" technical explanation, however, can only serve here to re-mark the coincidence of the coming of the talkie and the setting aside of depth, not to provide the reason for it. Although certain of its effects are, that reason is not technical. More than one sound film before *Citizen Kane* works with depth; the generalization of large aperture lenses even does not exclude its possibility: with the sensitivity of emulsions increasing and the quantity of light affordable, there was nothing to prevent – technically – the stopping down of these lenses (if indeed, as Renoir did, one could not find any others). So it is not as final "technical cause" that the talking picture must be brought into the argument; it is in that in a precise location of production–distribution (Hollywood) it re-models not just the systems of filmic writing but, with them and directing this bringing up to date, the ideological function of the cinema and the economic facts of its functioning.

It is not unimportant that it be – in Hollywood – at the moment when the rendering of the cinematic image becomes subtle, opens up to the shades of greys (monochrome translation of the range of colors), thus drawing nearer to a more faithful imitation of the photographic images promoted (fetishized) as the very norms of realism, that Speech and the speaking Subject come onto the scene. As soon as they are produced, sound and speech are plebiscited as *the "truth" which was lacking* in the silent film – the truth which is all of a sudden noticed, not without alarm and resistance, as having been lacking in the silent film. And at once this truth renders no longer valid all films which do not possess it, which do not produce it. The decisive supplement, the "ballast of reality" (Bazin) constituted by sound and speech intervenes straightaway, therefore, as *perfectionment and redefinition of the impression of reality.*

It is at the cost of a series of blindnesses (of disavowals) that the silent image was able to be taken for the reflection, the objective double of "life itself": disavowal of color, relief, sound. Founded on these lacks (as any representation is founded on a lack which governs it, a lack which is the very principle of any simulacrum: the spectator is anyhow well aware of the artifice but he/she prefers all the same to believe in it), filmic representation could find its production only by working to diminish its effects, to mask its very reality. Otherwise it would have been rejected as too visibly factitious: it was absolutely necessary that it facilitate the disavowal of the veritable sensory castrations which founded its specificity and that it not, by remarking them, prevent such disavowal. *Compromises* were necessary in order that the cinema could function as ideological apparatus, in order that its delusion could take place.

The work of suturing, of filling in, of patching up the lacks which ceaselessly recalled the radical difference of the cinematic image was not done all at one go but piece by piece, by the *patient accumulation of technical processes*. Directly and totally programmed by the ideology of resemblance, of the "objective" duplication of a "real" itself conceived as specular reflection, cinema technology occupied itself in improving and refining the initial imperfect *dispositif, always imperfect* by virtue of the ideological delusion produced by the film as "impression of reality". The lack of relief had been immediately compensated for (this is the original impression of reality) by movement and the depth of the image, inscribing the perspective code which in western cultures stands as principal emblem of spatial relief. The lack of color had to make do with panchromatic stock, pending the commercialization of three-color processes (1935–40). Neither the pianos nor the orchestras of the silent film could really substitute for "realistic sound": synchronized speech and sound – in spite of their imperfections, in truth of little weight at a time when it is the whole of sound reproduction, records, radios, which is affected by background noise and interference – thus considerably *displace the site and the means* (*until then strictly iconic*) of the production of the impression of reality.

Because the *ideological* conditions of production – consumption of the initial impression of reality (figurative analogy + movement + perspective) were changing (if only in function of the very dissemination of photo and film), it was necessary to tinker with its technical modalities in order that the act of disavowal renewing the deception could continue to be accomplished "automatically", in a reflex manner, without any disturbance of the spectacle, above all without any work or effort on the part of the spectator. The succession of technical advances cannot be read, in the manner of Bazin, as the progress towards a "realism plus" other than in that they accumulate realistic supplements which all aim at reproducing – in strengthening, diversifying, rendering more subtle – the impression of reality; which aim, that is, to reduce as much as possible, to minimize the gap which the "yes-I-know/but-all-the-same" has to fill.

What is at stake in deep focus, what is at stake in the historicity of the technique, are the codes and the modes of production of "realism", the transmission, renewal or transformation of the ideological systems of recognition, specularity, truth-to-lifeness.

"More real" or more visible?

The reinforcement of "effects of the real" is the first and foremost reason for Bazin's interest in deep focus. In a number of famous texts (notably *The evolution of cinematic language* and *William Wyler or the Jansenist of mise en scène*) and with reference essentially to the films of Orson Welles and William Wyler (a choice which is not without overdetermining Bazin's discourse), he makes deep focus the means and the symbol of the irreversible accomplishment of the "realist vocation of the cinema", of the "realist rejuvenation of narrative".

A series of principles are set up which follow from what is for Bazin a truly *first principle*: "the immanent ambiguity of reality", which montage and even classic Hollywood editing had reduced to a single meaning, to a single discourse (that of the filmmaker), "subjectivizing the event to an extreme, since every element is owing to the decision of the *metteur en scène*"; whereas filming with deep focus safeguards the ambiguity because it participates in "an aesthetic of reality" and offers the spectator "the possibility of carrying out at least the final stage of the editing him or herself".

Thus (a) the real is ambiguous; (b) to give a representation of it that is fragmented (because of montage or the work of the writing) is to reduce this ambiguity and replace it with a "subjectivity" (a meaning: a "view of the world", an ideology); (c) because deep focus brings the cinematic image closer to the "normal" retinal image, to "realist" vision, and shows literally *more* things, *more real*, it allows the reactivation of that "ambiguity" which leaves the spectator "free"; aims, that is, at abolishing the difference between film and reality, representation and real, at confirming the spectator in his or her "natural" relationship with the world, hence at reduplicating the conditions of his or her "spontaneous" vision and ideology. It is not for nothing that Bazin writes (not without humour) in the course of a discussion of *The Best Years of our Lives*: "Deep focus in Wyler's film is meant to be liberal and democratic like the consciousness of the American spectator and the film's heroes."

On the one hand, duplication of the ideological effects of the impression of reality, of the "normality" of specular representation; on the other, *revelation* (in its exact Christian sense) of "the natural ambiguity and unity" of the world.

To this "revelation" according to Bazin of "the immanent ambiguity of reality" by deep focus, Mitry opposes "the fact that the real of film is a mediated real: between the real world and us, there is the film, the camera, the representation, in the extreme case where there is not in addition an author". He writes:

> It is supremely naive to think (as Bazin does) that because the camera automatically records an element given in reality, it provides us with an objective and impartial image of that reality. . . . By the very fact that it is *given in an image*, the real captured by the camera lens is structured according to formalizing values which create a series of new relations and therefore a new reality – at very least a new appearance. The *represented* is seen via a *representation* which, necessarily, transforms it.

Secure in his insistence against Bazin on the distinction film/real, Mitry fails to see how, far from acknowledging the difference, film tends to reduce it by proposing itself as adequate to the norms of perception, by ceaselessly restoring the illusion of the homogeneous and the continuous, which is precisely the basis of Bazin's error – the postulation as the same value of the unifying functions of both perception and film representation. It was then inevitable that Mitry should end up sharing Bazin's view of deep focus. Against Bazin, he stresses the otherness of film to the real but fails to recognize the process of repression of which that otherness is the object and the place of the spectator in that process. The film is abstracted from its social inscription into an absolute realm where the "truth" of its nature ("fragmentation of the real into shots and sequences") takes precedence over that of its reading (reconstitution, suturation). Like Bazin – though not, of course, without shades of difference – he then comes to consider that, because it reduces such fragmentation, deep focus is indeed productive of an "increase in realism": it is seen as (ontological realism) capturing, as the classic shot does not, "the event globally, in its real space–time", restoring "to object and setting their density of existence, their weight of presence" (Bazin's formulations taken over by Mitry) and as (psychological realism) replacing "the spectator in the true conditions of perception"; that is to say, coherence, continuity and finally "ambiguity". On condition that deep focus does not become an omnivalent principle substitutive for every other formula of *mise en scène*, Mitry declares himself "perfectly in agreement with Bazin".

Nothing is less certain than that deep focus is in this way – particularly in the films of Welles and Wyler, the obligatory example since Bazin – responsible for an "increase in realism"; and this exactly in that it inscribes in the image, more successfully than any other filming process, the *representational code of linear perspective*.

We are thus faced with a contradiction: for Bazin the intervention of deep focus increases the realist coefficient of the cinematic image by completing the virtues (the virtualities) *already* inscribed in that image, by perfecting it, by giving literally *more field* to its "ontological realism". For Mitry this cannot be the case since by stressing the artificiality (the otherness) of the cinematic image, it is just such a "realism" that he refuses, merely conceding that deep focus – because it produces a "more global" and relatively less discontinuous space – comes closer to certain effects of ordinary perception; that is to say, it brings back and reinscribes in the image the (at least psychological) *conditions* of an increase in realism. For the first, this *more* is *added*; for the second, it tends to cancel out a *less*, to fill a lack. The contradiction between Bazin and Mitry is also a contradiction in Mitry, since the system of differences and specificities which constitutes the cinematic image as an other of the world, offered as its double, does not abolish the particular case of the deep focus image. In his illusion, Bazin is more coherent than Mitry, the person who denounces the illusion as such, for the stress on the constitutive differences and specific codings of the image must, as deep focus demonstrates, be accompanied by a simultaneous stress on the *work* of these codings (their *raison d'être* and their goal), which is to produce their own miscognition, to give themselves over as "natural" and hence to mask the play of differences.

It is from the basis of this *positive* contribution accorded deep focus by both Bazin and Mitry that the *double game* of the coding of the cinematic image (its "transparency", since it is not by being remarked as such that it functions) operates, insofar as the "supplement of realism" that deep focus is held to produce cannot be produced without distorting and emphasizing the codes of "realism" already "naturally" at work in the image: a supplement that is *excessive* in relation to the system of (perspective/cultural) norms which ground the impression of reality and maintain the category of "realism".

Denaturalizing depth

The theatre in *La Cecilia* as tipping over of the fiction, as superimposition, disphazing, dislocation of two representations, one over the other, one against the other.

This doubling-splitting of the scene that the inscription of the theater produces in the film is produced in the shot by deep focus. The decision was taken with the cameraperson Yann Le Masson, to use almost throughout short focal length lenses which give a field that is sharp in its distance, a space divided into planes set out in depth, backgrounds as legible as foregrounds. Paradoxically, this was not in order to strengthen the realism of the image (deep focus as "more real") but in order to make the shot theatrical: to act along the verticality of the image in the same way that in the theater one can perform along the vertical axis of the stage, in its depth, making dramatic use of what is the central condition of the Italian stage (governed by linear perspective): a theatrical space that is immediately and totally perceptible, a set given over straightaway and entirely to vision. With the proviso that what is arranged on the theatrical stage in the real depth of the given space necessarily becomes in the filmic image a spacing out in the plane of the frame, a lateral–vertical decentring of the "subjects" (otherwise what is in the foreground would always mask what comes behind). With the proviso also that the short focal lengths, which alone allow the apprehension of this depth, which do so with a forceful emphasis on perspective, bring with them at the same time as the background depth a more or less considerable deformation of the lateral edges of the field. This is why cinematic deep focus does not slip into the "naturalness" of linear perspective, but inevitably stresses that perspective, accentuates it, indicates its curvature, denounces the visual field it produces as a construction, a composition in which there is not simply "more real" but in which this more visible is spatially organized in the frame, dramatized. Deep focus does not wipe out perspective, does not pass it off as the "normality" of vision, but makes it readable as coding (exteriorization of the interiorized code); it de-naturalizes dramatizes it. The relationship which is established within the frame and in the duration of the scene between the actions or figures in the foreground and those in the background functions not only as a "montage within the shot" (opposed by Bazin to classic Hollywood editing) but also as the reinscription of a theatrical space and duration, in which the legibility of meanings goes via a movement of the eye, in which the playing of the actors is a playing of *relationship* to the others and to the elements of the decor, in which the bodies are always held in space and time, never abstract. (The abstraction is the method and the result of the analysis of the concrete contradictions: a body in a space, in relation to other bodies; speech first of all as accent, delivery, diction; a discourse as mode of behavior, symptom, relational crisis; political conflicts as dramatic conflicts – the political, in other words, not as (autonomous, free floating) discourse or (magisterial) lesson, but as movement, as trace, mark on faces, gestures, words; in short, theater).

Notes on representation

The most analogical representation of the world is still not, is never, its reduplication. Analogical repetition is a false repetition, staggered, displayed, deferred and different; but it produces *effects* of repetition and analogy which imply the disavowal (or the repression) of these differences and which thus make of the desire for identity, identification, recognition, of the desire for the *same*, one of the principal driving forces of analogical figuration. In other words the spectator, the ideological and social subject, and not just the technical apparatus, is the operator of the analogical mechanism.

There is a famous painting of the English school, *The Cholmondeley Sisters* (1600–10), which represents two sisters side by side, each holding a baby in her arms. The two sisters look very much alike, as do the babies, sisters and babies are dressed almost identically, and so on. Confronted with this canvas, one is disturbed by a repetition that is not a repetition, by a contradictory repetition. What is here painted is the very subject of figurative painting: repetition, *with*, in this repetition, all the play of the innumerable differences which at once *destroy* it (from one figure to the other, nothing is identical) and *assert* it as violent *effect*. Panic and confusion of the look doubled and split. The image is *in* the image, the double is not the same, the repetition is a fiction: it makes us believe that it repeats itself just because it does not repeat itself. It is in the most "analogical" representation (never completely so), the most "faithful", the most "realistic", that the *effects of representation* can be most easily read. One must be fooled by the image in order to see it as such (and no longer as a projection of the world).

Is it that cinema begins where *mise en scène* ends, when is broken or left behind the machinery of performance, of the actor and the scenario, when technical necessity takes off the mask of art? That is roughly what Vertov believed and what is repeated more or less by a whole avant-garde in his wake – with categories such as "pure cinema", "live cinema", *"cinéma vérité"* – right up to certain experimental films of today. It is not very difficult to see, however, that what is being celebrated in that tradition of "non-cinema" is a visible with no original blemish that will stand forth in its "purity" as soon as the cinema strips itself of the "literary" or "theatrical" artifices it inherited at its birth; a visible on the right side of things, manifesting their living authenticity. There is, of course, no visible not held in a look and, as it were, always already framed. Moreover, it is naive to locate *mise en scène* solely on the side of the camera: it is just as much, and even before the camera intervenes, everywhere where the social regulations order the place, the behavior and almost the "form" of subjects in the various configurations in which they are caught (and which do not demand the same type of performance: here authority, here submission; standing out or standing aside; etc.; from one system of social relation to another, the place of the subject changes and so does the subject's capture in the look of others). What Vertov films without *mise en scène* (as he believes) are the effects of other *mises en scène*. In other words, script, actors, *mise en scène* or not, all that is filmable is the changing, historical, determined relationship of men and things to the visible, are dispositions of representation.

However refined, analogy in the cinema is a deception, a lie, a fiction that must be straddled – in disavowing, knowing but not wanting to know – by the *will to believe* of the spectator, the spectator who expects to be fooled and wants to be fooled, thus becoming the first agent of his or her own fooling. The spectacle, and cinema itself, despite all the *reality effects* it may produce, always gives itself away *for what it is* to the spectators. There is no spectator other than one *aware* of the spectacle, even if (provisionally) allowing him or herself to be taken in by the fictioning machine, deluded by the simulacrum: it is precisely *for that* that he or she came. The certainty that we always have, in our heart of hearts, that the spectacle is not life, that the film is not reality, that the actor is not the character and that if we are present as spectators, it is because we know we are dealing with a semblance, this certainty must be capable of being doubted. It is only worth its risk; it interests us only if it can be (provisionally) cancelled out. The "yes, I know" calls irresistibly for the "but all the same", includes it as its value, its intensity. We know, but we want something else: to believe. We want to be fooled, while still knowing a little that we are so being. We want the one and the other, to be both fooled and not fooled, to oscillate, to swing from knowledge to belief, from distance to adherence, from criticism to fascination.

Which is why realist representations are successful: they allow this movement to and fro which ceaselessly sets off the intensity of the disavowal, they sustain the spectator's pleasure in being prisoner in a situation of conflict (I believe/I don't believe). They allow it because they lay out a contradictory, representative space, a space in which there are both effects of the real and effects of fiction, of repetition and difference, automatic devices of identification and significant resistances, recognition and seizure. In this sense, analogical fiction in the cinema is bound up with narrative fiction, and all cinematic fictions are tightened, more or less forcefully, by this knot of disavowal which ceaselessly starts and starts again with the continual *petitio principii* of the "impression of reality". The capturing power of a fiction, whether the fiction of the analogical reproduction of the visible or the fictions of cinematic narrative, depends always on its self-designation as such, on the fact that its fictive character is known and recognized from the start, that it presents itself as an artificial arrangement, that it does not hide that it is above all an apparatus of deception and thus that it postulates a spectator who is not easily but *difficultly* deceivable, not a spectator who is blindly condemned to fascination but one who is complicit, willing to "go along".

Fictional deceits, contrary to many other systems of illusions, are interesting in that they can function only from the clear designation of their deceptive character. There is no uncertainty, no mistake, no misunderstanding or manipulation. There is ambivalence, play. The spectacle is always a game, requiring the spectators' participation not as "passive", "alienated" consumers, but as players, accomplices, masters of the game even if they are also what is at stake. It is necessary to suppose spectators to be total imbeciles, completely alienated social beings, in order to believe that they are thoroughly deceived and deluded by simulacra. Different in this to ideological and political representations, spectatorial representations declare their existence as simulacrum and, on that contractual basis, invite the spectator to *use* the simulacrum to fool him or herself. Never "passive", the spectator, works. But that work is not only a work of decipherment, reading, elaboration of signs. It is first of all and just as much, if not more, to play the game, to fool him or herself out of pleasure, and in spite of those knowledges which reinforce his or her position of non-fool; it is to maintain – if the spectacle, its play makes it possible – the mechanism of disavowal at its highest level of intensity. The more one knows, the more difficult it is to believe, and the more it is worth it to manage to.

If there is in iconic analogy as operative in cinema the contradictory work of difference, non-similitude, false repetition which at once found and limit the deception, then it is the whole edifice of cinematic representation that finds itself affected with a fundamental lack: the negative index, the restriction the disavowal of which is the symptom and which it tries to fill while at the same time displaying it. More than the representative apparatuses that come before it (theater, painting, photography, etc.), cinema – precisely because it effects a greater approximation to the analogical reproduction of the visible, because it is carried along by that "realist vocation" so dear to Bazin – is no doubt more profoundly, more decisively undermined than those other apparatuses by everything that separates the real from the representable and even the visible from the represented. It is what resists cinematic representation, limiting it on all sides and from within, which constitutes equally its force; what makes it falter makes it go.

The cinematic image grasps only a small part of the visible; and it is a grasp which – provisional, contracted, fragmentary – bears in it its impossibility. At the same time, film images are only a small part in the multiplicity of the visible, even if they tend by their accumulation to cover it. Every image is thus doubly racked by disillusion: from within itself as machine for simulation, mechanical and deathly reproduction of the living; from without as single image only, and not all images, in that what fills it will never be but the present index of an absence, of the lack of another image. Yet it is also, of course, this structuring disillusion which offers the offensive strength of cinematic representation and allows it to work against the completing, reassuring, mystifying representations of ideology. It is that strength that is needed, and that work of disillusion, if cinematic representation is to do something other than pile visible on visible, if it is, in certain rares flashes, to produce in our sight the very blindness which is at the heart of this visible.

Notes

1   See "Technique et idéologie", *Cahiers du cinéma* no. 229 (May–June 1971), 9–15; translation "Technique and ideology: camera, perspective, depth of field", *Film Reader* no. 2 (1997), 132–8.
2   Gilles Deleuze and Claire Parnet, *Dialogues* (Paris: Flammarion 1977), 126–7.
3   With M. Pleynet – "Economique, idéologique, formel" (interview), *Cinéthique* no. 3 (1969) – the focus of attention is voluntarily and *first of all* on *one* of the component elements of the camera, the *lens*. For J.-P. Lebel – *Cinéma et idéologie* (Paris: Editions sociales 1971), chapter I – who cites the phenomenon of "persistence of vision", the rèference-Science, constantly invoked, is *geometrical optics*: the laws of the propagation of light.
4   Serge Daney, "Sur Salador", *Cahiers du cinéma* no. 222 (July 1970), 39.
5   In the general readjustment of codes of cinematic "realism" produced in Hollywood (according, of course, to its ideological and economic norms and objectives: for its profit and for that of bourgeois ideology) by the coming of sound, the codes of the strictly photographic "realism" of the filmic image are re-defined specifically (but not exclusively) in relation to the increasingly important place occupied by the photographic image in bourgeois societies in relation to mass consumption. This place has something to do with that of gold (of the fetish): the photo is the money of the "real" (of "life") assures its convenient circulation and appropriation. Thereby, the photo is unanimously con-secrated as general equivalent for, standard of, all "realism": the cinematic image could not, without losing its "power" (the power of its "credibility"), not align itself with the photographic norms. The "strictly technical" level of the improvements of optical apparatus and emulsions is thus totally programmed by the ideology of the "realistic" reproduction of the world at work in the constitution of the photographic image as the "objective representation" *par excellence*. Ideology system of coding, which in its turn that image renews.

The Coming of Sound

6

Technological Change
in the American Film Industry

DOUGLAS GOMERY

The coming of sound during the late 1920s climaxed a decade of significant change within the American industry. Following the lead of the innovators – Warner Bros. Pictures, Inc., and the Fox Film Corporation – all companies moved, virtually en masse, to convert to sound. By the autumn of 1930, Hollywood produced only talkies. The speed of conversion surprised almost everyone. Within twenty-four months a myriad of technical problems were surmounted, stages soundproofed, and theaters wired. Engineers invaded studios to coordinate sight with sound. Playwrights (from the East) replaced title writers; actors without stage experience rushed to sign up for voice lessons. At the time, chaos seemed to reign supreme. However, with some historical distance, we know that, although the switch-over to talkies seemed to come "overnight", no major company toppled. Indeed the coming of sound produced one of the more lucrative eras in US movie history. Speed of transformation must not be mistaken for disorder or confusion. On the contrary, the major film corporations – Paramount and Loew's (MGM) – were joined by Fox, Warner, and RKO in a surge of profits, instituting a grip on the marketplace which continues to the present day.

Moreover, sound films did not spring Minerva-like onto the movie screens of twenties America. Their antecedents reached back to the founding of the industry. We need a framework to structure this important thirty-year transformation. Here the neoclassical economic theory of technical change proves very useful. An enterprise introduces a new product (or process of production) in order to increase profits. Simplified somewhat, three distinct phases are involved: invention, innovation, and diffusion. Although many small-inventory entrepreneurs attempted to marry motion pictures and sound, it took two corporate giants, the American Telephone & Telegraph Corporation (AT&T), and the Radio Corporation of America (RCA), to develop the necessary technology. AT&T desired to make better phone equipment; RCA sought to improve its radio capabilities. As a secondary effect of such research, each perfected sound recording and reproduction equipment. With the inventions ready, two movie companies, Warner and Fox, adapted telephone and radio research for practical use. That is, they innovated sound movies. Each developed techniques to produce, distribute, and exhibit sound motion pictures. The final phase, diffusion, occurs when the product or process is adopted for widespread use. Initially, the movie industry giants hesitated to follow the lead of Warner and Fox but, after elaborate planning, decided to convert. All others followed. Because of the enormous economic power of the major firms, the diffusion proceeded quickly and smoothly. During each of the three phases, the movie studios and their suppliers of sound equipment formulated business decisions with a view toward maximizing long-run profits. This motivation propelled the American motion picture industry (as it had other industries) into a new era of growth and prosperity.

Invention

Attempts to link sound to motion pictures originated in the 1890s. Entrepreneurs experimented with mechanical means to combine the phonograph and motion pictures. For example, in 1895 Thomas Alva Edison introduced such a device, his Kinetophone. He did not try to synchronize sound and image; the Kinetophone merely supplied a musical accompaniment to which a customer listened as he or she viewed a "peep show". Edison's crude novelty met with public indifference. Yet, at the same time, many other inventors attempted to better Edison's effort. One of these, Léon Gaumont, demonstrated his Chronophone before the French Photographic Society in 1902. Gaumont's system linked a single projector to two phonographs by means of a series of cables. A dial adjustment synchronized the phonograph and motion picture. In an attempt to profit by his system, showman Gaumont filmed variety (vaudeville) acts. The premiere came in 1907 at the London Hippodrome. Impressed, the American monopoly, the Motion Picture Patents Company, licensed Chronophone for the United States. Within one year Gaumont's repertoire included opera, recitations, and even dramatic sketches. Despite initially bright prospects Chronophone failed to secure a niche in the marketplace because the system, relatively expensive to install, produced only coarse sounds, lacked the necessary amplification, and rarely remained synchronized for long. In 1913, Gaumont returned to the United States for a second try with what he claimed was an improved synchronizing mechanism and an advanced compressed air system for amplification. Exhibitors remembered Chronophone's earlier lackluster performance and ignored all advertised claims, and Gaumont moved on to other projects.

Gaumont and Edison did not represent the only phonograph sound systems on the market. More than a dozen others, all introduced between 1909 and 1913, shared common systems and problems. The only major rival was the Cameraphone, the invention of E. E. Norton, a former mechanical engineer with the American Gramophone Company. Even though in design the Cameraphone nearly replicated Gaumont's apparatus, Norton succeeded in installing his system in a handful of theaters. But like others who preceded him, he never solved three fundamental problems: (a) the apparatus was expensive; (b) the amplification could not reach all persons in a large hall; and (c) synchronization could not be maintained for long periods of time. In addition, since the Cameraphone system required a porous screen, the image retained a dingy gray quality. Therefore it was not surprising that Cameraphone (or Cinephone, Vivaphone, Synchroscope) was never successful.

It remained for one significant failure to eradicate any further commercial attempt to marry the motion picture and the phonograph. In 1913, Thomas Edison announced the second coming of the Kinetophone. This time, the Wizard of Menlo Park argued, he had perfected the talking motion picture! Edison's demonstration on 4 January 1913, impressed all present. The press noted that this system seemed more advanced than all predecessors. Its sensitive microphone obviated additional lip-sync difficulties for actors. An oversized phonograph supplied the maximum mechanical amplification. Finally, an intricate system of belts and pulleys erected between the projection booth and the stage could precisely coordinate the speed of the phonograph with the motion picture projector.

Because of the success of the demonstration, Edison was able to persuade vaudeville magnates John J. Murdock and Martin Beck to install the Kinetophone in four Keith-Orpheum theaters in New York. The commercial premiere took place on 13 February 1913, at Keith's Colonial. A curious audience viewed and listened to a lecturer who praised Edison's latest marvel. To provide dramatic evidence for his glowing tribute, the lecturer then smashed a plate, played the violin, and had his dog bark. After several music acts (recorded on the Kinetophone), a choral rendition of "The Star-Spangled Banner" stirringly closed the show. An enthusiastic audience stood and applauded for ten minutes. The wizard, Tom Edison, had done it again!

Unfortunately this initial performance would rank as the zenith for Kinetophone. For a majority of later presentations, the system functioned badly – for a variety of technical reasons. For example, at Keith's Union Square theater, the sound lost synchronization by as much as ten to twelve seconds. The audience booed the picture off the screen. By 1914, the Kinetophone had established a record so spotty that Murdock and Beck paid off their contract with Edison. Moreover, during that same year, fire destroyed Edison's West Orange factory. Although he quickly rebuilt, Edison chose not to reactivate the Kinetophone operation. The West Orange fire not only marked the end of the Kinetophone, but signaled the demise of all serious efforts to mechanically unite the phonograph with motion pictures. (The later disc system would use electronic connections.)

American moviegoers had to wait nine years for another workable sound system to emerge – and when it did, it was based on the principle of sound on film, not on discs. On 4 April 1923, noted electronics inventor Lee De Forest successfully exhibited his Phonofilm system to the New York Electrical Society. De Forest asserted that his system simply photographed the voice onto an ordinary film. In truth, Phonofilm's highly sophisticated design represented a major advance in electronics, begun when De Forest had patented the Audion amplifier tube in 1907. Two weeks later Phonofilm reached the public at large at New York's Rivoli theater. The program consisted of three shorts: a ballerina performing a "swan dance", a string quartet, and another dance number. Since the musical accompaniment for each was *non*synchronous, De Forest, whose brilliance shone in the laboratory rather than in show-manship or business, generated little interest. A *New York Times* reporter described a lukewarm audience response. No movie mogul saw enough of an advancement, given the repeated previous failures, to express more than a mild curiosity.

In fact, De Forest never wanted to work directly through a going motion picture concern, but go it alone. Consequently, legal and financial roadblocks continually hindered substantial progress. De Forest tried but could not establish anywhere near an adequate organization to market films or apparatus. Movie entrepreneurs feared, correctly, that the Phonofilm Corporation controlled too few patents ever to guarantee indemnity. Still, De Forest's greatest difficulties came when he attempted to generate financial backing. This brilliant individualist failed ever to master the intricacies of the world of modern finance. Between 1923 and 1925, Phonofilm, Inc., wired only thirty-four theaters in the United States, Europe, South Africa, Australia, and Japan. De Forest struggled on, but in September 1928, when he sold out to a group of South African businessmen, only three Phonofilm installations remained, all in the United States.

It took AT&T, the world's largest company, to succeed where others had failed. In 1912, AT&T's manufacturing subsidiary, Western Electric, secured the rights to De Forest's Audion tube to construct amplification repeaters for long-distance telephone transmission. In order to test such equipment the Western Electric Engineering Department, under Frank Jewett, needed a better method to test sound quality. After a brief interruption because of the First World War, Jewett and his scientists plunged ahead, concentrating on improving the disc method. Within three months of the armistice, one essential element for a sound system was ready, the loudspeaker. The loudspeaker was first used in the "Victory Day" parade on Park Avenue in 1919, but national notoriety came during the 1920 Republican and Democratic national conventions. A year later, by connecting this technology to its long-distance telephone network, AT&T broadcast President Harding's address at the burial of the Unknown Soldier simultaneously to overflowing crowds in New York's Madison Square Garden and San Francisco's Auditorium. Clear transmissions to large indoor audiences had become a reality. Other necessary components quickly flowed off Western Electric's research assembly line. The disc apparatus was improved by creating a single-drive shaft turntable using 33⅓ revolutions per minute. Ready in 1924, the complete new disc system included a high-quality microphone, a nondistortive amplifier, an electrically operated recorder and turntable, a high-quality loudspeaker, and a synchronizing system free from speed variation.

In 1922, in the midst of these developments, Western Electric began to consider commercial applications. Western Electric did advertise and sell the microphones, vacuum tubes, and loudspeakers in the radio field, but Jewett's assistant, Edward Craft, argued that more lucrative markets existed in "improved" phonographs and sound movies. Employing the sound-on-disc method, Craft produced the first motion picture using Western Electric's sound system. To *Audion*, an animated cartoon originally created as a silent public relations film, he added a synchronized score. Craft premiered *Audion* in Yale University's Woolsey Hall on 27 October 1922. He followed this first effort with more experiments. On 13 February 1924, at a dinner at New York's Astor Hotel, Craft presented *Hawthorne*. This public relations film showing Western Electric's plant in Chicago employed a perfectly synchronized sound track. By the fall of 1924, the sound-on-disc system seemed ready to market.

Laboratory success did not constitute the only criterion which distinguished Western Electric's efforts from those of De Forest and other inventors. Most important, Western Electric had almost unlimited financial muscle. In 1925, parent company AT&T ranked with US Steel as the largest private corporation in the world. Total assets numbered over $2.9 billion; revenues exceeded $800 million. At this time America's national income was only $76 billion, and government receipts totaled only $3.6 billion. Western Electric, although technically an AT&T subsidiary, ranked as a corporate giant in its own right with assets of $188 million and sales of $263 million, far in excess of even Paramount, the largest force in the motion picture industry at the time. If absolute economic power formed the greatest advantage, patent monopoly certainly added another. AT&T spent enormous sums to create basic patents in order to maintain its monopoly position in the telephone field. Moreover, AT&T's management actively encouraged the development of non-telephone patents to use for bargaining with competitors. For example, between 1920 and 1926 AT&T protected itself by cross-licensing its broadcasting-related patents with RCA. In turn, RCA and its allies agreed not to threaten AT&T's monopoly for wire communication. In particular, in the cross-licensing agreement of 1926, AT&T and RCA contracted to exchange information on sound motion pictures, if and when required. Thus by 1926, AT&T had control over its own patents, as well as any RCA created.

Using its economic power and patent position, Western Electric moved to reap large rewards for its sound-recording technology. As early as 1925, it had interested and licensed the key phonograph and record manufacturers Victor and Columbia. Movie executives proved more stubborn, so Western Electric hired an intermediary, Walter J. Rich. On 27 May 1925, Rich inked an agreement under which he agreed to commercially exploit the AT&T system for nine months.

Innovation

Warner Bros.

Warner Bros. would eventually be the company to innovate sound motion pictures. However, in 1925, Warner ranked low in the economic pecking order in the American film industry. Certainly brothers Harry, Albert, Sam, and Jack had come a long way since their days as nickelodeon operators in Ohio some two decades earlier. Yet in the mid-1920s, their future seemed severely constrained. Warner neither controlled an international system for distribution, nor owned a chain of first-run theaters. The brothers' most formidable rivals, Famous Players (soon to be renamed Paramount), Loew's, and First National did. Eldest brother Harry Warner remained optimistic and sought help.

In time, Harry Warner met Waddill Catchings, a financier with Wall Street's Goldman, Sachs. Catchings, boldest of the "New Era" Wall Street investors, agreed to take a flyer with this fledgling enterprise in the most speculative of entertainment fields. Catchings correctly reasoned that the consumer-oriented 1920s economy would provide a fertile atmosphere for boundless growth in the movie field. And Warner seemed progressive. The four brothers maintained strict cost accounting and budget controls, and seemed to have attracted more than competent managerial talent. Catchings agreed to finance Warner, only if it followed his master plan. The four brothers, sensing they would find no better alternative, readily agreed.

During the spring of 1925, Harry Warner, president of the firm, formally appointed Waddill Catchings to the board of directors, and elevated him to chairman of the finance committee. Catchings immediately established a $3 million revolving credit account through New York's National Bank of Commerce. Although this bank had never loaned a dollar to a motion picture company, not even the mighty Paramount, Catchings possessed enough clout to convince president James S. Alexander that Warner would be a good risk. Overnight Warner had acquired a permanent source for financing future productions. Simultaneously Warner took over the struggling Vitagraph Corporation, complete with its network of fifty distribution exchanges throughout the world. In this deal Warner also gained the pioneer company's two small studios, processing laboratory, and extensive film library. Finally, with four million more dollars that Catchings raised through bonds, Warner strengthened its distribution system, and even launched a ten-theater chain. Certainly by mid-1925 Warner was becoming a force to be reckoned with in the American movie business.

Warner's expansionary activities set the stage for the coming of sound. At the urging of Sam Warner, who was an electronics enthusiast, the company established radio station KFWB in Hollywood to promote Warner films. The equipment was secured from Western Electric. Soon Sam Warner and Nathan Levinson, Western's Los Angeles representative, became fast friends. Until then, Walter J. Rich had located no takers for Western Electric's sound inventions. Past failures had made a lasting and negative impression on the industry leaders, a belief shared by Harry Warner. Consequently, Sam had to trick his older brother into even attending a demonstration. That screening, in May 1925, included a recording of a five-piece jazz band. Quickly Harry and other Warner executives reasoned that if the company could equip their newly acquired theaters with sound and present vaudeville acts as part of their programs, they could successfully challenge the Big Three. Then, even Warner's smallest house could offer (a) famous vaudeville acts (on film); (b) silent features; and (c) the finest orchestral accompaniments (on disc). Warner, at this point, never considered feature-length talking pictures, only singing and musical films.

Catchings endorsed such reasoning and gave the go-ahead to open negotiations with Walter J. Rich. On 25 June 1925, Warner signed a letter of agreement with Western Electric calling for a period of joint experimentation. Western Electric would supply the engineers and sound equipment; Warner the camera operators, editors, and the supervisory talent of Sam Warner. Work commenced in September 1925 at the old Vitagraph studio in Brooklyn. Meanwhile, Warner continued to expand under Waddill Catchings' careful guidance. Although feature film output was reduced, more money was spent on each picture. In the spring of 1926, Warner opened a second radio station and an additional film-processing laboratory, and further expanded its foreign operations. As a result of this rapid growth, the firm expected a $1 million loss on its annual income statement issued in March 1926.

By December 1925, experiments were going so well that Rich proposed forming a permanent sound motion picture corporation. The contracts were prepared and the parties readied to sign, but negotiations ground to a halt as Western Electric underwent a management shuffle. Western placed John E. Otterson, an Annapolis graduate and career navy officer, in charge of exploiting nontelephone inventions. Otterson possessed nothing but contempt for Warner. He wanted to secure contracts with industry giants Paramount and Loew's, and then take direct control himself. Hitherto, Western Electric seemed content to function as a supplier of equipment. Catchings saw this dictatorial stance as typical of a man with a military background unable to adjust to the world of give-and-take in modern business and finance. Unfortunately for Warner, AT&T's corporate muscle backed Otterson's demands.

Only by going over Otterson's head to Western Electric's president, Edgar S. Bloom, was Catchings able to protect Warner interests and secure a reasonable contract. In April 1926, Warner, Walter J. Rich, and Western Electric formed the Vitaphone Corporation to develop sound motion pictures further. Warner and Rich furnished the capital. Western Electric granted Vitaphone an exclusive license to record and reproduce sound movies on its equipment. In return, Vitaphone agreed to lease a minimum number of sound systems each year and pay a royalty fee of 8 percent of gross revenues from sound motion pictures. Vitaphone's total equipment commitment became twenty-four hundred systems in four years.

As Variety and the other trade papers announced the formation of the alliance, Vitaphone began its assault on the marketplace. Its first goal was to acquire talent. Vitaphone contracted with the Victor Talking Machine Company for the right to bargain with its popular musical artists. A similar agreement was reached with the Metropolitan Opera Company. Vitaphone dealt directly with vaudeville stars. In a few short months it had contracted for the talent to produce the musical short subjects Harry Warner had envisioned. So confident was Vitaphone's management that the firm engaged the services of the New York Philharmonic Orchestra. Throughout the summer of 1926, Sam Warner and his crew labored feverishly to ready a Vitaphone program for a fall premiere, while the Warner publicity apparatus cranked out thousands of column inches for the nation's press.

Vitaphone unveiled its marvel on 6 August 1926, at the Warners' Theatre in New York. The first-nighters who packed the house paid up to $10 for tickets. The program began with eight "Vitaphone Preludes". In the first, Will Hays congratulated the brothers Warner and Western Electric for their pioneering efforts. At the end, to create the illusion of a stage appearance, Hays bowed to the audience, anticipating their applause. Next, conductor Henry Hadley led the New York Philharmonic in the Overture to *Tannhäuser*. He too bowed. The acts that followed consisted primarily of operatic and concert performances: tenor Giovanni Martinelli offered an aria from I *Pagliacci*, violinist Mischa Elman played "Humoresque", and soprano Anna Case sang, supported by the Metropolitan Opera Chorus. Only one "prelude" broke the serious tone of the evening and that featured Roy Smeck, a popular vaudeville comic-musician. Warner, playing it close to the vest, sought approval from all bodies of respectable critical opinion. The silent feature *Don Juan* followed a brief intermission. The musical accompaniment (sound-on-disc) caused no great stir because it "simply replaced" an absent live orchestra. All in all, Vitaphone, properly marketed, seemed to have a bright future.

That autumn, the *Don Juan* package played in Atlantic City, Chicago, and St Louis. Quickly Vitaphone organized a second program, but this time aimed at popular palates. The feature, *The Better 'Ole*, starred Charlie Chaplin's brother, Sydney. The shorts featured vaudeville "headliners" George Jessel, Irving Berlin, Elsie Janis, and Al Jolson. These performers would have charged more than any single theater owner could have afforded, if presented live. The trade press now began to see bright prospects for the invention that could place so much high-priced talent in towns like Akron, Ohio, and Richmond, Va. By the time Vitaphone's third program opened in February 1927, Warner had recorded fifty more acts.

As a result of the growing popularity of Vitaphone presentations, the company succeeded in installing nearly a hundred systems by the end of 1926. Most of these were located in the East. The installation in March 1927 of apparatus in the new Roxy theater and the attendant publicity served to spur business even more. Consequently, Warner's financial health showed signs of improvement. The corporation had invested over $3 million in Vitaphone alone, yet its quarterly losses had declined from about $334,000 in 1925 to less than $110,000 in 1926. It appeared that Catchings' master plan was working.

John Otterson remained unsatisfied. He sought to take control of Vitaphone so that Western Electric could deal directly with Paramount and Loew's. To accomplish this he initiated a harassment campaign by raising prices on Vitaphone equipment fourfold, and demanding a greater share of the revenues. By December 1926, Western Electric and Warner had broken off relations. Simultaneously, Otterson organized a special Western Electric subsidiary called Electrical Research Products, Inc. (ERPI), to conduct the company's nontelephone business – over 90 percent of which concerned motion picture sound equipment.

Realistically Warner, even with Catchings' assistance, could not prevent Otterson from talking with other companies – even though exclusive rights were contractually held by Warner. However, only Fox would initial an agreement. The majors adopted a wait-and-see stance. In fact, the five most important companies – Loew's (MGM), Universal, First National,

Paramount, and Producers Distributing Corporation – signed an accord in February 1927 to act together in regard to sound. The "Big Five Agreement", as it was called, recognized that since there were several sound systems on the market, inability to interchange this equipment could hinder wide distribution of pictures and therefore limit potential profits. These companies agreed to jointly adopt only the system that their specially appointed committee would certify, after one year of study, was the "best" for the industry. As further protection, they would employ no system unless it was made available to all producers, distributors, and exhibitors on "reasonable" terms.

Otterson needed to wrest away Warner's exclusive rights if he ever hoped to strike a deal with the Big Five. To this end, he threatened to declare Warner in default of its contractual obligations. Catchings, knowing such public statements would undermine his relations with the banks, persuaded Warner to accede to Otterson's wishes. In April 1927, ERPI paid Vitaphone $1,322,306 to terminate the old agreement. In May, after the two signed the so-called New License Agreement, Vitaphone, like Fox, became merely a licensee of ERPI. Warner had given up the exclusive franchise to exploit ERPI sound equipment and lost its share of a potential fortune in licensing fees.

Now on its own, Warner immediately moved all production to several new sound stages in Hollywood. While the parent company continued with its production program of silent features, Vitaphone regularly turned out five shorts a week, which became known in the industry as "canned vaudeville". Bryan Foy, an ex-vaudevillian and silent film director, now worked under Sam Warner to supervise the sound short subject unit. At this juncture, Vitaphone's most significant problem lay in a dearth of exhibition outlets for movies with sound. By the fall of 1927, six months since the signing of the New License Agreement, ERPI had installed only forty-four sound systems. ERPI was holding back on its sales campaign until the majors made a decision. Warner would later charge that ERPI had not used its best efforts to market the equipment and had itself defaulted. This accusation and others were brought to arbitration and, in a 1934 settlement, ERPI was forced to pay Vitaphone $5 million.

As the 1927–8 season opened, Vitaphone began to add new forms of sound films to its program. Though *The Jazz Singer* premiered on 6 October 1927, to lukewarm reviews, its four Vitaphoned segments of Al Jolson's songs proved very popular. Vitaphone contracted with Jolson immediately to make three more films for $100,000. (The four Warner brothers did not attend *The Jazz Singer*'s New York premiere because Sam Warner died in Los Angeles on 5 October. Jack Warner took over Sam's position as head of Vitaphone production.) Bryan Foy pushed his unit to create four new shorts each week, becoming more bold in program-ming strategies. On 4 December 1928, Vitaphone released the short *My Wife's Gone Away*, a ten-minute, all-talking comedy based on a vaudeville playlet developed by William Demarest. Critics praised this short; audiences flocked to it. Thus Foy, under Jack Warner's supervision, began to borrow even more from available vaudeville acts and "playlets" to create all-talking shorts. During Christmas week, 1927, Vitaphone released a twenty-minute, all-talking drama, *Solomon's Children*. Again revenues were high, and in January 1928, Foy moved to schedule production of two all-talking shorts per week.

Warner had begun to experiment with alternative types of shorts as a cheap way to maintain the novelty value of Vitaphone entertainment. Moreover, with such shorts it could develop talent, innovate new equipment, and create an audience for feature-length, all-sound films. In the spring of 1928, with the increased popularity of these shorts, Warner began to change its feature film offerings. On 14 March 1928, it released *Tenderloin* – an ordinary mystery that contained five segments in which the actors spoke all their lines (for twelve of the film's eighty-five minutes). More part-talkies soon followed that spring.

Harry Warner and Waddill Catchings knew the investment in sound was a success by April 1928. By then it had become clear that the *The Jazz Singer* show had become the most popular entertainment offering of the 1927–8 season. In cities that rarely held films for more than one week *The Jazz Singer* package set records for length of run: for example, five-week runs in Charlotte, NC, Reading, Pa., Seattle, and Baltimore. By mid-February 1928, *The Jazz Singer* and the shorts were in a (record) eighth week in Columbus, Ohio, St Louis, and Detroit, and a (record) seventh week in Seattle, Portland, Ore., and Los Angeles. The Roxy even booked *The Jazz Singer* package for an unprecedented second run in April 1928, where it grossed in excess of $100,000 each week, among that theater's best grosses for that season. Perhaps more important, all these first-run showings did not demand the usual expenses of a stage show and orchestra. It took Warner only until the fall of 1928 to convert to the complete production of talkies – both features and shorts. Catchings and Harry Warner had laid the foundation for this maximum exploitation of profit with their slow, steady expansion in production and distribution. In 1929, Warner would become the most profitable of any American motion picture company.

The Fox-Case Corporation

As noted above, only the Fox Film Corporation had also shown any interest in sound movies. Its chief, William Fox, had investigated the sound-on-film system developed by Theodore W. Case and Earl Sponable and found it to be potentially a great improvement over the cumbersome Western Electric disc system. Theodore Case and Earl Sponable were two recluse scientists. In 1913, the independently wealthy, Yale-trained physicist Case established a private laboratory in his hometown of Auburn, New York, a small city near Syracuse. Spurred on by recent breakthroughs in the telephone and radio fields, Case and his assistant, Sponable, sought to better the Audion tube. In 1917 they perfected the Thalofide cell, a highly improved vacuum tube, and began to integrate this invention into a system for recording sounds. As part of this work, Case met Lee De Forest. For personal reasons – envy perhaps – Case turned all his laboratory's efforts to besting De Forest. Within eighteen months, Case labs produced an improved sound-on-film system, based on the Thalofide cell. Naively, De Forest had openly shared with Case all his knowledge of sound-on-film technology. So as De Forest unsuccessfully attempted to market his Phonofilm system, Case quietly constructed – with his own funds – a complete sound studio and projection room adjacent to his laboratory.

In 1925, Case determined he was ready to try to market his inventions. Edward Craft of Western Electric journeyed to Auburn, and saw and heard a demonstration film. Craft left quite impressed. But after careful consideration, he and Frank Jewett decided that Case's patents added no substantial improvement to the Western Electric sound-on-disc system, then under exclusive contract to Warner. Rebuffed, Case decided to directly solicit a show business entrepreneur. He first approached John J. Murdock, the long-time general manager of the Keith-Albee vaudeville circuit. Case argued that his sound system could be used to record musical and comedy acts – the same idea Harry Warner had conceived six months earlier. Murdock blanched. He had been burned by Edison's hyperbole only a decade earlier, and De Forest a mere twenty-four months before. Keith-Albee would never be interested in talking movies! Executives from all the "Big Three" motion picture corporations, Paramount, Loew's (MGM), and First National, echoed Murdock's response. None saw the slightest benefit in this latest version of sight and sound.

Case moved to the second tier of the US film industry – Producers Distributing Company (PDC), Film Booking Office (FBO), Warner, Fox, and Universal. In 1926, Case signed with Fox because Courtland Smith, president of Fox Newsreels, reasoned that sound newsreels could push that branch of Fox Film to the forefront of the industry. In June 1926, Smith arranged a demonstration for company owner, founder, and president William Fox. The boss was pleased, and within a month helped create the Fox-Case Corporation to produce sound motion pictures. Case turned all patents over to the new corporation, and retired to his laboratory in upstate New York.

Initially, William Fox's approval of experiments with the Case technology constituted only a small portion of a comprehensive plan to thrust Fox Film into a preeminant position in the motion picture industry. Fox and his advisors had initiated an expansion campaign in 1925. By floating $6 million of common stock, they increased budgets for feature films and enlarged the newsreel division. (Courtland Smith was hired at this point.) Simultaneously Fox began building a chain of motion picture theaters. At that time Fox Film controlled only twenty small neighborhood houses in the New York City environs. By 1927, the Fox chain included houses in Philadelphia, Washington, DC, Brooklyn, New York City, St Louis, Detroit, Newark, Milwaukee, and a score of cities west of the Rockies. To finance these sizable investments, William Fox developed close ties to Harold Stuart, president of the Chicago investment house of Halsey, Stuart. Meanwhile, Courtland Smith had assumed control of Fox-Case, and, in 1926, initiated the innovation of the Case sound-on-film technology. At first all he could oversee were defensive actions designed to protect Fox-Case's patent position. In September 1926, exactly two months after incorporation, Fox-Case successfully thwarted claims by Lee De Forest, and a German concern, Tri-Ergon. For the latter, Fox-Case advanced $50,000 to check the future court action.

At last, Fox-Case could assault the marketplace. Although Smith pushed for immediate experimentation with sound newsreels, William Fox conservatively ordered Fox-Case to imitate the innovation strategy of Warner and film popular vaudeville acts. On 24 February 1927, Fox executives felt confident enough to stage a widely publicized demonstration of the newly christened Movietone system. At ten o'clock in the morning, fifty reporters entered the Fox studio near Times Square and were filmed by the miracle of Movietone. Four hours later these representatives of the press corps saw and heard themselves as part of a private screening. In addition, Fox-Case presented several vaudeville sound shorts: a banjo and piano act, a comedy sketch, and three songs by the then-popular cabaret performer Raquel Mueller. The strategy worked. Unanimous favorable commentary issued forth; the future seemed bright. Consequently, William Fox ordered sound systems for twenty-six of Fox's largest first-run theaters, including the recently acquired Roxy.

However, by this time Warner had signed nearly all popular entertainers to exclusive contracts. Smith pressed William Fox to again consider newsreels with sound. Then, Smith argued, Fox Film could offer a unique, economically viable alternative to Warner's presen-tations, and move into a heretofore unoccupied portion of the market for motion picture entertainment. Furthermore, sound newsreels would provide a logical method by which

Fox-Case could gradually perfect necessary new techniques of camerawork and editing. Convinced, William Fox ordered Smith to adopt this course for technological innovation. This decision would prove more successful for Fox Film's overall goal of corporate growth than either William Fox or Courtland Smith imagined at the time.

Smith moved quickly. The sound newsreel premiere came on 30 April 1927, at the Roxy in the form of a four-minute record of marching West Point cadets. And despite the lack of any buildup, this newsreel elicited an enthusiastic response from the trade press and New York-based motion picture reviewers. Quickly Smith seized upon one of the most important symbolic news events of the 1920s. At eight in the morning, on 20 May 1927, Charles Lindbergh departed for Paris. That evening Fox Movietone News presented footage of the takeoff – with sound – to a packed house at the Roxy. Six thousand persons stood and cheered for nearly ten minutes. The press saluted this new motion picture marvel and noted how it had brought alive the heroics of the "Lone Eagle". In June, when Lindbergh returned to a tumultuous welcome in New York City and Washington, DC, Movietone News cameramen also recorded portions of those celebrations. Both William Fox and Courtland Smith were now satisfied that the Fox-Case system had been launched on a propitious path.

That summer, Smith dispatched camera operators to all parts of the globe. They recorded the further heroics of aviators, beauty contests, and sporting events, as well as produced the earliest filmic records of statements by Benito Mussolini and Alfred Smith. Newspaper columnists, educators, and other opinion leaders lauded these latter short subjects for their didactic value. Fox Film's principal constraint now became a paucity of exhibition outlets. During the fall of 1927, Fox Film did make Movietone newsreels the standard in all Fox-owned theaters, but that represented less than 3 percent of the potential market. More extensive profits would come as Fox Film formed a larger chain of first-run theaters. In the meantime, Courtland Smith established a regular pattern for release of Movietone newsreels, one ten-minute reel per week. He also increased the permanent staff and established a worldwide network of stringers.

In addition, Smith and William Fox decided again to try to produce vaudeville shorts and silent feature films accompanied by synchronized music on disc. Before 1928, Fox-Case released only one scored feature, *Sunrise*. The two executives moved quickly. By January 1928, Fox had filmed ten vaudeville shorts and a part-talkie feature, *Blossom Time*. During the spring of 1928, these efforts, Fox's newsreels, and Warner's shorts and part-talkies proved to be the hits of the season. Thus in May 1928, William Fox declared that 100 percent of the upcoming production schedule would be "Movietoned". Simultaneously Fox Film continued to wire, as quickly as possible, all the houses in its ever-expanding chain and draw up plans for an all-sound Hollywood-based studio. Fox's innovation of sound neared completion; colossal profits loomed on the horizon.

The rise of RKO

Only RCA offered Warner, Western Electric, or Fox any serious competition. In 1919, General Electric and Westinghouse had created RCA to control America's patents for radio broadcasting. Like rival AT&T, GE conducted fundamental research in radio technology. The necessary inventions for what would become RCA's Photophone sound-on-film system originated when, during the First World War, the US Navy sought a high-speed recorder of radio signals. GE scientist Charles A. Hoxie perfected such a device. After the war, Hoxie pressed to extend his work. Within three years, having incorporated a photoelectric cell and a vibrating mirror, he could record a wide variety of complex sounds. In December 1921, GE executives labeled the new invention the Pallo-Photophone.

To test it, Willis R. Whitney, head of the GE Research Laboratory, successfully recorded speeches by Vice-President Calvin Coolidge and several Harding Administration cabinet members. At this point, GE executives conceived of the Pallo-Photophone as a marketable substitute for the phonograph. During 1922 and 1923, Hoxie and his assistants continued to perfect the invention. For example, they discovered that the recording band need not be 35 millimeters wide. A track as narrow as 1.5 millimeters proved sufficient, and thus freed sound to accompany a motion picture image. Simultaneously other GE scientists, Chester W. Rise and Edward W. Kellogg, developed a new type of loudspeaker to improve reception for the radio sets General Electric manufactured for RCA. Late in 1922, Whitney learned of Lee De Forest's efforts to record sound on film. Not to be outdone, Whitney ordered Hoxie and his research team to develop a sound reproducer that could be attached to a standard motion picture projector. In November 1923, Hoxie demonstrated such a system for GE's top executives in an almost perfect state. However, by that time, Whitney and his superiors sensed that De Forest's failure to innovate sound motion pictures proved there existed no market for Hoxie's invention. Whitney promptly transferred all efforts toward the development of a marketable all-electric phonograph. GE successfully placed its new phonograph before the public during the summer of 1925.

One year later, because of Warner's success, Whitney reactivated the sound movie experiments. At this point he christened the system "Photophone". By the end of that year, 1926, GE's publicity department had created several experimental short subjects. Quickly GE executives pondered how to approach a sales campaign. However before they could institute any action, Fox sought a license in order to utilize GE's amplification patents. Contemplating the request, David Sarnoff, RCA's general manager, convinced his superiors at GE that RCA should go out on its own, sign up the large movie producers Paramount and Loew's, and not worry about Fox. The GE high brass agreed and assigned Sarnoff the task of commercially exploiting GE's sound movie patents.

Sarnoff easily convinced Paramount and Loew executives to seriously consider RCA's alternative to Western Electric's then monopoly, even though RCA had yet to publicly demonstrate Photophone. Presently the "Big Five Agreement" was signed. Sarnoff immediately went public. On 2 February 1927, Sarnoff demonstrated Photophone for invited guests and the press at the State theater in GE's home city of Schenectady, New York. Musical short subjects featuring a hundredpiece orchestra impressed all present. Nine days later Sarnoff recreated the event for more reporters at New York's Rivoli theater. Here two reels of MGM's *The Flesh and the Devil* were accompanied by a Photophone recording of the Capital theater orchestra. Then three shorts featured the Van Curler Hotel Orchestra of Schenectady, an unnamed baritone, and a quartet of singers recruited from General Electric employees. A *New York Times* reporter praised the synchronization, volume, and tone. Sarnoff, in turn, lauded Photophone's ease of installation and simplicity of operation.

In private, Sarnoff tried to convince the producers' committee of his company's technical and financial advantages. The producers had established three specific criteria for selection: (a) the equipment had to be technically adequate; (b) the manufacturer had to control all required patents; and (c) the manufacturer had to have substantial resources and financial strength. Only two systems qualified: RCA's Photophone and Western Electric's Vitaphone. At first, the producers favored RCA because it had not licensed any movie concern, whereas Western Electric had formal links to Warner and Fox. In October 1927, Sarnoff proposed an agreement which called for a holding company, one-half owned by RCA and one-half by the five motion picture producers. All of GE's sound patents would be vested in this one corporation. Sarnoff demanded 8 percent of all gross revenues from sound movies as a royalty. The producers countered. They sought individual licenses and fees set at $500 per reel. For a typical eight-reel film (90 minutes) with gross revenues of $500,000, the 8 percent royalty would be $40,000; at the new rate the amount came to $4,000, a savings of $36,000.

Sarnoff reluctantly acceded to the per reel method of royalty calculation, but stubbornly refused to grant individual licenses. On the other hand, the motion picture corporations held fast to their belief that they should play no role in the manufacture of the apparatus. They wanted a license only to produce and distribute sound films. For two months the two parties stalemated over this issue. Late in November 1927, John Otterson of Western Electric stepped forward and offered individual licenses. Western Electric's engineers had made great progress with their sound-on-film system, and there no longer existed exclusive ties to Warner. Consequently, in March 1928, the movie producers, with all the relevant information in hand, selected Western Electric. Each producer – Paramount, United Artists, Loew's, and First National – secured an individual license and would pay $500 per reel of negative footage. All four signed on 11 May 1928. Universal, Columbia and other companies quickly followed. The movie producers had adroitly played the two electrical giants off each other and secured reasonably favorable terms.

Sarnoff reacted quickly as the tide turned toward Western Electric. First General Electric purchased (for nearly $500,000) 14,000 shares of stock of the Film Booking Office from a syndicate headed by Joseph P. Kennedy. This acquisition guaranteed Photophone a studio outlet. FBO was the only producer with national distribution which was not linked in talks with Western Electric. Next Sarnoff formed RCA Photophone, Inc. Sarnoff now controlled production facilities and the necessary sound technology. To generate significant profits, RCA needed a chain of theaters.

In 1928, the Keith-Albee vaudeville chain controlled such a chain. Faced with declining business in vaudeville, Keith-Albee executives developed two approaches. First they took over the Orpheum vaudeville chain, and thus merged all major American vaudeville under one umbrella. The new Keith Albee-Orpheum controlled two hundred large downtown theaters. Second, Keith-Albee acquired a small movie company, Pathé, just to hedge its bets. When Sarnoff approached the owners of the new Keith-Albee-Orpheum they were more than ready to sell. Sarnoff quickly moved to consolidate his empire. FBO and Pathé formally acquired licenses for Photophone. FBO and Pathé executives supervised the addition of music-on-film to three features, *King of Kings*, *The Godless Girl*, and *The Perfect Crime*. Upcoming sound newsreels and vaudeville shorts were promised. However, these films would be useless unless Sarnoff could wire the Keith-Albee-Orpheum theaters with Photophone equipment. Warner, Fox, and Western Electric had taken almost two years to eliminate all the problems of presenting clear sounds of sufficient volume in large movie palaces. As of this point Photophone had yet to be tested in a commercial situation. And Sarnoff and his staff would need at least six months to iron out technological problems. Promised first in April, then July, commercial installations commenced in October 1928. In the meantime, Sarnoff used a low installation price and sweeping prognostications of future greatness to persuade a shrinking number of prospective clients to wait for Photophone equipment.

That October, Sarnoff legally consolidated RCA's motion picture interests by creating a holding company, Radio-Keith-Orpheum (RKO). Sarnoff became president of the film industry's newest vertically integrated combine. The merger united theaters (Keith-Albee-Orpheum), radio (NBC), and motion pictures (FBO and Pathé, subsequently renamed Radio Pictures in May 1929). Although late on the scene, RCA had established a secure place in the motion picture industry. RKO released its first talkies in the spring of 1929, and Photophone could battle Western Electric for contracts with the remaining unwired houses. Gradually during the 1930s, RCA Photophone would become as widely accepted as Western Electric's system.

Diffusion

The widespread adoption of sound – its diffusion – took place quickly and smoothly, principally because of the extensive planning of the producers' committee. Since an enormous potential for profits existed, it was incumbent on the majors to make the switchover as rapidly as possible. Paramount released its first films with musical accompaniment in August 1928; by September its pictures contained talking sequences; and by January 1929, it sent out its first all-talking production. By May, one year after signing with ERPI, Paramount produced talkies exclusively and was operating on a level with Warner and Fox. In September 1929, MGM, Fox, RKO, Universal, and United Artists completed their transitions. Those independent production companies which survived took, on average, one year longer.

Elaborate plans had been laid by the industry to facilitate diffusion. In Hollywood, the Academy of Motion Picture Arts and Sciences was designated as a clearing house for information relating to production problems. The local film boards of trade handled changes in distribution trade practices. And a special lawyers' committee representing the major producers was appointed to handle disputes and contractual matters with equipment manufacturers. For example, when ERPI announced a royalty hike, the committee initiated a protest, seeking lower rates. Unions presented no difficulties. The American Federation of Musicians unsuccessfully tried to prevent the wholesale firing of theatrical musicians; Actors' Equity, now that professionals from the Broadway stage began to flock west, failed to establish a union shop in the studios. All problems were resolved within a single year; the industry never left an even keel.

ERPI's task all the while was to keep up with the demand for apparatus. It wired the large, first-run theaters first and then, as equipment became available, subsequent-run houses. Installations were made usually from midnight to nine in the morning. For example, in January 1930, ERPI installed more than nine systems each day. To facilitate the switchover, Western Electric expanded its Hawthorne, Illinois, plant, and ERPI established training schools for projectionists in seventeen cities and opened fifty district offices to service and repair equipment. Many smaller theaters, especially in the South and Southwest, could not afford ERPI's prices and signed with RCA, or De Forest. As late as July 1930, fully 22 percent of all US theaters still presented silent versions of talkies. That figure neared zero two years later.

The public's infatuation with sound ushered in another boom period for the industry. Paramount's profits jumped $7 million between 1928 and 1929, Fox's $3.5 million, and Loew's

$3 million. Warner, however, set the record; its profits increased $12 million, from a base of only $2 million. A 600 percent leap! Conditions were ripe for consolidation, and Warner, with its early start in sound, set the pace. It began by acquiring the Stanley Company, which owned a chain of three hundred theaters along the East Coast, and First National. In 1925, when Waddill Catchings joined the Warner board of directors, the company's assets were valued at a little over $5 million; in 1930 they totaled $230 million. In five short years, Warner had become one of the largest and most profitable companies in the American film industry.

Not content merely to establish RKO, David Sarnoff of RCA set out to sever all connections with General Electric and Westinghouse and acquire sound manufacturing facilities of his own. The first step in this direction was the acquisition in March 1929 of Victor Talking Machine Company and its huge plant in Camden, New Jersey. In the process, RCA secured Victor's exclusive contracts with many of the biggest stars in the musical world. By December 1929 Sarnoff had reached his goal. RCA was now a powerful independent entertainment giant with holdings in the broadcasting, vaudeville, phonograph, and motion picture industries.

William Fox had the most grandiose plan of all. In March 1929, he acquired controlling interest in Loew's, the parent company of MGM. Founder Marcus Loew had died in 1927 and left his widow and sons one-third of the company's stock. Nicholas Schenck, the new president, pooled his stock and that belonging to corporate officers with the family's and sold out to Fox at 25 percent above the market price. The new Fox-Loew's merger created the largest motion picture complex in the world. Its assets totaled more than $200 million and an annual earning potential existed of $20 million. Fox assumed a substantial short-term debt obligation in the process, but during the bull market of the late twenties he could simply float more stock and bonds to meet his needs.

Adolph Zukor of Paramount, meanwhile, added more theaters, bringing Paramount's total to almost one thousand. He also acquired a 49 percent interest in the Columbia Broadcasting System. Then, in the fall of 1929, he proposed a merger with Warner that would create a motion picture and entertainment complex larger than Fox-Loew's and RCA combined. Catchings and Harry Warner were agreeable, but the new US attorney general, William D. Mitchell, raised the red flag. If that merger went through, the industry would be dominated by three firms. As it happened, though, it was to be dominated by five. After the stock market crash, William Fox was unable to meet his short-term debts and had to relinquish ownership of Loew's. The oligopolistic structure of the industry, now formed by Warner, Paramount, Fox, Loew's, and RKO, would continue to operate well into the 1950s. The coming of sound had produced important forces for industry consolidation, immediately prior to the motion picture industry's first crisis of retrenchment – the Great Depression.

PART THREE

PROJECTIONS AND AESTHETICS

Introduction

Theorists and filmmakers alike have endeavored to identify those instances where cinema's thematic and aesthetic formations extend towards a revised consciousness, reflecting and adopting the essential principles of technologies and technological cultural contexts other than its own.

Responding in part to Donna Haraway's "A Manifesto for Cyborgs: Science, Technology, and Socialist Feminism in the 1980s",[1] Claudia Springer examines a series of films that magnify and in turn negotiate cultural attitudes to the possibility of a future where bodies are threatened by the prospect of obsolescence. What emerges, she suggests, is a contradictory response, one that oscillates between technophilia and technophobia. On the one hand, there is the potential pleasure of the interface, "the thrill of escape from the confines of the body and from the boundaries that have separated organic from inorganic matter". On the other, the gender distinctions that one would expect to vanish when dispensing with the biological body in fact persist in popular cyborg narratives.

The vision of artificial life that Springer identifies is projected according to a demarcation not solely of cybernetic and organic, but of gender roles associated with reproduction and sexuality. "What is really being debated in the discourses surrounding a cyborg future", she explains, "are contemporary disputes concerning gender and sexuality, with the future providing a clean slate, or a blank screen, onto which we can project our fascination and fears." This psychic imaginary becomes an expression of patriarchal fears concerning female sexuality, manifested in the relationship between technological and biological reproduction.

As Dogme 95, Lars von Trier and Thomas Vinterberg propose a series of parameters designed to counter the type of filmmaking associated with the ease of use and stylistic presets of consumer electronics. "Today", they pronounce, "a technological storm is raging of which the result is the elevation of cosmetics to God. By using new technology anyone at any time can wash the last grains of truth away in the deadly embrace of sensation."

The rules and restrictions of "The Vow of Chastity", by contrast, are deliberately austere: a film must be shot on location, sound must be recorded with the image, the camera must be held by hand, and so on. As much a provocative gesture as it is a sustainable movement, Dogme 95 has nevertheless given rise to a series of feature films – including *The Celebration*

(Dogme 1: Festen) (1998) and *The Idiots (Dogme 2: Idioterne)* (1998) – that subscribe to its ascetic rulebook.

Patricia R. Zimmermann explores the liberatory potential of digital technologies in terms of the aesthetics of deconstruction they engender. Despite utopian claims, inequalities in the dissemination of technologies have resulted in what theorists describe as a digital divide, a new class distinction that separates the digital haves (exemplified by globalized corporations such as Microsoft) and the digital have-nots (those without the means to participate in the hype of technological revolution, or who seek to challenge its political underpinnings).

In this context, strategies of ownership take on amplified political meaning. Zimmermann identifies how technologies, or rather counter-technologies, can be employed to deconstruct the ideological implications of a global trade in moving images. Where the processes of digital dissemination differ from those of previous eras is in the sheer malleability of digital data. Zeroes and ones, the constituent elements of digital information, can be replicated, and therefore deconstructed, with unprecedented ease. Having hijacked an original, its meaning can be pirated, sabotaged, jammed or subverted for the purpose of reorienting its political status.

In different ways and to different extents, cinema has responded, and continues to respond, to the regimes of technology located within society. The nature by which these various strategies are realized reveals a shift in cinematic form, a refraction whose sounds and images replicate, and in turn shape, the conditions of an evolving technological culture.

Note

1   Haraway, D. (1985) "A Manifesto for Cyborgs: Science, Technology, and Socialist Feminism in the 1980s" in *Socialist Review* 80: 65–107.

The Pleasure of the Interface

7

CLAUDIA SPRINGER

Sex times technology equals the future.
J. G. Ballard[1]

A discourse describing the union of humans and electronic technology currently circulates in the scientific community and in popular culture texts such as films, television, video games, magazines, cyberpunk fiction and comic books. Much of the discourse represents the possibility of human fusion with computer technology in positive terms, conceiving of a hybrid computer/human that displays highly evolved intelligence and escapes the imperfections of the human body. And yet, while disparaging the imperfect human body, the discourse simultaneously uses language and imagery associated with the body and bodily functions to represent its vision of human/technological perfection. Computer technologies thus occupy a contradictory discursive position where they represent both escape from the physical body and fulfilment of erotic desire. To quote science fiction author J. G. Ballard again:

> I believe that organic sex, body against body, skin area against skin area, is becoming no longer possible. . . . What we're getting is a whole new order of sexual fantasies, involving a different order of experiences, like car crashes, like traveling in jet aircraft, the whole overlay of new technologies, architecture, interior design, communications, transport, merchandising. These things are beginning to reach into our lives and change the interior design of our sexual fantasies.[2]

The language and imagery of technological bodies exist across a variety of diverse texts. Scientists who are currently designing ways to integrate human consciousness with computers (as opposed to creating Artificial Intelligence) describe a future in which human bodies will be obsolete, replaced by computers that retain human intelligence on software.[3] *Omni* magazine postulates a "postbiological era". The *Whole Earth Review* publishes a forum titled "Is the body obsolete?" Jean-François Lyotard asks, "Can thought go on without a body?"[4] Popular culture has appropriated the scientific project; but instead of effacing the human body, these texts intensify corporeality in their representation of cyborgs. A mostly technological system is represented as its opposite: a muscular human body with robotic parts that heighten physicality and sexuality. In other words, these contemporary texts represent a future where human bodies are on the verge of becoming obsolete but sexuality nevertheless prevails.

The contradictory discourse on cyborgs reveals a new manifestation of the simultaneous revulsion and fascination with the human body that has existed throughout the western cultural tradition. Ambivalence toward the body has traditionally been played out most explicitly in texts labelled pornographic, in which the construction of desire often depends upon an element of aversion. That which has been prohibited by censorship, for example, frequently becomes highly desirable. It was only in the nineteenth century, however, that pornography was introduced as a concept and a word, though its etymology dates back to the Greek πορνογραφος: writing about prostitutes. In his book *The Secret Museum*, Walter Kendrick argues that the signifier "pornography" has never had a specific signified, but constitutes a shifting ideological framework that has been imposed on a variety of texts since its inception.[5] He suggests that after the years between 1966 and 1970 we entered a post-pornographic era heralded by the publication of *The Report of the Commission on Obscenity and Pornography*.[6] I would like to propose that if we are in a post-pornographic era, it is most aptly distinguished by the dispersion of sexual representation across boundaries that previously separated the organic from the technological. As Donna Haraway writes:

> Late twentieth-century machines have made thoroughly ambiguous the difference between natural and artificial, mind and body, self-developing and externally designed, and many other distinctions that used to apply to organisms and machines. Our machines are disturbingly lively, and we ourselves frighteningly inert.[7]

Sexual images of technology are by no means new: modernist texts in the early twentieth century frequently eroticized technology. As K. C. D'Alessandro argues:

> Sexual metaphor in the description of locomotives, automobiles, pistons, and turbines; machine cults and the Futurist movement, *Man With a Movie Camera*, and *Scorpio Rising* – these are some of the ways technophiliacs have expressed their passion for technology. For technophiliacs, technology provides an erotic thrill – control over massive power, which can itself be used to control others. . . . The physical manifestations of these machines – size, heft, shape, motions that thrust, pause and press again – represent human sexual responses on a grand scale. There is much to venerate in the technology of the Industrial age.[8]

The film *Metropolis* (Fritz Lang 1926) is a classic example of the early twentieth-century fascination with technology. It combines celebration of technological efficiency with fear of technology's power to destroy humanity by running out of control. This dual response is expressed by the film in sexual terms: a robot shaped like a human woman represents technology's simultaneous allure and powerful threat. The robot is distinguished by its overt sexuality, for it is its seductive manner that triggers a chaotic worker revolt. Andreas Huyssen argues that modernist texts tend to equate machines with women, displacing and projecting fears of overpowering technology onto patriarchal fears of female sexuality.[9] Huyssen contends that historically, technology was not always linked to female sexuality: the two became associated after the beginning of the nineteenth century just as machines came to be perceived as threatening entities capable of vast, uncontrollable destruction. In nineteenth-century literature, human life appears often to be vulnerable to the massive destructive potential of machines. Earlier, in the eighteenth century, before the Industrial Revolution installed machinery in the workplace on a grand scale, mechanization offered merely a playful diversion in the form of the mechanical figures, designed to look male as often as female, that achieved great popularity in the European cities where they were displayed.[10]

Cyborgs, however, belong to the information age, where, as D'Alessandro writes, "huge, thrusting machines have been replaced with the circuitry maze of the microchip, the minimal curve of aerodynamic design".[11] Indeed, machines have been replaced by systems, and the microelectronic circuitry of computers bears little resemblance to the thrusting pistons and grinding gears that characterized industrial machinery. D'Alessandro asks: "What is sensual, erotic, or exciting about electronic tech?" She answers by suggesting that cybernetics makes possible the thrill of control over information and, for the corporate executives who own the technology, control over the consumer classes. What popular culture's cyborg imagery suggests is that electronic technology also makes possible the thrill of escape from the confines of the body and from the boundaries that have separated organic from inorganic matter.

While robots represent the acclaim and fear evoked by industrial age machines for their ability to function independently of humans, cyborgs incorporate rather than exclude humans, and in so doing erase the distinctions previously assumed to distinguish humanity from technology. Transgressed boundaries, in fact, define the cyborg, making it the con-summate postmodern concept. When humans interface with computer technology in popular culture texts, the process consists of more than just adding external robotic prostheses to their bodies. It involves transforming the self into something entirely new, combining technological with human identity. Although human subjectivity is not lost in the process, it is significantly altered.

Rather than portraying human fusion with electronic technology as terrifying, popular culture frequently represents it as a pleasurable experience. The pleasure of the interface, in Lacanian terms, results from the computer's offer to lead us into a microelectronic Imaginary where our bodies are obliterated and our consciousness integrated into the matrix. The word matrix, in fact, originates in the Latin *mater* (meaning both mother and womb), and the first of its several definitions in *Websters* is "something within which something else originates or develops". Computers in popular culture's cyborg imagery extend to us the thrill of meta-phoric escape into the comforting security of our mother's womb, which, as Freud explained, represents our earliest *Heim* (home).[12] According to Freud, when we have an *unheimlich* (uncanny) response to something, we are feeling the simultaneous attraction and dread evoked by the womb, where we experienced our earliest living moment at the same time that our insentience resembled death. It was Freud's contention that we are constituted by a death wish as well as by the pleasure principle; and popular culture's cyborg imagery effectively fuses the two desires.

Indeed, collapsing the boundary between what is human and what is technological is often represented as a sexual act in popular culture. By associating a deathlike loss of identity with sexuality, popular culture's cyborg imagery upholds a longstanding tradition of using loss of self as a metaphor for orgasm. It is well known that love and death are inextricably linked in the western cultural tradition, as Denis de Rougemont shows in his book *Love in the Western World*.[13] The equation of death with love has been accompanied in literature by the idea of bodiless sexuality: two united souls represent the purest form of romance. De Rougemont considers the Tristan legend to be western culture's paradigmatic romantic myth, from the twelfth century into the twentieth century; and it persists in the late twentieth century in cyborg imagery that associates the human/computer interface with sexual pleasure.

Instead of losing our consciousness and experiencing bodily pleasures, cyborg imagery in popular culture invites us to experience sexuality by losing our bodies and becoming pure consciousness. One of many examples is provided by the comic book *Cyberpunk*,[14] whose protagonist, Topo, mentally enters the Playing Field – a consensual hallucination where all the world's data exists in three-dimensional abstraction (called cyberspace in the cyberpunk novels of William Gibson) – saying "it's the most beautiful thing in the human universe. If I could leave my meat behind and just live here. If I could just be pure conscious-ness I could be happy." While in the Playing Field he meets Neon Rose, a plant/woman with a rose for a head and two thorny tendrils for arms (and like Topo, only present through hallucination). Even her name inscribes the collapse of boundaries between organic plant life and a technological construct. He engages her in a contest of wills, represented as their bodies entwined around each other while he narrates: "In here, you're what you will. Time and space at our command. No limits, except how good your software is. No restraints." Topo's spoken desire – to leave his meat behind and become pure consciousness, which is in fact what he has done – is contradicted by the imagery: his body – his meat – wrapped around another body.

The word "meat" is widely used to refer to the human body in cyberpunk texts. Cyberpunk, a movement in science fiction dating from the early 1980s, combines an aggressive punk sensibility rooted in urban street culture with a highly technological future where distinctions between technology and humanity have dissolved. In this context, meat typically carries a negative connotation along with its conventional association with the penis. It is an insult to be called meat in these texts, and to be meat is to be vulnerable. And yet despite its aversion to meat, *Cyberpunk* visually depicts Topo's body after he has abandoned it to float through the Playing Field's ever-changing topography. His body, however, only seems to be inside the Playing Field because of an illusion, and he is capable of transforming it in any way he desires. As he sees Neon Rose approach, he transforms himself into mechanical parts shaped like his own human body, but more formidable. He has lost his flesh and become steel. Only his face remains unchanged, and it is protected by a helmet. Topo's new powerful body, a product of his fantasy, inscribes the conventional signifiers of masculinity: he is angular with broad shoulders and chest; and, most importantly, he is hard. It is no accident that he adopts this appearance in order to greet Neon Rose, who is coded in stereotypical feminine fashion as a sinewy plant who throws her tendrils like lassos to wrap them around him. In case the reader is still in doubt about Neon Rose's gender, *Cyberpunk* shows her as a human woman after Topo defeats her in their mock battle.

This example from *Cyberpunk* indicates that while popular culture texts enthusiastically explore boundary breakdowns between humans and computers, gender boundaries are treated less flexibly. Cyberbodies, in fact, tend to appear masculine or feminine to an exag-gerated degree. We find giant pumped-up pectoral muscles on the males and enormous breasts on the females; or, in the case of Neon Rose, cliched flower imagery meant to represent female consciousness adrift in the computer matrix. Cyborg imagery has not so far realized the ungendered ideal theorized by Donna Haraway.[15] Haraway praises the cyborg as a potentially liberatory concept, one that could release women from their inequality under patriarchy by making genders obsolete. When gender difference ceases to be an issue, she explains, then equality becomes possible. Janet Bergstrom points out that exaggerated genders dominate in science fiction because

> where the basic fact of identity as a human is suspect and subject to transformation into its opposite, the representation of sexual identity carries a potentially heightened significance, because it can be used as the primary marker of difference in a world otherwise beyond our norms.[16]

In heightening gender difference, popular culture's cyborg imagery has not caught up with scientist Hans Moravec, who tells us that there will be no genders in the mobile computers that will retain human mental functions on software once the human body has become obsolete: "not unless for some theatrical reason. I expect there'll be play, which will be just another kind of simulation, and play may include costume parties."[17] According to Lyotard, on the other hand, the most complex and transcendent thought is made possible by the force of desire, and therefore "thinking machines will have to be nourished not just on radiation but on irremediable gender difference".[18]   *Monsters are Z*

Jean Baudrillard takes a similar position when he suggests that its inability to feel pleasure makes Artificial Intelligence incapable of replicating human intelligence.[19] But Baudrillard, unlike Lyotard, does not insist that gender difference is indispensable. Instead, he sees the collapse of clear boundaries between humans and machines as part of the same post-modern move toward uncertainty that characterizes the collapse of difference between genders. Baudrillard asserts that "science has anticipated this panic-like situation of uncertainty by making a principle of it".[20] Indeed, uncertainty is a central characteristic of postmodernism and the essence of the cyborg. But since most cyborgs in popular culture exhibit definite gender difference, it is apparent that, despite its willingness to relinquish other previously sacrosanct categories, patriarchy continues to uphold gender difference.

Despite the fact that cyborg imagery in popular culture often exaggerates conventional gender difference, however, it does not always conform entirely to traditional sexual repre-sentations. Contrary to the way most sexual imagery has been designed for a male gaze and has privileged heterosexual encounters, cyborg imagery, taken as a whole, implies a wider range of sexualities. Erotic interfacing is, after all, purely mental and nonphysical; it theoretically allows a free play of imagination. Accordingly, not all cyborg imagery adheres strictly to the standardized male fantasies celebrated in *Playboy*. Nor does it simply posit the computer as female in the manner that *Metropolis* associates technology with female sexuality and represents men as vulnerable to both. Instead, computers in popular culture's cyborg imagery represent sexual release of various kinds for both genders.

In some examples, the act of interfacing with a computer matrix is acknowledged to be solitary, but it is nonetheless represented as a sexual act, a masturbatory fantasy expressed in terms of entering something, but lacking the presence of another human body or mind. In the comic book *Interface*, the interfacing experience of a woman named Linda Williams is coded as masturbation, which becomes linked to the process of thinking.[21] Williams is seen from a high angle lying on her bed on her back, saying, "I relax my body. My mind starts to caress the frequencies around me. There. That's better. I'm one with the super-spectrum now. I'm interfaced with the world." In the last panel, she is seen doubled, her second self rising nude from the bed with head thrown back and arms outstretched in a sexual pose.

Linda Williams's mental journey through the computer matrix in search of valuable files is drawn so as to show her nude body diving through oceans of electronic circuitry and a jumble of cliched newspaper headlines. Although female masturbation is a staple of conventional pornography for a male spectator, Williams's interface/masturbation is drawn differently from the pornographic norm: her body is ghostly white and in constant motion as she swoops through the matrix surrounded by a watery mist. In two panels, her body is merely an indistinct blur. Its activity distinguishes her from the conventional passive female object of pornography, and her masturbation is not a prelude to heterosexual sex. Later in the evening, after she has returned from the matrix (sighing, "coming down from the interface makes me feel dizzy") and is once again fully clothed, she rejects the sexual advances of a male character. She tells him, "I need some time to myself right now." When he tries to persuade her, she responds,

> Not tonight. I know you were expecting me to sleep with you, to make you want to stay. But I don't do that sort of thing. Look, I'm attracted to you. So maybe you'll get lucky sometime. Right now, I've got a lot on my mind. There's so much I have to think about.

Williams takes control over her own sexuality, which embodies the cyborgian condition as represented in popular culture by being purely cerebral and simultaneously sexual. When she says she wants to be alone because there is so much she has to think about, the reader may infer that her private thoughts will be expressed sexually, as they were when she mentally entered the computer matrix.

Imaginary sex – sex without physically touching another human – prevails in cyborg discourses, though bodily sex is not altogether absent. The emphasis on cerebral sexuality suggests that while pain is a meat thing, sex is not. Historical, economic, and cultural conditions have facilitated human isolation and the evolution of cerebral sex. Capitalism has always separated people from one another with its ideology of rugged individualism. Its primary form of sanctioned unity – the nuclear family – has traditionally decreed that one person, usually the woman, relinquish her individuality in order to support in the private realm the public endeavors of the other. Public relations under capitalism are characterized by competition and its attendant suspicions. In late capitalism, social relations are mediated not only by money, but also by the media with its simulations. Rather than communicate, we spectate. Computer technology offers greater opportunities for dialogue – through modem hookup and electronic mail, for example – than does television, and can be thought of as a way to reestablish the human contact that was lost during the television decades. It is hardly astonishing that, at a time when paranoia over human contact in response to the AIDS virus is common, human interaction should occur through computerized communication, with the participants far apart and unable to touch each other.

To say that people communicate via their computers is not to say that the act of communication has remained unchanged from the pre-computer era. The term "communication" is in fact imprecise, according to Baudrillard. He writes that in the interface with the computer

> the Other, the sexual or cognitive interlocuter, is never really aimed at – crossing the screen evokes the crossing of the mirror. The screen itself is targeted as the point of interface. The machine (the interactive screen) transforms the process of communication,

the relation from one to the other, into a process of commutation, i.e. the process of reversability from the same to the same. The secret of the interface is that the Other is within it virtually the Same – otherness being surreptitiously confiscated by the machine.[22]

Although the computer invites us to discard our identities and embrace an Imaginary unity, like a mirror it also reminds us of our presence by displaying our words back to us. What Baudrillard argues is that this intensely private experience precludes actual interaction with another person and turns all computerized communication into a kind of autocommunication which may contain elements of autoeroticism.

In an example of solitary sexual communion with technology, William Gibson, one of the founding authors of cyberpunk fiction, uses the term "jack in" in his writing to describe the moment when a "cowboy" sitting at a "deck" enters his command to be mentally transported into cyberspace: he wanted to title his first novel "Jacked In", but the publisher refused on the grounds that it sounded too much like "Jacked Off".[23] Gibson's trilogy – *Neuromancer*, *Count Zero* and *Mona Lisa Overdrive* – evokes a dystopian future where isolated individuals drift in and out of each others' lives and often escape into fantasy.[24] Not unlike television's mass-produced fantasies of today, Gibson's "simstim" (simulated stimulation) feeds entertaining narratives directly into people's minds. Cyberspace, too, is a place of the mind, but it feels like three-dimensional space to those who enter it:

> Cyberspace. A consensual hallucination experienced daily by billions of legitimate operators, in every nation, by children being taught mathematical concepts. . . . A graphic representation of data abstracted from the banks of every computer in the human system. Unthinkable complexity. Lines of light ranged in the nonspace of the mind, clusters and constellations of data. Like city lights, receding. . . . [25]

Gibson's evocation of cyberspace has influenced the way people think about Virtual Reality, a concept dating back to the late 1960s which has become fashionable in the 1990s, receiving widespread media coverage while several companies develop its capabilities and design marketing strategies. Virtual Reality creates a computer-generated space that a person perceives as three-dimensional through goggles fitted with small video monitors. Gloves connected to the computer allow users to interact with the space and feel as though they are performing such activities as picking up objects, driving or flying. It would be inappropriate to call Virtual Reality an escape from reality, since what it does is provide an alternative reality where "being" somewhere does not require physical presence and "doing" something does not result in any changes in the physical world. Virtual Reality undermines certainty over the term reality, ultimately abandoning it altogether along with all the other certainties that have been discarded in postmodern times. John Perry Barlow, who writes about the cyberworld and is cofounder of the Electronic Frontier Foundation (an organization that tries to protect those working in electronic communications from governmental repression), calls Virtual Reality "a Disneyland for epistemologists", declaring that it will "further expose the conceit that 'reality' is a fact . . . delivering another major hit to the old fraud of objectivity".[26]

In published descriptions of Virtual Reality there are frequent references to its erotic potential. One concept in the works is "teledildonics", which puts the user in a bodysuit lined with tiny vibrators.[27] The user would telephone others who are similarly outfitted. Their telephone conversations would be accompanied by computerized visual representations, displayed to them on headsets, of their bodies engaged in sexual activities. As Howard Rheingold, author of the book *Virtual Reality*,[28] points out, teledildonics would revolutionize sexual encounters as well as our definitions of self:

> Clearly we are on the verge of a whole new semiotics of mating. Privacy and identity and intimacy will become tightly coupled into something we don't have a name for yet. . . . What happens to the self? Where does identity lie? And with our information machines so deeply intertwingled [*sic*] with our bodily sensations, as Ted Nelson might say, will our communication devices be regarded as "its" . . . or will they be part of "us"?[29]

Confusion over the boundaries between the self and technological systems is already evident. Virtual Reality, according to some of its proponents, will be able to eliminate the interface, the "mind-machine information barrier".[30] According to Baudrillard, uncertainty over the boundary between humanity and technology originates in our relationship to the new technological systems, not to traditional machines:

> Am I a man, am I a machine? In the relationship between workers and traditional machines, there is no ambiguity whatsoever. The worker is always estranged from the machine, and is therefore alienated by it. He keeps his precious quality of alienated man to himself. Whilst new technology, new machines, new images, interactive screens, do not alienate me at all. With me they form an integrated circuit.[31]

Nowhere is the confusion of boundaries between humanity and electronic technology more apparent than in films involving cyborg imagery: here cyborgs are often indistinguishable from humans. The Terminator (*The Terminator* [James Cameron 1984]), for example, can be recognized as nonhuman only by dogs, not by humans. Even when cyborgs in films look different from humans, they are often represented as fundamentally human. In *Robocop* (Paul Verhoeven 1987), Robocop is created by fusing electronic technology and robotic prostheses with the face of a policeman, Alex J. Murphy, after he has died from multiple gunshot wounds. He clearly looks technological, while at the same time he retains a human shape. His most recognizably human feature is his face, with its flesh still intact, while the rest of his body is entirely constructed of metal and electronic circuitry. The film shows that despite his creators' attempts to fashion him into a purely mechanical tool, his humanity keeps surfacing. He seeks information about Murphy, his human precursor; and increasingly identifies with him, particularly since he retains memories of the attack that killed Murphy. At the end of the film, Robocop identifies himself, when asked for his name, as Murphy. In the sequel, *Robocop II* (Irvin Kershner 1990), Robocop's basic humanity is further confirmed when he is continually stirred by memories of Murphy's wife and young son, and takes to watching them from the street outside their new home. Robocop's inability to act on his human desires constitutes the tragic theme of the film, which takes for granted that Robocop is basically human.

If there is a single feature that consistently separates cyborgs from humans in these films, it is the cyborg's greater capacity for violence, combined with enormous physical prowess. Instead of representing cyborgs as intellectual wizards whose bodies have withered away and been replaced by computer terminals, popular culture gives us muscular hulks distinguished by their superior fighting skills. To some extent the phenomenon of the rampaging cyborg in films suggests a residual fear of technology of the sort that found similar expression in older films like *Metropolis*. Electronic technology's incredible capabilities can certainly evoke fear and awe, which can be translated in fictional representation into massive bodies that overpower human characters.

But fear of the computer's abilities does not entirely explain why cyborgs are consistently associated with violence. Significantly, musclebound cyborgs in films are informed by a tradition of muscular comic-book superheroes; and, like the superheroes, their erotic appeal lies in the promise of power they embody. Their heightened physicality culminates not in sexual climax but in acts of violence. Violence substitutes for sexual release. Steve Neale has theorized that violence displaces male sexuality in films in response to a cultural taboo against a homoerotic gaze.[32] Certain narrative films continue to be made for a presumed male audience, and homophobia exerts a strong influence on cinematic techniques. For example, closeup shots that caress the male body on screen might encourage a homoerotic response from the male spectator. But, as Neale explains, the spectacle of a passive and desirable male body is typically undermined by the narrative, which intervenes to make him the object or the perpetrator of violence, thereby justifying the camera's objectification of his body.

In the opening sequence of *The Terminator*, for example, the shot of the cyborg's (Arnold Schwarzenegger) beautifully sculpted nude body standing on a hill above night-time Los Angeles, city lights twinkling like ornaments behind him, is quickly followed by his bloody attack on three punk youths in order to steal their clothes. His attire then consists of hard leather and metal studs, concealing his flesh and giving his sexuality a veneer of violence. As in similar examples from other films, an invitation to the spectator to admire the beauty of a male body is followed by the body's participation in violence. The male body is restored to action to deny its status as passive object of desire, and the camera's scrutiny of the body receives narrative justification.

Klaus Theweleit, in his two-volume study of fascist soldier males (specifically, men of the German *Freikorps* between the World Wars), writes that their psychological state indicates an intense misogyny and an overwhelming desire to maintain a sense of self in the face of anything they perceive might threaten their bodily boundaries.[33] Theweleit draws on the theories of psychologist Margaret Mahler to argue that fascist males have never developed an identity (they are "not-yet-fully-born"), and thus invest all of their energies into maintaining a fragile edifice of selfhood. Their failure to disengage from their mothers during infancy results in a fear that women will dissolve their identities; hence the frequency with which women are associated in fascist rhetoric with raging floods that threaten to engulf their victims. In order to protect themselves from women, onto whom they project the watery weakness they despise in themselves, fascist males encase themselves in body armor, both literally and figuratively. The machine body becomes the ideal tool for ego maintenance.

For the fascist male, additionally, the sexual act evokes loss of self and becomes displaced onto violence. The act of killing, especially by beating the victim into a bloody pulp, functions to externalize the dissolution of self that he fears, and assures him of his relative solidity. He reaffirms his physical and psychological coherence every time he kills. Acts of violence also serve to release some of his enormous tension, for the task of maintaining a sense of self when a self barely exists is excruciating, and the soldier male does not allow himself to experience release through sexual union. As Theweleit writes, "heroic acts of killing take the place of the sexual act", and the ecstasy of killing substitutes for sexual climax.[34]

Cyborg imagery in films is remarkably consistent with Theweleit's description of the fascist soldier male. If anything, cyborg imagery epitomizes the fascist ideal of an invincible armoured fighting machine. In *Robocop*, Robocop's armour is external and protects him from gunshots and other assaults that would kill a human. He strides fearlessly into a blaze of gunfire as bullets bounce off his armoured body. In *The Terminator*, the cyborg's armour is inside his body and therefore not visible, but it makes him virtually indestructible. Near the end of the film, after the Terminator's flesh has been burnt away, he is revealed to be a metal construct that, despite the loss of all its flesh, continues methodically to stalk its victim.

Cyborg imagery, therefore, represents more than just a recognition that humanity has already become integrated with technology to the point of indistinguishability; it also reveals an intense crisis in the construction of masculinity. Shoring up the masculine subject against the onslaught of a femininity feared by patriarchy now involves transforming the male body into something only minimally human. Whereas traditional constructions of masculinity in film often relied on external technological props (guns, armored costumes, motorcycles, fast cars, cameras, and so on)[35] to defend against disintegration, the cinematic cyborg heralds the fusion of the body with the technological prop.

Ironically, the attempt to preserve the masculine subject as a cyborg requires destroying the coherence of the male body and replacing it with electronic parts; either physically – using hardware or psychologically – using software. The construction of masculinity as cyborg requires its simultaneous deconstruction. And yet, by escaping from its close identification with the male body, masculine subjectivity has been reconstituted, suggesting that there is an essential masculinity that transcends bodily presence. In a world without human bodies, the films tell us, technological things will be gendered and there will still be a patriarchal hierarchy. What this reconfiguration of masculinity indicates is that patriarchy is more willing to dispense with human life than with male superiority.

However, the sacrifice of the male body is disguised in cyborg films by emphasizing physicality and intensifying gender difference. Pumping up the cyborg into an exaggerated version of the muscular male physique hides the fact that electronic technology has no gender. In *Total Recall* (Paul Verhoeven 1990), for example, the fact that Doug Quaid's identity is merely an electronic implant is counteracted by his massive physical presence, once again made possible by casting Arnold Schwarzenegger in the role of Quaid. Muscular cyborgs in films thus assert and simultaneously disguise the dispersion of masculine subjectivity beyond the male body.

The paradox that preserving masculine subjectivity in the figure of the cyborg requires destroying the male body accounts in part for the extreme violence associated with cyborgs in films: they represent an impossible desire for strength through disintegration; and, like the fascist soldier males, their frustration finds expression in killing. The Terminator, for example, is programmed to kill and in fact has no other function than to kill humans. He has been sent into the past by his machine masters expressly to kill a young woman, Sarah Connor. His adversary Kyle Reese tells Connor that the Terminator "can't be bargained with, it can't be reasoned with, it doesn't feel pity or remorse or fear and it absolutely will not stop, ever, until you are dead", recalling Theweleit's observation that the fascist soldier male has no moral qualms about killing.

Robocop is also an expert killer, but the two *Robocop* films, unlike *The Terminator*, justify the hero's acts of killing by putting him on the side of law enforcement and showing his victims caught in the act of committing crimes. In *Robocop* II, Robocop is programmed to apprehend criminals without killing them by a smarmy woman psychologist who preaches nonviolence and is made to appear ridiculous. The film indicates, however, that the software program that prevents Robocop from killing hinders his effectiveness; and the film celebrates his acts of killing when he manages to overcome the restraining program. In *Total Recall*, Doug Quaid is attacked nearly every time he turns a corner, and he responds by killing all of his attackers with a show of incredible strength and brutality.

Not only does cyborg imagery in films extol the human killing machine, it also expresses the concomitant fear of sexuality theorized by Theweleit. In the film *Hardware* (Richard Stanley 1990), for example, the cyborg is dormant until activated by the sight of a young woman, Jill, having sex with her boyfriend. After the boyfriend has left the apartment and Jill has hung the cyborg on the wall as part of a scrap metal sculpture, the cyborg watches her sleeping body for a while and then emerges to attack her; for, like the Terminator, it has been created to destroy humans.

Sexuality is feared by fascist soldier males not only because it signifies loss of personal boundaries, writes Theweleit, but also because sexuality evokes the creation of life, and the soldier male is bent on destroying all signs of life before they can destroy him. Pregnant women, according to Theweleit, are treated with revulsion in his rhetoric. Like fascist soldier males, cyborgs in films are often determined to prevent birth. In *Hardware*, it turns out that the cyborg that kills all the life forms it encounters is a secret weapon in the government's birth control programme. The Terminator, likewise, has been programmed to travel back through time to kill Sarah Connor in order to prevent her giving birth to her son John, who, forty years into the future, will lead the few humans who have survived a nuclear war in defeating the machines that threaten humanity with annihilation.

Creation versus destruction of life is not only a central thematic concern but also a site of dispute in cyborg texts. The ability to engender life is divided between men and women and between humans and technology. Women are typically associated with biological reproduction while men are involved in technological reproduction. In the film *Demon Seed* (Donald Cammell 1977), for example, a scientist creates an Artificial Intelligence in a sophisticated computer laboratory where teams of specialists educate their artificial child. The scientist's wife, Susan (Julie Christie), is a psychiatrist, a member of a humanistic profession that opposes her husband's technophilia. She complains about his emotional coldness, illustrating the film's stereotypically phallocentric definition of gender roles: men are scientific and aloof while women are humanistic and emotional.

Demon Seed reinforces its version of gender difference by taking for granted that the AI, a form of pure consciousness, is male. Masculine subjectivity has dispensed entirely with the need to construct a body in this film, existing instead as bodiless intellect. And the woman's role is even further confined when Susan is raped by the AI, whose pure intellect is the antithesis of Susan's reduction to a reproductive vessel. Since the Artificial Intelligence has no physical form (its name is Proteus IV, after the Greek sea god capable of assuming different forms), it relies on a robot and a giant mutating geometric shape under its command to rape Susan. Its orgasm while impregnating her is represented as a trip into the far reaches of the cosmos. ("I'll show you things only I have seen", it tells her.) Motivated by a desire to produce a child and thereby experience emotions and physical sensations, the AI attempts to take control over the reproductive process; in effect vying with Susan's husband for power over creation, but going back to a biological definition of reproduction and a phallocentric definition of woman as childbearer. Susan is a mere womb in the AI's scheme. When the film ends with the birth of the child conceived by the AI and Susan, it leaves ambiguous whether the cyborg child, a union of a disembodied intellect and a human woman, will be demonic or benign.

Men are also the creators of life in *Weird Science* (John Hughes 1985), a throwback to *Metropolis* with its representation of a woman artificially designed to fulfil a male fantasy. Two unpopular high school boys program a computer to create their perfect woman, assembled from fragmented body parts selected from *Playboy* magazines. Her role, like the robot's in *Metropolis*, at first appears to be sexual: the boys' initial desire is to take a shower with her. Also as in *Metropolis*, the woman's sexuality is too powerful for the boys who are incapable of doing more than just kissing her. However, unlike *Metropolis*, she takes on a big sisterly role that involves instructing her creators in the finer points of talking to girls. Her guidance boosts their self-confidence and allows them to win over the two most popular high school girls, whom earlier they could only admire from afar. The film uses the concept of computer-generated life only to further its conventional coming-of-age narrative, and does nothing to question either gender roles or the implications of nonbiological reproduction.

Eve of Destruction (Duncan Gibbins 1991) complicates the theme of creation versus destruction, but only to punish the woman protagonist for her sexuality and for engaging in technological rather than biological reproduction. A scientist named Eve creates a cyborg, also named Eve, who looks exactly like her and is programmed with her memories. The cyborg escapes from the scientist and goes on a killing spree. Rather than engaging in random destruction, however, the cyborg Eve lives out the scientist Eve's repressed fantasies of sex and revenge against men. Thus the cyborg kills the scientist's father, whom the scientist has hated since childhood because he brutalized and caused the death of her mother. The cyborg's first victim is a redneck at a country saloon that the scientist had fantasized frequenting for casual sex. The cyborg takes the man to a motel room and, when he taunts her with his erection, bites his penis.

The film's castration anxiety escalates, for it turns out that the cyborg has something much more dangerous than a vagina dentata: a nuclear vagina. We learn that the Defense Department funded the cyborg project to create a secret military weapon, complete with nuclear capabilities. In a computer graphics display of the cyborg's design, we see that the nuclear explosive is located at the end of a tunnel inside her vagina. Sure enough, the countdown to a nuclear explosion begins when the cyborg has an orgasm as she destroys another man by crashing her car into his. Patriarchal fear of female sexuality has clearly raised the stakes since the 1920s when *Metropolis* showed unleashed female sexuality leading to the collapse of a city. *Eve of Destruction* puts the entire planet at risk.

Having established that female sexuality leads to uncontrollable destruction, the film suggests that what the scientist placed in danger by creating artificial life was her role as biological mother: for the cyborg kidnaps the scientist's young son. Only then does the scientist cooperate with the military officer whose job it is to destroy the cyborg before it detonates. Earlier, they had an antagonistic relationship revolving around contempt for each other's profession. His attempts to destroy her cool professional demeanour finally succeed, and at the end it is she who destroys the cyborg only seconds before zero hour in order to save the lives of her son and the military officer. The scientist in effect destroys her repressed sexuality and anger towards men, and accepts her primary status as biological mother.

As *Eve of Destruction* illustrates, artificial life in films continues, in the Frankenstein tradition, to threaten the lives of its creators; but it also continues to hold out the promise of immortality. A yearning for immortality runs throughout cyborg discourses. In cyberpunk fiction, taking the postmodern principle of uncertainty to its radical extreme, not even death is a certainty. Cyberpunk fiction writers William Gibson and Rudy Rucker[36] have made immortality a central theme in their books, raising questions about whether nonphysical existence constitutes life and, especially in Gibson's novels, examining how capitalism would allow only the extremely wealthy class to attain immortality by using technology inaccessible to the lower classes. But cyberpunk fiction is not without recognition of the paradoxes and dangers of immortality. In both Gibson's and Rucker's work, characters who attempt to become immortal are usually surrounded by a tragic aura of loneliness and decay.

Even Topo, in the comic book *Cyberpunk*, rejects the idea of leaving his meat behind and remaining permanently in the Playing Field when he is offered the opportunity.[37] What he rejects is immortality. But the comic book reveals that the loss of his human body would be tantamount to death; for the invitation to join those who have permanently abandoned their bodies comes from a death mask, called The Head, that addresses him from atop a pedestal. During their conversation, disembodied skulls swoop by around them, reinforcing the death imagery. When, in the next issue, Topo loses his human body and becomes a cyberghost trapped in the Playing Field, the line between life and death becomes more ambiguous.[38] There is much speculation among his friends, who remain outside of the computer matrix, about whether Topo is dead or alive. Topo himself says "after all, I'm only a data construct myself, now. Nothing equivocal about it. We live. We are forms of life, based on electrical impulses. Instead of carbon or other physical matter. We are the next step."

These examples show that cyborg imagery revolves around the opposition between creation and destruction of life, expressing ambivalence about the future of human existence and also, as with the fascist soldier males, uncertainty about the stability of masculine subjectivity. Fusion with electronic technology thus represents a paradoxical desire to preserve human life by destroying it. The concept of abandoning the body with pleasure arises in part from late twentieth-century post-nuclear threats to the body: nuclear annihilation, AIDS, and environmental disasters. Devising plans to preserve human consciousness outside of the body indicates a desire to redefine the self in an age when human bodies are vulnerable in unprecedented ways. Contemporary concern with the integrity of the body is only the latest manifestation of postwar anxiety over the body's fragility.

Neither alive nor dead, the cyborg in popular culture is constituted by paradoxes: its contradictions are its essence, and its vision of a discordant future is in fact a projection of our own conflictual present. What is really being debated in the discourses surrounding a cyborg future are contemporary disputes concerning gender and sexuality, with the future providing a clean slate, or a blank screen, onto which we can project our fascination and fears. While some texts cling to traditional gender roles and circumscribed sexual relations, others experiment with alternatives. It is perhaps ironic, though, that a debate over gender and sexuality finds expression in the context of the cyborg, an entity that makes sexuality, gender, even humankind itself, anachronistic. Foucault's statement that "man is an invention of recent date. And one perhaps nearing its end" prefigures the consequences of a cyborg future.[39] But, as Foucault also argues, it is precisely during a time of discursive crisis, when categories previously taken for granted become subject to dispute, that new concepts emerge. Late twentieth-century debates over sexuality and gender roles have thus contributed to producing the concept of the cyborg. And, depending on one's stake in the outcome, one can look to the cyborg to provide either liberation or annihilation.

Notes

1 J. G. Ballard, interviewed by Peter Linnett, *Corridor*, (1974), no. 5; reprinted in *Re/Search*, nos 8–9 (San Francisco: Re/Search Publications 1984), 164.

2 J. G. Ballard, interviewed by Lynn Barber, *Penthouse*, September 1970; reprinted in *Re/Search*, nos 8–9, 157.

3 Hans Moravec, director of the Mobile Robot Laboratory at Carnegie-Mellon University, is at the forefront of cyborg development: see his book *Mind Children: The Future of Robot and Human Intelligence* (Cambridge: Harvard University Press 1988). For a journalistic account of Moravec's research projects and his concept of a cyborg future, see Grant Fjermedal, *The Tomorrow Makers: A Brave New World of Living-Brain Machines* (New York: Macmillan 1986).

4 "Interview with Hans Moravec", *omni*, (1989), vol. 11, no. 11: 88; "Is the body obsolete? A forum", *Whole Earth Review*, (1989), no. 63: 34–55; Lyotard, J.-F., "Can thought go on without a body?", *Discourse*, (1988–9), vol. 11, no. 1: 74–87.

5 Walter Kendrick, *The Secret Museum: Pornography in Modern Culture* (New York: Penguin Books 1987), 31.

6 Commission on Obscenity and Pornography, *Report of the Commission on Obscenity and Pornography* (Toronto, New York and London: Bantam 1970). The Commission was established by the US Congress in October 1967 to define "pornography" and "obscenity", to determine the nature and extent of their distribution, to study their effects upon the public, and to recommend legislation action. The Commission's report did not define obscenity and pornography and stated that no empirical evidence existed to link criminal behaviour to sexually explicit material. It also recommended against any legislative action and proposed that all existing prohibitive laws be repealed. Soon after its release, the report was rejected by the US Senate and by President Nixon.

7 Donna Haraway, "A manifesto for cyborgs: science, technology, and socialist feminism in the 1980s", *Socialist Review*, (1985), no. 80: 65–107; reprinted in Elizabeth Weed (ed.), *Coming to Terms: Feminism, Theory, and Practice* (New York: Routledge 1989), 173–204: the quotation is from 176.

8 K. C. D'Alessandro, "Technophilia: cyberpunk and cinema", a paper presented at the Society for Cinema Studies conference, Bozeman, Montana (July 1988), 1.

9 Andreas Huyssen, "The vamp and the machine: technology and sexuality in Fritz Lang's *Metropolis*", *New German Critique*, (1981–2), nos 24–25: 221–37.

10 Ibid., 226.

11 D'Alessandro, "Technophilia: cyberpunk and cinema", 1.

12 Sigmund Freud, "The 'Uncanny'" (1919), *The Standard Edition of the Complete Psychological Works of Sigmund Freud*, vol. 17, trans. and ed. James Strachey (London: The Hogarth Press 1973), 219–52.

13 Denis de Rougemont, *Love in the Western World* (New York: Harper & Row 1956).

14 Scott Rockwell, *Cyberpunk*, book one, vol. 1, no. 1 (Wheeling, West Virginia: Innovative Corporation 1989).

15 Haraway, "A manifesto for cyborgs".

16 Janet Bergstrom, "Androids and androgyny", *Camera Obscura*, (1986), 15: 39.

17 "Interview with Hans Moravec", 88.

18 Lyotard, "Can thought go on without a body?", 86.

19 Jean Baudrillard, *Xerox and Infinity*, trans. Agitac (Paris: Touchepas 1988), 3.

20 Ibid., 16.

21 James D. Hudnall, *Interface*, vol. 1, no. 1 (New York: Epic Comics 1989).

22 Baudrillard, *Xerox and Infinity*, 5–6.

23 William Gibson and Timothy Leary in conversation, "High tech/high life", *Mondo* 2000, no. 1 (Berkeley, CA: Fun City Megamedia 1989), 61.

24 William Gibson, *Neuromancer* (New York: Ace Books 1984); *Count Zero* (New York: Ace Books 1986); *Mona Lisa Overdrive* (New York: Bantam Books 1988).

25 Gibson, *Neuromancer*, 51.

26 John Perry Barlow, "Being in nothingness", *Mondo* 2000, no. 2 (Berkeley, CA: Fun City Megamedia 1990), 39, 41.

27 Howard Rheingold, "Teledildonics: reach out and touch someone", *Mondo* 2000, no. 2 (Berkeley, CA: Fun City Megamedia 1990), 52–4.

28 Howard Rheingold, *Virtual Reality* (New York: Simon & Schuster 1991).

29 Rheingold, "Teledildonics", 54.

30 Barlow, "Being in nothingness", 38.

31 Baudrillard, *Xerox and Infinity*, 14.

32 Steve Neale, "Masculinity as spectacle: reflections on men and mainstream cinema", *Screen*, (1983), vol. 24, no. 6: 2–16.

33 Klaus Theweleit, *Male Fantasies*, vol. 1 (Minneapolis: University of Minnesota Press 1987); *Male Fantasies*, vol. 2 (Minneapolis: University of Minnesota Press 1989).

34 Theweleit, *Male Fantasies*, vol. 2, 276, 279.

35 For a discussion of how constructions of the masculine subject have relied on technological props, see Sabrina Barton, "The apparatus of masculinity" in *Shane* and *Sex, Lies, and Videotape*, a paper presented at the Society for Cinema Studies Conference, Washington DC (May 1990); Constance Penley, "Feminism, film theory, and the bachelor machines", *The Future of an Illusion: Film, Feminism, and Psychoanalysis* (Minneapolis: University of Minnesota Press 1989), ch. 4. In the context of the war film, see Susan Jeffords, *Remasculinization of America: Gender and the Vietnam War* (Bloomington: Indiana University Press 1989).

36 Rudy Rucker, *Software* (New York: Avon Books 1982); *Hardware* (New York: Avon Books 1988).

37 Scott Rockwell, *Cyberpunk*, book two, vol. 1, no. 1 (Wheeling, West Virginia: Innovative Corporation 1990).

38 Scott Rockwell, *Cyberpunk*, book two, vol. 1, no. 2 (Wheeling, West Virginia: Innovative Corporation 1990).

39 Michel Foucault, *The Order of Things. An Archaeology of the Human Sciences* (New York: Vintage Books 1973), 387.

Dogme 95

8

The Vow of Chastity

LARS VON TRIER AND THOMAS VINTERBERG

Dogme 95 . . . is a collective of film directors founded in Copenhagen in spring 1995.

Dogme 95 has the expressed goal of countering "certain tendencies" in the cinema today.

Dogme 95 is a rescue action!

In 1960 enough was enough! The movie was dead and called for resurrection. The goal was correct but the means were not! The new wave proved to be a ripple that washed ashore and turned to muck.

Slogans of individualism and freedom created works for a while, but no changes. The wave was up for grabs, like the directors themselves. The wave was never stronger than the men behind it. The anti-bourgeois cinema itself became bourgeois, because the foundations upon which its theories were based was the bourgeois perception of art. The *auteur* concept was bourgeois romanticism from the very start and thereby . . . false!

To Dogme 95 cinema is not individual!

Today a technological storm is raging, the result of which will be the ultimate democratization of the cinema. For the first time, anyone can make movies. But the more accessible the media becomes, the more important the avant-garde. It is no accident that the phrase "avant-garde" has military connotations. Discipline is the answer . . . we must put our films into uniform, because the individual film will be decadent by definition!

Dogme 95 counters the individual film by the principle of presenting an indisputable set of rules known as The Vow of Chastity.

In 1960 enough was enough! The movie had been cosmeticized to death, they said; yet since then the use of cosmetics has exploded.

The "supreme" task of the decadent film-makers is to fool the audience. Is that what we are so proud of? Is that what the "100 years" have brought us? Illusions via which emotions can be communicated? . . . By the individual artist's free choice of trickery?

Predictability (dramaturgy) has become the golden calf around which we dance. Having the characters' inner lives justify the plot is too complicated, and not "high art". As never before, the superficial action and the superficial movie are receiving all the praise.

The result is barren. An illusion of pathos and an illusion of love.

To Dogme 95 the movie is not illusion!

Today a technological storm is raging of which the result is the elevation of cosmetics to God. By using new technology anyone at any time can wash the last grains of truth away in the deadly embrace of sensation. The illusions are everything the movie can hide behind.

Dogme 95 counters the film of illusion by the presentation of an indisputable set of rules known as The Vow of Chastity.

"I swear to submit to the following set of rules drawn up and confirmed by Dogme 95:

1   Shooting must be done on location. Props and sets must not be brought in (if a particular prop is necessary for the story, a location must be chosen where this prop is to be found).
2   The sound must never be produced apart from the images, or vice versa. (Music must not be used unless it occurs where the scene is being shot.)
3   The camera must be hand-held. Any movement or immobility attainable in the hand is permitted. (The film must not take place where the camera is standing; shooting must take place where the film takes place.)
4   The film must be in color. Special lighting is not acceptable. (If there is too little light for exposure the scene must be cut or a single lamp be attached to the camera.)
5   Optical work and filters are forbidden.
6   The film must not contain superficial action. (Murders, weapons, etc. must not occur.)
7   Temporal and geographical alienation are forbidden. (That is to say that the film takes place here and now.)
8   Genre movies are not acceptable.
9   The film format must be Academy 35 mm.
10   The director must not be credited.

Furthermore, I swear as a director to refrain from personal taste! I am no longer an artist. I swear to refrain from creating a "work", as I regard the instant as more important than the whole. My supreme goal is to force the truth out of my characters and settings. I swear to do so by all the means available and at the cost of any good taste and any aesthetic considerations.
Thus I make my Vow of Chastity".

Copenhagen, Monday, 13 March 1995
On behalf of Dogme 95
Lars von Trier, Thomas Vinterberg

9

Pirates of the New World Image Orders

PATRICIA R. ZIMMERMANN

Pirates, not plagiarists

[. . .]

The word *piracy* rouses many different forms, fictions, and fantasies. I use the term *piracy* as itself a hybrid of history, fact, fiction, and fantasy, a practice that defines itself in rewriting borders and fantasizing new futures. I recuperate the term and decriminalize it. Media pirates, those who recycle images from other sources, are distinguished from plagiarists in two ways: first, the plagiarist uses images or words in their entirety, whereas the pirate decontextualizes images and words in order to recontextualize them; second, the plagiarist renders the copying process invisible and seamless, whereas the pirate foregrounds the process of snatching as a disruptive act and intervention, a rerouting of media tributaries. For example, a pirate editorial titled "So You Want to Be a Pirate?" explains, "So what's a pirate? A pirate is somebody who believes that information belongs to the people. Just as a book can be zeroed or placed in a library to be shared, pirates provide a type of library service."[1]

The post-1989 economic and technological realignments have precipitated a variety of new formations of piracy. The conflicts among the countries of the North and South and West and East have transformed from militarization to mediazation. State power has been realigned along economic lines more than ever before, shifting the location of culture from a state prerogative for national history building to a narrative of transnational consumption of stateless, globalized commodities dependent on the circulation of image culture. As the CIA tracked weapons and nuclear capacity during the Cold War, the Motion Picture Association of America (MPAA) now pursues illegal pirating of Hollywood films to force nations to adopt stricter copyright legislation. The newly emerging democracies of Eastern Europe and China have spawned commercial pirates in droves; they copy and sell everything from *Forrest Gump* to Windows 95, Madonna CDs, and downlinked satellite broadcasts of *Friends*. As Gordon Graham noted in *Publishers Weekly* in 1990, "Piracy, as we know it today, is an eruption of the world post-colonial era."[2]

If the commercial pirate copies for profit, the media pirate copies for the pleasure of profaning the dominant commercial media discourse and turning it against itself. The commercial pirate operates in the realm of exchange value, trading money for a material commodity, whereas the media pirate functions outside and in between exchange relations, forging new ideas by cutting apart and twisting the old parts into something new that exchanges ideas in a circulatory system rather than products.

If the commercial pirate is a counterfeiter, the media pirate is a counter-discourser. The former produces an object; the latter produces new subjects. Media pirates conduct subversive art maneuvers that alter the material of the image by fragmenting it, whereas criminal pirates basically reproduce films, CDs, and software without any alteration of the material object or representational mode. Pirate media are the ultimate form of recycling in the transnational era: they salvage corporatized images for compost to grow something new out of the old.

Subcomandante Marcos, the leader of the Zapatista insurrection in Chiapas, Mexico, exemplifies this new piracy strategy. He commenced his offensive on the day the North American Free Trade Agreement (NAFTA) was signed, giving equal importance to media tactics and war strategy. Guillermo Gómez-Peña has dubbed Marcos "a consummate performancero" who "utilized performance and media strategies to enter in the political 'wrestling arena' of contemporary Mexico".[3] In an address broadcast via satellite to the "Freeing the Media" teach-in held in New York City on 31 January 1997, Subcomandante Marcos remarked:

> Independent media tries to save history: the present history – saving it and trying to share it, so it will not disappear, moreover to distribute it to other places, so that this history is not limited to one country, to one region, to one city or social group.[4]

Guillermo Gómez-Peña, also responding to the NAFTA provision that allows capital but not labor to move freely across the borders that separate the United States from Canada and Mexico, has also written about how expropriation of media and cultural elements is necessary in the new world orders to create more open and fluid systems, with art spaces creating what he calls "demilitarized zones". Describing the new hybridized cultural worker, he says:

> S/he performs multiple roles in multiple contexts. At times, s/he can operate as a cross-cultural diplomat, as an intellectual coyote (smuggler of ideas), or a media pirate. At other times, s/he assumes the role of nomadic chronicler, intercultural translator, or political trickster.[5]

John Fiske, in a 1989 essay titled "Popular News", anticipated Marcos and Gómez-Peña. In contradistinction to the homogenizing and narcotizing structure of commercial news, he imagined a formally open, participatory news boiling over with contradictions that provoke public discussions and minimize distinctions among author, text, and reader.[6] Media piracy, as a form of popular news, deploys digitality and new technologies to open up previously closed and encoded formal systems, going beyond Fiske by materializing his ideas. Yet it also, in a crucial distinction from the postmodern inflection, collapses the frontier between author and consumer, between writer and reader. The media pirate, then, rejects the exchange value of the image and rescues its use value for new uses.

A 1992 Paper Tiger program called *Low Power Empowerment*, for example, chronicles low-power radio produced by women in Galway, Ireland, and by Black Liberation Radio in

Springfield, Illinois, with inexpensive audio technology that creates community-based talk around significant issues such as women's work and housing. However, the tape is not simply a celebration of the appropriation of low-end consumer technologies for clandestine radio broadcasts; it also functions as a how-to primer on pirate radio: it provides viewers with tips on where to shop for components and instructions on how to rig a system.

Pirate radio operations around the globe foreground the confrontations among diffusion of new technologies, the surveillance of the nation-state, and democracy. The case of Radio Free Berkeley illustrates these points of rupture. In 1996, the Federal Communications Commission (FCC) fined pirate radio producer Steven Dunifer twenty thousand dollars for broadcasting without a license. Dunifer contends that the FCC investigated him after he shipped transmitter parts for low-power radio stations to villages in Mexico, Guatemala, El Salvador, Chiapas, and Haiti. The FCC countered that Radio Free Berkeley posed a threat to VHF emergency frequencies, aircraft navigation, civil defense, and law enforcement communications. In a *New York Times* story outlining the case, Dunifer explained, "You really can't have true democracy until there's equal access to all means of communication."[7]

In *The Complete Manual of Pirate Radio*, a technical how-to book on constructing a low-power transmitter, Zeke Teflon extends this analysis of democratic agendas and their inhibition by the growth of media concentration and corporate power. He says: "In theory, freedom of the press exists in this country. (Freedom of the airwaves doesn't even exist in theory.) In practice, only those individuals and groups with very large amounts of money can use print media effectively."[8] In his introductory chapter, he argues that all forms of media, from commercial to public television, to cable access, to print, require large amounts of capital and time investment, therefore making the means of communication completely inaccessible to most citizens. Teflon sees hope, however, in the diffusion of low-end technologies, which destroy the barriers to entry erected by more corporate media.

Media piracy, then, is a high-stakes affair of global proportions, manufacturing sanctuaries from the privatization of public culture by democratizing the means of production, now refashioned as a mode of information and image making. It is not the same thing as post-modernism, although they share some formal strategies. If postmodernist documentary appropriates images for deconstruction, pirate media appropriate both images and technologies, infiltrating old spaces and producing new spaces, consuming and producing, deconstructing and reconstructing. It moves between history and the future in a double move, as exemplified by pirate radio broadcasts.

In *Media Virus!* Douglas Rushkoff discusses media pranks by environmentalist organizations such as Earth First! and AIDS activist groups like ACT UP as metamedia in the dadaist tradition, a form of symbolic warfare that has the ability to penetrate dominant media systems.[9] Piracy, then, is not exactly new, but a great-granddaughter of Dada, Soviet constructivism, and the anti-Nazi photomontagist, John Heartfield, all movements that sought "a provocative dismembering of reality" through the recycling of media images married with a distribution system that infiltrated mass media.[10] In this sense, then, images are not just reappropriated and analyzed; in their new formations, they infiltrate dominant media systems, produce space, and make histories.

The BLO Nightly News (1994), produced by the Barbie Liberation Organization, is itself a media prank that hijacks network news. The tape discloses how activists switched the voice boxes on three hundred Barbie dolls and GI Joes in forty-three states in the fall of 1993 to "culture jam" gender stereotyping in children's toys. GI Joes say "Let's go shopping", and Barbie dolls speak of war tactics. The dolls were altered by BLO operatives, then returned to stores in what the BLO calls "shopgiving". Parents unknowingly bought the dolls as Christmas gifts for their surprised children. Local and network news covered the story of the dolls, themselves pulled into the web of the ingenious media prank to expose how toy manufacturers produce gender bias. The BLO even sent press releases to news organizations and ran a toll-free telephone number in a parody of public relations spin efforts.

The BLO Nightly News sabotages the objectivity of network news in a variety of ways. It reuses the conventional news coverage from NBC and CNN as clips, thereby turning the corporate commercial media into producers for the activists' agenda. It fabricates a fake television newscast replete with a sports announcer describing the advance of the altered Barbies over archival sports footage and a science reporter investigating the "corrective surgery" techniques employed in the transgendered alterations. At one point, a stolen image of President Clinton is keyed behind the fake news anchor.

The BLO Nightly News, then, instigates a two-way dialogue between the activists and the corporate media by means of the prank: the activists gain access to dominant media through gender bending and then reuse those news stories in their own tape. The dominant media are recast as penetrable to raids, and usable. The division between producer and consumer is blurred. The mass-media coverage of the pranks opened up a small discussion on sexism in children's toys through humor at a particularly heated time of the year for toy purchases. At the same time, the tape itself apes the slickness of corporate news visual models, but bends them with a transvestite weatherperson, montage editing that exposes the corporate media agenda, and a style of news reporting that highlights the performative pose of corporate media reporters.

The tape does not stop at documenting the Barbie and GI Joe voice box surgery, however; it also serves as an instruction manual on how to change the dolls. Through these multiple moves, the tape turns all consumption into production of ideologies, deconstructions, practices, or subject positions. Even the viewing of the tape itself changes spectatorship, assuming that the how-to aspect of the Barbie caper is as crucial as the why. The BLO Nightly News presumes that all technologies are infinitely malleable, from toll-free telephone numbers to computer chip voice boxes in dolls, to television, to videotape, to satellite feeds, to the mail, to surveillance cameras, to ChromaKey technology.

To survive these new nearly debilitating structural realignments in public culture, democratic media strategy needs to deterritorialize, to adopt a more mobile, more multiple, more clever performance that is a productive relation on spatiality. It needs to embrace hybridity, rejecting the essentialism of identity politics, but also rebuffing formal purity, combining tools – from film to video to digitality – styles, and distribution systems. It needs to dispose of such concepts as guerrilla or alternative filmmaking, hangovers from older periods with quite different political debates and historical contexts. A theory of piracy and pirates offers a sailing ship with which to navigate the new world orders with new epistemological structures and political tactics.

In the 1970s, it was fashionable to refer to radical media practice as guerrilla filmmaking, a concept borrowed from Third World liberation struggles that sought to overthrow the colonization of territories. The guerrilla media maker operated outside, marooned in the margins, fighting for territory in an underground way. The term guerrilla suggests that media practice was itself militarized, armed, ready to bomb out the opposition, seeking discursive and geographic territory. A signifier condensing this strategy resides in the logo of the Newsreel collective: quick flashes of the name Newsreel with bursts of machine-gun sounds.

In the transnational era of mobile capital, fluidity, global communication flows, digitality, and diaspora, any concept of radical media practice that is lashed to binary oppositions between demonized corporate media and sanctified pure independent media is bound to fail at creating more democratic spaces. A more complex, constantly shape-shifting hybridity of strategies, technologies, and textual interventions is urgently necessary if there is to be any struggle for independent media at all.

As David Cordingly has argued in *Under the Black Flag*, the construct of the pirate has intertwined fact and fiction: in the seventeenth and eighteenth centuries, many pirates were criminal outcasts who chose to reject the naval operations of the nation-state for economic gain, but not all; in literature and Hollywood film, many pirates have been romanticized as dazzlingly handsome action-adventure heroes who lived a life of sailing, but not all.[11] Nearly a century before the French Revolution, pirate ships were democracies dedicated to liberty, equality, and brotherhood.[12]

In her novel *The Holder of the World*, a feminist novel about the transnational movement of a young woman in the seventeenth century who moves from the American colonies to England and then to India, novelist Bharati Mukherjee summons the image of the pirate ship. In narrativizing and reimagining the pirate ship, Mukherjee casts away its criminality, refashioning it as a mobile boat of resistance to capitalist companies, the state, colonization, and slavery. In *The Holder of the World*, pirates freed the slaves in Madagascar. In contemporary practice, media pirates free the media from its transnational corporate location.

Piracy is identified with an earlier period of mercantilism, when capital was in a similar era of change and growth internationally. Always on a boat, on water, moving in and out to raid and steal, the pirates were not moored to one nation. Pirate ships, as Mukherjee imagines them, had crews composed of many nationalities; they were ships of deterritorialized bodies, moving in and out of ports.

The information age, with its global flows in the vast ocean of cyberspace and its infinite reproduction of images, marks another era of great economic shifts. If piracy can be theorized as a media form that is fluid, mobile, and hybrid, then it can perhaps provide a way to rethink this new period of exploration and capital growth not as something huge, impenetrable, dominating, and depressing, but as an archive to be raided, its contents borrowed, mutated, digitized. Jacques Derrida has noted the indeterminacy and openness of the archive, its endless productive capacities in the period of digitality: "The archivist produces more archive, and that is why the archive is never closed. It opens out of the future."[13]

If piracy can be conceptualized as a new media strategy, it then becomes an insignia for difference(s), multiple layers of critique(s), intervention(s), and space(s). Theorizing piracy means disengaging from territories, deconstructing the binary opposition fueling most of a quarter of a century of independent media, and entering the global flows not as consumers, but as producers-in-dialogue. A notion of piracy refuses to recognize images as property, but instead collectivizes the images in the global image flows, severing them from ownership by the transnationals.

In rejecting the binary opposition between Afrocentrist essentialism and black nationalist pluralism, Paul Gilroy has also summoned the image of the ship as a central metaphor for hybridity, displacement, border crossing, circulatory systems, transformation, and reinscription. In his conception of the "Black Atlantic", he explains how sailors moved between nations on ships that were "microsystems of linguistic and political hybridity".[14] Gilroy's emphasis on movement, border crossing, plurality of forms, and open textuality as modalities of resistant cultural practice is materialized in the dubbing, scratching, and remixing of digitally sampled hip-hop music, a form of black music that ransacks other musical forms in order to refashion them into a new musical language.[15]

Media piracy, which reinscribes racializing and engendering discourses on dominant media that privilege whiteness and maleness, similarly refutes the binary oppositions between dominant and radical media by creating a hybrid structure that graphs together old media and new forms, a sampling and remixing of culture. Gilroy deploys the term *antiphony* to describe the democratic model emerging in African American call-and-response musical forms, a term that collapses the binary oppositions between producer and consumer, author and reader, into intersubjectivity and interaction.[16] Media piracy, then, can be theorized as an antiphonic relation, rather than as simply a marginal or resistant position. The former implies motion, whereas the latter suggests stasis.

Pirate antiphony, however, is not simply a productive relation, but a virtuoso invention of new social spaces designed with recuperated imagery and tactical practices. In *The Practice of Everyday Life*, Michel de Certeau theorizes space and its relation to poaching, a tactic of the dispossessed to change the register of totalitarian regimes by concocting a creative utopia through wit, trickery, and art, reversing the power relations. An example of this poaching emerges in folktales and legends, where the story enunciates this inversion: the disempowered trick giants and other ogres, signifying impregnable power and triumph, a pedagogy of utopianism and hope.[17] For de Certeau, space differs from place in that it is "composed of intersections of mobile elements", whereas place is bounded, fixed, located.[18] These notions of space and tactics rather than place and strategies are central to rethinking how to deal with the post-Cold War new world communication orders, which have simultaneously centralized (with mergers across industries) and decentralized (diffusion of new technologies such as camcorders and computers). Media piracy, then, produces mobile space through tactics in which, as de Certeau has said, "order is tricked by an art".[19]

[. . .]

Notes

1 Pirate Editorial, "So You Want to Be a Pirate?" in *High Noon on the Electronic Frontier: Conceptual Issues in Cyberspace*, ed. Peter Ludlow (Cambridge: MIT Press 1996), 110. I thank Chuck Kleinhans for provoking my thinking on piracy by asking me why PBS and CPB matter anymore for political documentary.

2 Gordon Graham, "Progress in a Quiet War", *Publishers Weekly*, 12 January 1990, S4.

3 Guillermo Gómez-Peña, "The Subcomandante of Performance" in *First World, Ha Ha Ha: The Zapatista Challenge*, ed. Elaine Katzenberger (San Francisco: City Lights 1995), 90–91.

4 "Statement of Subcomandante Marcos" satellite broadcast, *Freeing the Media Teach-In*, organized by the Learning Alliance, Paper Tiger Television, and FAIR in Cooperation with the Media and Democracy Congress, 31 January 1997, New York.

5 Guillermo Gómez-Peña, "The Free Trade Art Agreement/El Tratado De Libre Cultura" in *The New World Border* (San Francisco: City Lights 1996), 12.

6 John Fiske, "Popular News" in *Reading the Popular* (Boston: Unwin Hyman 1989), 185–197.

7 Quoted in Kenneth B. Noble, "Defying Airwave Rules and Exporting the Way", *New York Times*, 2 January 1996, A10.

8 Zeke Teflon, *The Complete Manual of Pirate Radio* (Tucson, Ariz.: See Sharp 1993), 5.

9 Douglas Rushkoff, *Media Virus! Hidden Agendas in Popular Culture* (New York: Ballantine 1994), 258–316.

10 Dawn Ades, *Photomontage* (New York: Thames & Hudson 1973), 12–13; see also Douglas Kahn, *John Heartfield: Art and Mass Media* (New York: Tanam 1985).

11 David Cordingly, *Under the Black Flag: The Romance and Reality of Life among the Pirates* (New York: Random House 1995), 1–75.

12 Ibid., 96.

13 Jacques Derrida, *Archive Fever: A Freudian Impression*, trans. Eric Prenowitz (Chicago: University of Chicago Press 1996), 68.

14 Paul Gilroy, *The Black Atlantic: Modernity and Double Consciousness* (Cambridge: Harvard University Press 1994), 12, 73–106, 190–200.

15 Ibid., 100–106.

16 Ibid., 200–202.

17 Michel de Certeau, *The Practice of Everyday Life* (Berkeley: University of California Press 1984), 23–25.

18 Ibid., 117.

19 Ibid., 26.

PART FOUR

CONTEXTS AND CONSEQUENCES

Introduction

While the wider world impacts on cinema, this dynamic of exchange is mutual. At various historical moments, the technologies of cinema have figured both in contemporary discourses and in transformations in the social sphere.

This type of engagement, for Dziga Vertov, can be achieved through the symbiosis of technology and the body, as a way of creating new ways of seeing that transcend the limits of the human eye. Most notable, in this respect, is Vertov's theory of the kino-eye – a symbolic melding of ocular perception and the expanded, technologized vistas of cinematic vision. The camera, and later the devices of sound recording, are presented by Vertov as prosthetic devices, mechanical augmentation at the service of political transformation. "I am a mechanical eye", he asserts, outlining this rhetorical shift from human to machinic consciousness, "I, a machine, show you the world as only I can see it."

One film, in particular, *Man with a Movie Camera* (*Chevlovek s kinoapparatom*) (1929), puts Vertov's proto-cyborgian manifesto into practice. Through superimposition and montage, images of the human eye are aligned, both graphically and operationally, with the lens and iris of the film camera. For the eponymous figure of the man with a movie camera, body and machine become a singular entity at the service of the Cultural Revolution.

Walter Benjamin explores the reverberations of cinema's technologies in terms of the politics of accelerated reproduction. The technological status of cinema, he argues, represents a shift from the status of an original work of art, such as a painting hung in a gallery, to the systems of mass reproduction on which cinema is predicated. For Benjamin, the quality of this reproduction and the speed with which it could be achieved had increased exponentially when compared with the progress of previous centuries.

The differences between manual and mechanical modes of reproduction are presented as facilitating a fundamental change in the function of art, with political imperative supplanting ritual appreciation. "Mechanical reproduction of art", Benjamin argues, "changes the reaction of the masses", giving rise to simultaneous shared experiences that constitute a new form of perception. By contrast to studied concentration, "the distracted mass absorbs the work of art", participating in what becomes a form of consensual illusion. This dynamic of distraction and control takes on heightened meaning if we consider the historical context (1930s Germany amidst the rise of Fascism) to which Benjamin, a Jew, was responding. Cinema, as a form aimed precisely at mass reproduction, was considered especially susceptible to exploitation.

Where Vertov's concern is with the fusion of human and machine as creative labor, Vivian Sobchack situates the act of viewing as constructing an interface between cybernetic and organic. "We are all part of a moving-image culture", she suggests, "and we live cinematic and electronic lives." To an unprecedented degree, our daily routines engage with networks of moving image communication and the texts they produce. Whether watching, playing or using, these encounters impinge on our existence and collectively transform us as subjects. "As they have mediated our engagement with the world, with others, and with ourselves", she argues, "cinematic and electronic technologies have transformed us so that we currently see, sense, and make sense of ourselves as quite other than we were before them."

While cinematic and electronic technologies both contribute to the moving image culture we inhabit, Sobchack proposes they each impact differently on how we perceive our sense of self and bodily presence. Unlike cinematic representation, the spatial projection and materiality of which fosters an inherent sense of dimension, electronic representation is predisposed towards the symbolic surface of the screen. Writing in the wake of Cyberpunk, a subculture that popularized narratives of leaving behind the body in order to pass beyond the screen, Sobchack contends that what gets left behind in such scenarios – "AIDS, homelessness, hunger, torture, and all the other ills the flesh is heir to" – are precisely the conditions in most need of our attention. Most alarmingly, she warns, by "devaluing the physical lived body and the concrete materiality of the world, electronic presence suggests that we are all in imminent danger of becoming merely ghosts in the machine".

The technologies and representations of cinema are the result of, and feed into, a whole range of contexts and consequences that exist beyond the cinematic. Just as cinema's history cannot be told apart from its technologies, nor can the history of technological culture be viewed in isolation from the contribution of cinema.

Kinoks

10

A Revolution

DZIGA VERTOV

(From an appeal at the beginning of 1922)

You – filmmakers, you directors and artists with nothing to do, all you confused cameramen and writers scattered throughout the world,

You – theater audiences, patient as mules beneath the burden of the emotional experiences offered you,

You – impatient proprietors of theaters not yet bankrupt, greedily snatching at leftovers from the German, or more rarely, the American table –

You – exhausted by memories, await with dreamy sighs the moon of some new six-act production . . . (nervous folk are requested to shut their eyes).

You're waiting for something that will not come; the wait is pointless.

A friendly warning:
Don't hide your heads like ostriches.
Raise your eyes,
Look around you –
There!
It's obvious to me
as to any child
The innards,
the guts of strong sensations
are tumbling out
of cinema's belly,
ripped open on the reef of revolution.
See them dragging along,
leaving a bloody trail on the earth
that quivers with horror and disgust.
It's all over.

(From a stenographic record)
To the Council of Three – Dziga Vertov

Psychological, detective, satirical, travel film – it doesn't matter what kind – if we cut out all the themes, leaving only the captions, we get the picture's literary skeleton. We can shoot other themes to go with that literary skeleton – realist, symbolist, expressionist – what have you. This situation will not change. The correlation is the same: a literary skeleton plus film-illustrations – such, almost without exception, are all films, ours and those from abroad.

(From an appeal of 20 January 1923)
To cinematographers – the Council of Three

Five seething years of universal daring have passed through you and gone leaving no trace. You keep prerevolutionary "artistic" models hanging like ikons within you, and it is to them alone that your inner piety has been directed. Foreign countries support you in your errors, sending to a renewed Russia the imperishable relics of film-drama done up in splendid, technical sauce.

Spring arrives. The film-factories are expected to resume work. The Council of Three observes with unconcealed regret film production workers leafing through literary texts in search of suitable dramatizations. Names of theatrical dramas and epics proposed for adaptation are already in the air. In the Ukraine, and here in Moscow, several pictures with all the signs of impotence are already in production.

A strong technological lag; a loss of active thinking, lost during a period of idleness; an orientation toward the six-act psychodrama – i.e. an orientation toward what's behind you – all these factors doom each attempt [at adaptation] to failure. Cinema's system is poisoned with the terrible toxin of routine. We demand the opportunity to test the antidote we've found upon its dying body. We ask the unbelievers to see for themselves: we agree to test our medicine beforehand on "guinea pigs" – film études . . .

The resolution of the Council of Three, 10 April 1923

The situation on the film front must be considered inauspicious.

As was to be expected, the first new Russian productions shown recall the old "artistic" models just as Nepmen recall the old bourgeoisie.

The repertoire planned for summer production, both here and in the Ukraine, does not inspire the least confidence.

The proposals for broad experimental work have been passed over.

All efforts, sighs, tears, and expectations, all prayers – are directed toward it – the six-act film-drama.

Therefore the Council of Three without waiting for the kinoks to be assigned work and ignoring the latter's desire to realize their own projects, are temporarily disregarding authorship rights and resolve to immediately publish for general use the common principles and slogans of the future revolution-through-newsreel; for which purpose, first and foremost, kinok Dziga Vertov is directed, in accordance with party discipline, to publish certain excerpts from the pamphlet *Kinoks: A Revolution*, which shall sufficiently clarify the nature of that revolution.

The Council of Three

In fulfillment of the resolution of the Council of Three on 10 April of this year, I am publishing the following excerpts:

Upon observing the films that have arrived from America and the West and taking into account available information on work and artistic experimentation at home and abroad, I arrive at the following conclusion:

The death sentence passed in 1919 by the kinoks on all films, with no exceptions, holds for the present as well. The most scrupulous examination does not reveal a single film, a single artistic experiment, properly directed to the emancipation of the camera, which is reduced to a state of pitiable slavery, of subordination to the imperfections and the shortsightedness of the human eye.

We do not object to cinema's undermining of literature and the theater; we wholly approve of the use of cinema in every branch of knowledge, but we define these functions as accessory, as secondary offshoots of cinema.

The main and essential thing is:

The sensory exploration of the world through film.

We therefore take as the point of departure the use of the camera as a kino-eye, more perfect than the human eye, for the exploration of the chaos of visual phenomena that fills space.

The kino-eye lives and moves in time and space: it gathers and records impressions in a manner wholly different from that of the human eye. The position of our bodies while observing or our perception of a certain number of features of a visual phenomenon in a given instant are by no means obligatory limitations for the camera which, since it is perfected, perceives more and better.

We cannot improve the making of our eyes, but we can endlessly perfect the camera.

Until now many a cameraman has been criticized for having filmed a running horse moving with unnatural slowness on the screen (rapid cranking of the camera) – or for the opposite, a tractor plowing a field too swiftly (slow cranking of the camera), and the like.

These are chance occurrences, of course, but we are preparing a system, a deliberate system of such occurrences, a system of seeming irregularities to investigate and organize phenomena.

Until now, we have violated the movie camera and forced it to copy the work of our eye. And the better the copy, the better the shooting was thought to be. Starting today we are liberating the camera and making it work in the opposite direction – away from copying.

The weakness of the human eye is manifest. We affirm the kino-eye, discovering within the chaos of movement the result of the kino-eye's own movement; we affirm the kino-eye with its own dimensions of time and space, growing in strength and potential to the point of self-affirmation.

I make the viewer see in the manner best suited to my presentation of this or that visual phenomenon. The eye submits to the will of the camera and is directed by it to those successive points of the action that, most succinctly and vividly, bring the film phrase to the height or depth of resolution.

Example: shooting a boxing match, not from the point of view of a spectator present, but shooting the successive movements (the blows) of the contenders.

Example: the filming of a group of dancers, not from the point of view of a spectator sitting in the auditorium with a ballet on the stage before him.

After all, the spectator at a ballet follows, in confusion, now the combined group of dancers, now random individual figures, now someone's legs – a series of scattered perceptions, different for each spectator.

One can't present this to the film viewer. A system of successive movements requires the filming of dancers or boxers in the order of their actions, one after another . . . by forceful transfer of the viewer's eye to the successive details that must be seen.

The camera "carries" the film viewer's eyes from arms to legs, from legs to eyes and so on, in the most advantageous sequence, and organizes the details into an orderly montage study.

You're walking down a Chicago street today in 1923, but I make you greet Comrade Volodarsky, walking down a Petrograd street in 1918, and he returns your greeting.

Another example: the coffins of national heroes are lowered into the grave (shot in Astrakhan in 1918); the grave is filled in (Kronstadt 1921); cannon salute (Petrograd 1920); memorial service, hats are removed (Moscow 1922) – such things go together, even with thankless footage not specifically shot for this purpose (cf. *Kinopravda* no. 13). The montage of crowds and of machines greeting Comrade Lenin (*Kinopravda* no. 14), filmed in different places at different times, belongs to this category.

I am kino-eye. I am a builder. I have placed you, whom I've created today, in an extraordinary room which did not exist until just now when I also created it. In this room there are twelve walls shot by me in various parts of the world. In bringing together shots of walls and details I've managed to arrange them in an order that is pleasing and to construct with intervals, correctly, a film-phrase which is the room.

I am kino-eye, I create a man more perfect than Adam, I create thousands of different people in accordance with preliminary blueprints and diagrams of different kinds.

I am kino-eye.

From one person I take the hands, the strongest and most dexterous; from another I take the legs, the swiftest and most shapely; from a third, the most beautiful and expressive head – and through montage I create a new, perfect man.

I am kino-eye, I am a mechanical eye. I, a machine, show you the world as only I can see it.

Now and forever, I free myself from human immobility, I am in constant motion, I draw near, then away from objects, I crawl under, I climb onto them. I move apace with the muzzle of a galloping horse, I plunge full speed into a crowd, I outstrip running soldiers, I fall on my back, I ascend with an airplane, I plunge and soar together with plunging and soaring bodies. Now I, a camera, fling myself along their resultant, maneuvering in the chaos of movement, recording movement, starting with movements composed of the most complex combinations.

Freed from the rule of sixteen–seventeen frames per second, free of the limits of time and space, I put together any given points in the universe, no matter where I've recorded them.

My path leads to the creation of a fresh perception of the world. I decipher in a new way a world unknown to you.

Once more let us agree: the eye and the ear. The ear does not spy, the eye does not eavesdrop.

Separation of functions.

Radio-ear – the montage "I hear!"

Kino-eye – the montage "I see!"

There you have it, citizens, for the first time: instead of music, painting, theater, cinematography, and other castrated outpourings.

Within the chaos of movements, running past, away, running into and colliding – the eye, all by itself, enters life.

A day of visual impressions has passed. How is one to construct the impressions of the day into an effective whole, a visual study? If one films everything the eye has seen, the result, of course, will be a jumble. If one skillfully edits what's been photographed, the result will be clearer. If one scraps bothersome waste, it will be better still. One obtains an organized memo of the ordinary eye's impressions.

The mechanical eye, the camera, rejecting the human eye as crib sheet, gropes its way through the chaos of visual events, letting itself be drawn or repelled by movement, probing, as it goes, the path of its own movement. It experiments, distending time, dissecting movement, or, in contrary fashion, absorbing time within itself, swallowing years, thus schematizing processes of long duration inaccessible to the normal eye.

Aiding the machine-eye is the kinok-pilot, who not only controls the camera's movements, but entrusts himself to it during experiments in space. And at a later time the kinok-engineer, with remote control of cameras.

The result of this concerted action of the liberated and perfected camera and the strategic brain of man directing, observing, and gauging – the presentation of even the most ordinary things will take on an exceptionally fresh and interesting aspect.

How many people, starved for spectacles, are wearing away the seats of their pants in theaters?

They flee from the humdrum, from the "prose" of life. And meanwhile the theater is almost always just a lousy imitation of that same life, plus an idiotic conglomerate of balletic affectation, musical squeaks, tricks of lighting, stage sets (from daubs to constructivism), and occasionally the work of a talented writer distorted by all that nonsense. Certain masters of the theater are destroying the theater from within, shattering old forms, and advancing new slogans for theatrical work; to further their rescue they've enlisted biomechanics (in itself a worthy pursuit), and cinema (honor and glory to it), and writers (not bad in themselves), and constructions (there are some good ones), and automobiles (how can one not admire the automobile?), and gunfire (something dangerous and impressive at the front); and by and large not a damned thing comes of it.

Theater and nothing more.

Not only is this no synthesis; it's not even a legitimate mixture.

And it cannot be otherwise.

We kinoks, as firm opponents of premature synthesis ("For synthesis must come at the summit of achievement!"), understand that it's pointless to mix scraps of achievement: the little ones will immediately perish from overcrowding and disorder. And in general –

The arena's small. Come out, please, into life.

This is where we work – we, the masters of vision, the organizers of visible life, armed with the omnipresent kino-eye. This is where the masters of word and sound, the most skillful editors of audible life, work. And I make bold to slip them the ubiquitous mechanical ear and megaphone – the radiotelephone.

This is:

newsreel,

radio-news.

I promise to drum up a parade of kinoks on Red Square on the day when the futurists release the first issue of a radio-news montage.

Not the newsreels from Pathé or Gaumont (newspaper chronicle), not even *Kinopravda* (political newsreel), but a real kinok newsreel – an impetuous survey of visual events deciphered by the camera, bits of real energy (as opposed to theater) joined through intervals into a tectonic whole by the great craft of montage.

Such structuring of the film-object enables one to develop any given theme, be it comic, tragic, one of special effects, or some other type.

It's entirely a question of the particular juxtaposition of visual details, of intervals.

The unusual flexibility of montage construction enables one to introduce into a film study any given motif – political, economic, or other. And therefore:

- As of now, neither psychological nor detective dramas are needed in cinema,
- As of now, theatrical productions transferred to film are no longer needed,
- As of now, neither Dostoyevsky nor Nat Pinkerton are to be put on the screen.
- Everything is included in the new conception of the newsreel. Into the jumble of life resolutely enter:

1   kino-eye, challenging the human eye's visual representation of the world and offering its own "I see", and
2   the kinok-editor, organizing the minutes of the life-structure seen *this way* for the first time.

The Work of Art in the Age of Mechanical Reproduction

11

WALTER BENJAMIN

Our fine arts were developed, their types and uses were established, in times very different from the present by men whose power of action upon things was insignificant in comparison with ours. But the amazing growth of our techniques, the adaptability and precision they have attained, the ideas and habits they are creating, make it a certainty that profound changes are impending in the ancient craft of the Beautiful. In all the arts there is a physical component which can no longer be considered or treated as it used to be, which cannot remain unaffected by our modern knowledge and power. For the last twenty years neither matter nor space nor time has been what it was from time immemorial. We must expect great innovations to transform the entire technique of the arts, thereby affecting artistic invention itself and perhaps even bringing about an amazing change in our very notion of art.[1]

Paul Valéry, *Pièces sur l'art*,
"La Conquète de l'ubiquité", Paris

Preface

When Marx undertook his critique of the capitalistic mode of production, this mode was in its infancy. Marx directed his efforts in such a way as to give them prognostic value. He went back to the basic conditions underlying capitalistic production and through his presentation showed what could be expected of capitalism in the future. The result was that one could expect it not only to exploit the proletariat with increasing intensity, but ultimately to create conditions which would make it possible to abolish capitalism itself.

The transformation of the superstructure, which takes place far more slowly than that of the substructure, has taken more than half a century to manifest in all areas of culture the change in the conditions of production. Only today can it be indicated what form this has taken. Certain prognostic requirements should be met by these statements. However, theses about the art of the proletariat after its assumption of power or about the art of a classless society would have less bearing on these demands than theses about the developmental tendencies of art under present conditions of production. Their dialectic is no less noticeable in the superstructure than in the economy. It would therefore be wrong to underestimate the value of such theses as a weapon. They brush aside a number of outmoded concepts, such as creativity and genius, eternal value and mystery – concepts whose uncontrolled (and at present almost uncontrollable) application would lead to a processing of data in the Fascist sense. The concepts which are introduced into the theory of art in what follows differ from the more familiar terms in that they are completely useless for the purposes of Fascism. They are, on the other hand, useful for the formulation of revolutionary demands in the politics of art.

I

In principle a work of art has always been reproducible. Man-made artifacts could always be imitated by men. Replicas were made by pupils in practice of their craft, by masters for diffusing their works, and, finally, by third parties in the pursuit of gain. Mechanical reproduction of a work of art, however, represents something new. Historically, it advanced intermittently and in leaps at long intervals, but with accelerated intensity. The Greeks knew only two procedures of technically reproducing works of art: founding and stamping. Bronzes, terracottas, and coins were the only art works which they could produce in quantity. All others were unique and could not be mechanically reproduced. With the woodcut graphic art became mechanically reproducible for the first time, long before script became reproducible by print. The enormous changes which printing, the mechanical reproduction of writing, has brought about in literature are a familiar story. However, within the phenomenon which we are here examining from the perspective of world history, print is merely a special, though particularly important, case. During the Middle Ages engraving and etching were added to the woodcut; at the beginning of the nineteenth century lithography made its appearance.

With lithography the technique of reproduction reached an essentially new stage. This much more direct process was distinguished by the tracing of the design on a stone rather than its incision on a block of wood or its etching on a copperplate and permitted graphic art for the first time to put its products on the market, not only in large numbers as hitherto, but also in daily changing forms. Lithography enabled graphic art to illustrate everyday life, and it began to keep pace with printing. But only a few decades after its invention, lithography was surpassed by photography. For the first time in the process of pictorial reproduction, photography freed the hand of the most important artistic functions which henceforth devolved only upon the eye looking into a lens. Since the eye perceives more swiftly than the hand can draw, the process of pictorial reproduction was accelerated so enormously that it could keep pace with speech. A film operator shooting a scene in the studio captures the images at the speed of an actor's speech. Just as lithography virtually implied the illustrated newspaper, so did photography foreshadow the sound film. The technical reproduction of sound was tackled at the end of the last century. These convergent endeavors made predictable a situation which Paul Valéry pointed up in this sentence:

> Just as water, gas, and electricity are brought into our houses from far off to satisfy our needs in response to a minimal effort, so we shall be supplied with visual or auditory images, which will appear and disappear at a simple movement of the hand, hardly more than a sign.[2]

Around 1900 technical reproduction had reached a standard that not only permitted it to reproduce all transmitted works of art and thus to cause the most profound change in their impact upon the public; it also had captured a place of its own among the artistic processes. For the study of this standard nothing is more revealing than the nature of the repercussions that these two different manifestations – the reproduction of works of art and the art of the film – have had on art in its traditional form.

II

Even the most perfect reproduction of a work of art is lacking in one element: its presence in time and space, its unique existence at the place where it happens to be. This unique existence of the work of art determined the history to which it was subject throughout the time of its existence. This includes the changes which it may have suffered in physical condition over the years as well as the various changes in its ownership.[3] The traces of the first can be revealed only by chemical or physical analyses which it is impossible to perform on a reproduction; changes of ownership are subject to a tradition which must be traced from the situation of the original.

The presence of the original is the prerequisite to the concept of authenticity. Chemical analyses of the patina of a bronze can help to establish this, as does the proof that a given manuscript of the Middle Ages stems from an archive of the fifteenth century. The whole sphere of authenticity is outside technical – and, of course, not only technical – reproducibility.[4] Confronted with its manual reproduction, which was usually branded as a forgery, the original preserved all its authority; not so *vis à vis* technical reproduction. The reason is twofold. First, process reproduction is more independent of the original than manual reproduction. For example, in photography, process reproduction can bring out those aspects of the original that are unattainable to the naked eye yet accessible to the lens, which is adjustable and chooses its angle at will. And photographic reproduction, with the aid of certain processes, such as enlargement or slow motion, can capture images which escape natural vision. Second, technical reproduction can put the copy of the original into situations which would be out of reach for the original itself. Above all, it enables the original to meet the beholder halfway, be it in the form of a photograph or a phonograph record. The cathedral leaves its locale to be received in the studio of a lover of art; the choral production, performed in an auditortum or in the open air, resounds in the drawing room.

The situations into which the product of mechanical reproduction can be brought may not touch the actual work of art, yet the quality of its presence is always depreciated. This holds not only for the art work but also, for instance, for a landscape which passes in review before the spectator in a movie. In the case of the art object, a most sensitive nucleus – namely, its authenticity – is interfered with whereas no natural object is vulnerable on that score. The authenticity of a thing is the essence of all that is transmissible from its beginning, ranging from its substantive duration to its testimony to the history which it has experienced. Since the historical testimony rests on the authenticity, the former, too, is jeopardized by reproduction when substantive duration ceases to matter. And what is really jeopardized when the historical testimony is affected, is the authority of the object.[5]

One might subsume the eliminated element in the term "aura" and go on to say: that which withers in the age of mechanical reproduction is the aura of the work of art. This is a symptomatic process whose significance points beyond the realm of art. One might generalize by saying: the technique of reproduction detaches the reproduced object from the domain of tradition. By making many reproductions it substitutes a plurality of copies for a unique existence. And in permitting the reproduction to meet the beholder or listener in his own particular situation, it reactivates the object reproduced. These two processes lead to a tremendous shattering of tradition which is the obverse of the contemporary crisis and renewal of mankind. Both processes are intimately connected with the contemporary mass movements. Their most powerful agent is the film. Its social significance, particularly in its most positive form, is inconceivable without its destructive, cathartic aspect, that is, the liquidation of the traditional value of the cultural heritage. This phenomenon is most palpable in the great historical films. It extends to ever new positions. In 1927 Abel Gance exclaimed enthusiastically: "Shakespeare, Rembrandt, Beethoven will make films . . . all legends, all mythologies and all myths, all founders of religion, and the very religions . . . await their exposed resurrection, and the heroes crowd each other at the gate."[6] Presumably without intending it, he issued an invitation to a far-reaching liquidation.

III

During long periods of history, the mode of human sense perception changes with humanity's entire mode of existence. The manner in which human sense perception is organized, the medium in which it is accomplished, is determined not only by nature but by historical circumstances as well. The fifth century, with its great shifts of population, saw the birth of the late Roman art industry and the Vienna Genesis, and there developed not only an art different from that of antiquity but also a new kind of perception. The scholars of the Viennese school, Riegl and Wickhoff, who resisted the weight of classical tradition under which these later art forms had been buried, were the first to draw conclusions from them concerning the organization of perception at the time. However far-reaching their insight, these scholars limited themselves to showing the significant, formal hallmark which characterized perception in late Roman times. They did not attempt – and, perhaps, saw no way – to show the social transformations expressed by these changes of perception. The conditions for an analogous insight are more favorable in the present. And if changes in the medium of contemporary perception can be comprehended as decay of the aura, it is possible to show its social causes.

The concept of aura which was proposed above with reference to historical objects may usefully be illustrated with reference to the aura of natural ones. We define the aura of the latter as the unique phenomenon of a distance, however close it may be. If, while resting on a summer afternoon, you follow with your eyes a mountain range on the horizon or a branch which casts its shadow over you, you experience the aura of those mountains, of that branch. This image makes it easy to comprehend the social bases of the contemporary decay of the aura. It rests on two circumstances, both of which are related to the increasing significance of the masses in contemporary life. Namely, the desire of contemporary masses to bring things "closer" spatially and humanly, which is just as ardent as their bent toward overcoming the uniqueness of every reality by accepting its reproduction.[7] Every day the urge grows stronger to get hold of an object at very close range by way of its likeness, its reproduction. Unmistakably, reproduction as offered by picture magazines and newsreels differs from the image seen by the unarmed eye. Uniqueness and permanence are as closely linked in the latter as are transitoriness and reproducibility in the former. To pry an object from its shell, to destroy its aura, is the mark of a perception whose "sense of the universal equality of things" has increased to such a degree that it extracts it even from a unique object by means of reproduction. Thus is manifested in the field of perception what in the theoretical sphere is noticeable in the increasing importance of statistics. The adjustment of reality to the masses and of the masses to reality is a process of unlimited scope, as much for thinking as for perception.

IV

The uniqueness of a work of art is inseparable from its being imbedded in the fabric of tradition. This tradition itself is thoroughly alive and extremely changeable. An ancient statue of Venus, for example, stood in a different traditional context with the Greeks, who made it an object of veneration, than with the clerics of the Middle Ages, who viewed it as an ominous idol. Both of them, however, were equally confronted with its uniqueness, that is, its aura. Originally the contextual integration of art in tradition found its expression in the cult. We know that the earliest art works originated in the service of a ritual – first the magical, then the religious kind. It is significant that the existence of the work of art with reference to its aura is never entirely separated from its ritual function.[8] In other words, the unique value of the "authentic" work of art has its basis in ritual, the location of its original use value. This ritualistic basis, however remote, is still recognizable as secularized ritual even in the most profane forms of the cult of beauty.[9] The secular cult of beauty, developed during the Renaissance and prevailing for three centuries, clearly showed that ritualistic basis in its decline and the first deep crisis which befell it. With the advent of the first truly revolutionary means of reproduction, photography, simultaneously with the rise of socialism, art sensed the approaching crisis which has become evident a century later. At the time, art reacted with the doctrine of *l'art pour l'art*, that is, with a theology of art. This gave rise to what might be called a negative theology in the form of the idea of "pure" art, which not only denied any social function of art but also any categorizing by subject matter. (In poetry, Mallarmé was the first to take this position.)

An analysis of art in the age of mechanical reproduction must do justice to these relationships, for they lead us to an all-important insight: for the first time in world history, mechanical reproduction emancipates the work of art from its parasitical dependence on ritual. To an ever greater degree the work of art reproduced becomes the work of art designed for reproducibility.[10] From a photographic negative, for example, one can make any number of prints; to ask for the "authentic" print makes no sense. But the instant the criterion of authenticity ceases to be applicable to artistic production, the total function of art is reversed. Instead of being based on ritual, it begins to be based on another practice – politics.

V

Works of art are received and valued on different planes. Two polar types stand out: with one, the accent is on the cult value; with the other, on the exhibition value of the work.[11] Artistic production begins with ceremonial objects destined to serve in a cult. One may assume that what mattered was their existence, not their being on view. The elk portrayed by the man of the Stone Age on the walls of his cave was an instrument of magic. He did expose it to his fellow men, but in the main it was meant for the spirits. Today the cult value would seem to demand that the work of art remain hidden. Certain statues of gods are accessible only to the priest in the cella; certain Madonnas remain covered nearly all year round; certain sculptures on medieval cathedrals are invisible to the spectator on ground level. With the emancipation of the various art practices from ritual go increasing opportunities for the exhibition of their products. It is easier to exhibit a portrait bust that can be sent here and there than to exhibit the statue of a divinity that has its fixed place in the interior of a temple. The same holds for the painting as against the mosaic or fresco that preceded it. And even though the public presentability of a mass originally may have been just as great as that of a symphony, the latter originated at the moment when its public presentability promised to surpass that of the mass.

With the different methods of technical reproduction of a work of art, its fitness for exhibition increased to such an extent that the quantitative shift between its two poles turned into a qualitative transformation of its nature. This is comparable to the situation of the work of art in prehistoric times when, by the absolute emphasis on its cult value, it was, first and foremost, an instrument of magic. Only later did it come to be recognized as a work of art. In the same way today, by the absolute emphasis on its exhibition value, the work of art becomes a creation with entirely new functions, among which the one we are conscious of, the artistic function, later may be recognized as incidental.[12] This much is certain: today photography and the film are the most serviceable exemplifications of this new function.

VI

In photography, exhibition value begins to displace cult value all along the line. But cult value does not give way without resistance. It retires into an ultimate retrenchment: the human countenance. It is no accident that the portrait was the focal point of early photography. The cult of remembrance of loved ones, absent or dead, offers a last refuge for the cult value of the picture. For the last time the aura emanates from the early photographs in the fleeting expression of a human face. This is what constitutes their melancholy, incomparable beauty. But as man withdraws from the photographic image, the exhibition value for the first time shows its superiority to the ritual value. To have pinpointed this new stage constitutes the incomparable significance of Atget, who, around 1900, took photographs of deserted Paris streets. It has quite justly been said of him that he photographed them like scenes of crime. The scene of a crime, too, is deserted; it is photographed for the purpose of establishing evidence. With Atget, photographs become standard evidence for historical occurrences, and acquire a hidden political significance. They demand a specific kind of approach; free floating contemplation is not appropriate to them. They stir the viewer; he feels challenged by them in a new way. At the same time picture magazines begin to put up signposts for him, right ones or wrong ones, no matter. For the first time, captions have become obligatory. And it is clear that they have an altogether different character than the title of a painting. The directives which the captions give to those looking at pictures in illustrated magazines soon become even more explicit and more imperative in the film where the meaning of each single picture appears to be prescribed by the sequence of all preceding ones.

VII

The nineteenth-century dispute as to the artistic value of painting versus photography today seems devious and confused. This does not diminish its importance, however; if anything, it underlines it. The dispute was in fact the symptom of a historical transformation the universal impact of which was not realized by either of the rivals. When the age of mechanical reproduction separated art from its basis in cult, the semblance of its autonomy disappeared forever. The resulting change in the function of art transcended the perspective of the century; for a long time it even escaped that of the twentieth century, which experienced the development of the film.

Earlier much futile thought had been devoted to the question of whether photography is an art. The primary question – whether the very invention of photography had not transformed the entire nature of art – was not raised. Soon the film theoreticians asked the same ill-considered question with regard to the film. But the difficulties which photography caused traditional aesthetics were mere child's play as compared to those raised by the film. Whence the insensitive and forced character of early theories of the film. Abel Gance, for instance, compares the film with hieroglyphs:

> Here, by a remarkable regression, we have come back to the level of expression of the Egyptians. . . . Pictorial language has not yet matured because our eyes have not yet adjusted to it. There is as yet insufficient respect for, insufficient cult of, what it expresses.[13]

Or, in the words of Séverin-Mars:

> What art has been granted a dream more poetical and more real at the same time! Approached in this fashion the film might represent an incomparable means of expression. Only the most high-minded persons, in the most perfect and mysterious moments of their lives, should be allowed to enter its ambience.[14]

Alexandre Arnoux concludes his fantasy about the silent film with the question: "Do not all the bold descriptions we have given amount to the definition of prayer?"[15] It is instructive to note how their desire to class the film among the "arts" forces these theoreticians to read ritual elements into it – with a striking lack of discretion. Yet when these speculations were published, films like L'Opinion publique and The Gold Rush had already appeared. This, however, did not keep Abel Gance from adducing hieroglyphs for purposes of comparison, nor Séverin-Mars from speaking of the film as one might speak of paintings by Fra Angelico. Characteristically, even today ultrareactionary authors give the film a similar contextual significance – if not an outright sacred one, then at least a supernatural one. Commenting on Max Reinhardt's film version of A Midsummer Night's Dream, Werfel states that undoubtedly it was the sterile copying of the exterior world with its streets, interiors, railroad stations, restaurants, motorcars, and beaches which until now had obstructed the elevation of the film to the realm of art. "The film has not yet realized its true meaning, its real possibilities . . . these consist in its unique faculty to express by natural means and with incomparable persuasiveness all that is fairylike, marvelous, supernatural."[16]

VIII

The artistic performance of a stage actor is definitely presented to the public by the actor in person; that of the screen actor, however, is presented by a camera, with a twofold consequence. The camera that presents the performance of the film actor to the public need not respect the performance as an integral whole. Guided by the cameraman, the camera continually changes its position with respect to the performance. The sequence of positional views which the editor composes from the material supplied him constitutes the completed film. It comprises certain factors of movement which are in reality those of the camera, not to mention special camera angles, close-ups, etc. Hence, the performance of the actor is subjected to a series of optical tests. This is the first consequence of the fact that the actor's performance is presented by means of a camera. Also, the film actor lacks the opportunity of the stage actor to adjust to the audience during his performance, since he does not present his performance to the audience in person. This permits the audience to take the position of a critic, without experiencing any personal contact with the actor. The audience's identification with the actor is really an identification with the camera. Consequently the audience takes the position of the camera; its approach is that of testing.[17] This is not the approach to which cult values may be exposed.

IX

For the film, what matters primarily is that the actor represents himself to the public before the camera, rather than representing someone else. One of the first to sense the actor's metamorphosis by this form of testing was Pirandello. Though his remarks on the subject in his novel Si Gira were limited to the negative aspects of the question and to the silent film only, this hardly impairs their validity. For in this respect, the sound film did not change anything essential. What matters is that the part is acted not for an audience but for a mechanical contrivance – in the case of the sound film, for two of them. "The film actor", wrote Pirandello,

> feels as if in exile – exiled not only from the stage but also from himself. With a vague sense of discomfort he feels inexplicable emptiness: his body loses its corporeality, it evaporates, it is deprived of reality, life, voice, and the noises caused by his moving about, in order to be changed into a mute image, flickering an instant on the screen, then vanishing into silence. . . . The projector will play with his shadow before the public, and he himself must be content to play before the camera.[18]

This situation might also be characterized as follows: for the first time – and this is the effect of the film – man has to operate with his whole living person, yet forgoing its aura. For aura is tied to his presence; there can be no replica of it. The aura which, on the stage, emanates from Macbeth, cannot be separated for the spectators from that of the actor. However, the singularity of the shot in the studio is that the camera is substituted for the public. Consequently, the aura that envelops the actor vanishes, and with it the aura of the figure he portrays.

It is not surprising that it should be a dramatist such as Pirandello who, in characterizing the film, inadvertently touches on the very crisis in which we see the theater. Any thorough study proves that there is indeed no greater contrast than that of the stage play to a work of art that is completely subject to or, like the film, founded in, mechanical reproduction. Experts have long recognized that in the film "the greatest effects are almost always obtained by 'acting' as little as possible. . . ." In 1932 Rudolf Arnheim saw "the latest trend . . . in treating the actor as a stage prop chosen for its characteristics and . . . inserted at the proper place".[19] With this idea something else is closely connected. The stage actor identifies himself with the character of his role. The film actor very often is denied this opportunity. His creation is by no means all of a piece; it is composed of many separate performances. Besides certain fortuitous considerations, such as cost of studio, availability of fellow players, décor, etc., there are elementary necessities of equipment that split the actor's work into a series of mountable episodes. In particular, lighting and its installation require the presentation of an event that, on the screen, unfolds as a rapid and unified scene, in a sequence of separate shootings which may take hours at the studio; not to mention more obvious montage. Thus a jump from the window can be shot in the studio as a jump from a scaffold, and the ensuing flight, if need be, can be shot weeks later when outdoor scenes are taken. Far more paradoxical cases can easily be construed. Let us assume that an actor is supposed to be startled by a knock at the door. If his reaction is not satisfactory, the director can resort to an expedient: when the actor happens to be at the studio again he has a shot fired behind him without his being forewarned of it. The frightened reaction can be shot now and be cut into the screen version. Nothing more strikingly shows that art has left the realm of the "beautiful semblance" which, so far, had been taken to be the only sphere where art could thrive.

X

The feeling of strangeness that overcomes the actor before the camera, as Pirandello describes it, is basically of the same kind as the estrangement felt before one's own image in the mirror. But now the reflected image has become separable, transportable. And where is it transported? Before the public.[20] Never for a moment does the screen actor cease to be conscious of this fact. While facing the camera he knows that ultimately he will face the public, the consumers who constitute the market. This market, where he offers not only his labor but also his whole self, his heart and soul, is beyond his reach. During the shooting he has as little contact with it as any article made in a factory. This may contribute to that oppression, that new anxiety which, according to Pirandello, grips the actor before the camera. The film responds to the shriveling of the aura with an artificial build-up of the "personality" outside the studio. The cult of the movie star, fostered by the money of the film industry, preserves not the unique aura of the person but the "spell of the personality", the phony spell of a commodity. So long as the movie-makers' capital sets the fashion, as a rule no other revolutionary merit can be accredited to today's film than the promotion of a revolutionary criticism of traditional concepts of art. We do not deny that in some cases today's films can also promote revolutionary criticism of social conditions, even of the distribution of property. However, our present study is no more specifically concerned with this than is the film production of Western Europe.

It is inherent in the technique of the film as well as that of sports that everybody who witnesses its accomplishments is somewhat of an expert. This is obvious to anyone listening to a group of newspaper boys leaning on their bicycles and discussing the outcome of a bicycle race. It is not for nothing that newspaper publishers arrange races for their delivery boys. These arouse great interest among the participants, for the victor has an opportunity to rise from delivery boy to professional racer. Similarly, the newsreel offers everyone the opportunity to rise from passer-by to movie extra. In this way any man might even find himself part of a work of art, as witness Vertov's *Three Songs About Lenin* or Ivens' *Borinage*. Any man today can lay claim to being filmed. This claim can best be elucidated by a comparative look at the historical situation of contemporary literature.

For centuries a small number of writers were confronted by many thousands of readers. This changed toward the end of the last century. With the increasing extension of the press, which kept placing new political, religious, scientific, professional, and local organs before the readers, an increasing number of readers became writers – at first, occasional ones. It began with the daily press opening to its readers space for "letters to the editor". And today there is hardly a gainfully employed European who could not, in principle, find an opportunity to publish somewhere or other comments on his work, grievances, documentary reports, or that sort of thing. Thus, the distinction between author and public is about to lose its basic character. The difference becomes merely functional, it may vary from case to case. At any moment the reader is ready to turn into a writer. As expert, which he had to become willy-nilly in an extremely specialized work process, even if only in some minor respect, the reader gains access to authorship. In the Soviet Union work itself is given a voice. To present it verbally is part of a man's ability to perform the work. Literary license is now founded on polytechnic rather than specialized training and thus becomes common property.[21]

All this can easily be applied to the film, where transitions that in literature took centuries have come about in a decade. In cinematic practice, particularly in Russia, this changeover has partially become established reality. Some of the players whom we meet in Russian films are not actors in our sense but people who portray *themselves* – and primarily in their own work process. In Western Europe the capitalistic exploitation of the film denies consideration to modern man's legitimate claim to being reproduced. Under these circumstances the film industry is trying hard to spur the interest of the masses through illusion-promoting spectacles and dubious speculations.

XI

The shooting of a film, especially of a sound film, affords a spectacle unimaginable anywhere at any time before this. It presents a process in which it is impossible to assign to a spectator a viewpoint which would exclude from the actual scene such extraneous accessories as camera equipment, lighting machinery, staff assistance, etc. – unless his eye were on a line parallel with the lens. This circumstance, more than any other, renders superficial and insignificant any possible similarity between a scene in the studio and one on the stage. In the theater one is well aware of the place from which the play cannot immediately be detected as illusionary. There is no such place for the movie scene that is being shot. Its illusionary nature is that of the second degree, the result of cutting. That is to say, in the studio the mechanical equipment has penetrated so deeply into reality that its pure aspect freed from the foreign substance of equipment is the result of a special procedure, namely, the shooting by the specially adjusted camera and the mounting of the shot together with other similar ones. The equipment-free aspect of reality here has become the height of artifice; the sight of immediate reality has become an orchid in the land of technology.

Even more revealing is the comparison of these circumstances, which differ so much from those of the theater, with the situation in painting. Here the question is: how does the camera-man compare with the painter? To answer this we take recourse to an analogy with a surgical operation. The surgeon represents the polar opposite of the magician. The magician heals a sick person by the laying on of hands; the surgeon cuts into the patient's body. The magician maintains the natural distance between the patient and himself; though he reduces it very slightly by the laying on of hands, he greatly increases it by virtue of his authority. The surgeon does exactly the reverse; he greatly diminishes the distance between himself and the patient by penetrating into the patient's body, and increases it but little by the caution with which his hand moves among the organs. In short, in contrast to the magician – who is still hidden in the medical practitioner – the surgeon at the decisive moment abstains from facing the patient man to man; rather, it is through the operation that he penetrates into him.

Magician and surgeon compare to painter and cameraman. The painter maintains in his work a natural distance from reality, the cameraman penetrates deeply into its web.[22] There is a tremendous difference between the pictures they obtain. That of the painter is a total one, that of the cameraman consists of multiple fragments which are assembled under a new law. Thus, for contemporary man the representation of reality by the film is incomparably more significant than that of the painter, since it offers, precisely because of the thorough-going permeation of reality with mechanical equipment, an aspect of reality which is free of all equipment. And that is what one is entitled to ask from a work of art.

XII

Mechanical reproduction of art changes the reaction of the masses toward art. The reactionary attitude toward a Picasso painting changes into the progressive reaction toward a Chaplin movie. The progressive reaction is characterized by the direct, intimate fusion of visual and emotional enjoyment with the orientation of the expert. Such fusion is of great social significance. The greater the decrease in the social significance of an art form, the sharper the distinction between criticism and enjoyment by the public. The conventional is uncritically enjoyed, and the truly new is criticized with aversion. With regard to the screen, the critical and the receptive attitudes of the public coincide. The decisive reason for this is that individual reactions are predetermined by the mass audience response they are about to produce, and this is nowhere more pronounced than in the film. The moment these responses become manifest they control each other. Again, the comparison with painting is fruitful. A painting has always had an excellent chance to be viewed by one person or by a few. The simultaneous contemplation of paintings by a large public, such as developed in the nineteenth century, is an early symptom of the crisis of painting, a crisis which was by no means occasioned exclusively by photography but rather in a relatively independent manner by the appeal of art works to the masses.

Painting simply is in no position to present an object for simultaneous collective experience, as it was possible for architecture at all times, for the epic poem in the past, and for the movie today. Although this circumstance in itself should not lead one to conclusions about the social role of painting, it does constitute a serious threat as soon as painting, under special conditions and, as it were, against its nature, is confronted directly by the masses. In the churches and monasteries of the Middle Ages and at the princely courts up to the end of the eighteenth century, a collective reception of paintings did not occur simultaneously, but by graduated and hierarchized mediation. The change that has come about is an expression of the particular conflict in which painting was implicated by the mechanical reproducibility of paintings. Although paintings began to be publicly exhibited in galleries and salons, there was no way for the masses to organize and control themselves in their reception.[23] Thus the same public which responds in a progressive manner toward a grotesque film is bound to respond in a reactionary manner to surrealism.

XIII

The characteristics of the film lie not only in the manner in which man presents himself to mechanical equipment but also in the manner in which, by means of this apparatus, man can represent his environment. A glance at occupational psychology illustrates the testing capacity of the equipment. Psychoanalysis illustrates it in a different perspective. The film has enriched our field of perception with methods which can be illustrated by those of Freudian theory. Fifty years ago, a slip of the tongue passed more or less unnoticed. Only exceptionally may such a slip have revealed dimensions of depth in a conversation which had seemed to be taking its course on the surface. Since the *Psychopathology of Everyday Life* things have changed. This book isolated and made analyzable things which had heretofore floated along unnoticed in the broad stream of perception. For the entire spectrum of optical, and now also acoustical, perception the film has brought about a similar deepening of apperception. It is only an obverse of this fact that behavior items shown in a movie can be analyzed much more precisely and from more points of view than those presented on paintings or on the stage. As compared with painting, filmed behavior lends itself more readily to analysis because of its incomparably more precise statements of the situation. In comparison with the stage scene, the filmed behavior item lends itself more readily to analysis because it can be isolated more easily. This circumstance derives its chief importance from its tendency to promote the mutual penetration of art and science. Actually, of a screened behavior item which is neatly brought out in a certain situation, like a muscle of a body, it is difficult to say which is more fascinating, its artistic value or its value for science. To demonstrate the identity of the artistic and scientific uses of photography which heretofore usually were separated will be one of the revolutionary functions of the film.[24]

By close-ups of the things around us, by focusing on hidden details of familiar objects, by exploring commonplace milieux under the ingenious guidance of the camera, the film, on the one hand, extends our comprehension of the necessities which rule our lives; on the other hand, it manages to assure us of an immense and unexpected field of action. Our taverns and our metropolitan streets, our offices and furnished rooms, our railroad stations and our factories appeared to have us locked up hopelessly. Then came the film and burst this prison-world asunder by the dynamite of the tenth of a second, so that now, in the midst of its far-flung ruins and debris, we calmly and adventurously go traveling. With the close-up, space expands; with slow motion, movement is extended. The enlargement of a snapshot does not simply render more precise what in any case was visible, though unclear: it reveals entirely new structural formations of the subject. So, too, slow motion not only presents familiar qualities of movement but reveals in them entirely unknown ones "which, far from looking like retarded rapid movements, give the effect of singularly gliding, floating, supernatural motions".[25] Evidently a different nature opens itself to the camera than opens to the naked eye – if only because an unconsciously penetrated space is substituted for a space consciously explored by man. Even if one has a general knowledge of the way people walk, one knows nothing of a person's posture during the fractional second of a stride. The act of reaching for a lighter or a spoon is familiar routine, yet we hardly know what really goes on between hand and metal, not to mention how this fluctuates with our moods. Here the camera intervenes with the resources of its lowerings and liftings, its interruptions and isolations, its extensions and accelerations, its enlargements and reductions. The camera introduces us to unconscious optics as does psychoanalysis to unconscious impulses.

XIV

One of the foremost tasks of art has always been the creation of a demand which could be fully satisfied only later.[26] The history of every art form shows critical epochs in which a certain art form aspires to effects which could be fully obtained only with a changed technical standard, that is to say, in a new art form. The extravagances and crudities of art which thus appear, particularly in the so-called decadent epochs, actually arise from the nucleus of its richest historical energies. In recent years, such barbarisms were abundant in Dadaism. It is only now that its impulse becomes discernible: Dadaism attempted to create by pictorial – and literary – means the effects which the public today seeks in the film.

Every fundamentally new, pioneering creation of demands will carry beyond its goal. Dadaism did so to the extent that it sacrificed the market values which are so characteristic of the film in favor of higher ambitions – though of course it was not conscious of such intentions as here described. The Dadaists attached much less importance to the sales value of their work than to its uselessness for contemplative immersion. The studied degradation of their material was not the least of their means to achieve this uselessness. Their poems are "word salad" containing obscenities and every imaginable waste product of language. The same is true of their paintings, on which they mounted buttons and tickets. What they intended and achieved was a relentless destruction of the aura of their creations, which they branded as reproductions with the very means of production. Before a painting of Arp's or a poem by August Stramm it is impossible to take time for contemplation and evaluation as one would before a canvas of Derain's or a poem by Rilke. In the decline of middle-class society, contemplation became a school for asocial behavior; it was countered by distraction as a variant of social conduct.[27] Dadaistic activities actually assured a rather vehement distraction by making works of art the center of scandal. One requirement was foremost: to outrage the public.

From an alluring appearance or persuasive structure of sound the work of art of the Dadaists became an instrument of ballistics. It hit the spectator like a bullet, it happened to him, thus acquiring a tactile quality. It promoted a demand for the film, the distracting element of which is also primarily tactile, being based on changes of place and focus which periodically assail the spectator. Let us compare the screen on which a film unfolds with the canvas of a painting. The painting invites the spectator to contemplation; before it the spectator can abandon himself to his associations. Before the movie frame he cannot do so. No sooner has his eye grasped a scene than it is already changed. It cannot be arrested. Duhamel, who detests the film and knows nothing of its significance, though something of its structure, notes this circumstance as follows: "I can no longer think what I want to think. My thoughts have been replaced by moving images."[28] The spectator's process of association in view of these images is indeed interrupted by their constant, sudden change. This constitutes the shock effect of the film, which, like all shocks, should be cushioned by heightened presence of mind.[29] By means of its technical structure, the film has taken the physical shock effect out of the wrappers in which Dadaism had, as it were, kept it inside the moral shock effect.[30]

XV

The mass is a matrix from which all traditional behavior toward works of art issues today in a new form. Quantity has been transmuted into quality. The greatly increased mass of participants has produced a change in the mode of participation. The fact that the new mode of participation first appeared in a disreputable form must not confuse the spectator. Yet some people have launched spirited attacks against precisely this superficial aspect. Among these, Duhamel has expressed himself in the most radical manner. What he objects to most is the kind of participation which the movie elicits from the masses. Duhamel calls the movie

> a pastime for helots, a diversion for uneducated, wretched, worn-out creatures who are consumed by their worries . . . a spectacle which requires no concentration and presupposes no intelligence . . . which kindles no light in the heart and awakens no hope other than the ridiculous one of someday becoming a "star" in Los Angeles.[31]

Clearly, this is at bottom the same ancient lament that the masses seek distraction whereas art demands concentration from the spectator. That is a commonplace. The question remains whether it provides a platform for the analysis of the film. A closer look is needed here. Distraction and concentration form polar opposites which may be stated as follows: a man who concentrates before a work of art is absorbed by it. He enters into this work of art the way legend tells of the Chinese painter when he viewed his finished painting. In contrast, the distracted mass absorbs the work of art. This is most obvious with regard to buildings. Architecture has always represented the prototype of a work of art the reception of which is consummated by a collectivity in a state of distraction. The laws of its reception are most instructive.

Buildings have been man's companions since primeval times. Many art forms have developed and perished. Tragedy begins with the Greeks, is extinguished with them, and after centuries its "rules" only are revived. The epic poem, which had its origin in the youth of nations, expires in Europe at the end of the Renaissance. Panel painting is a creation of the Middle Ages, and nothing guarantees its uninterrupted existence. But the human need for shelter is lasting. Architecture has never been idle. Its history is more ancient than that of any other art, and its claim to being a living force has significance in every attempt to comprehend the relationship of the masses to art. Buildings are appropriated in a twofold manner: by use and by perception – or rather, by touch and sight. Such appropriation cannot be understood in terms of the attentive concentration of a tourist before a famous building. On the tactile side there is no counterpart to contemplation on the optical side. Tactile appropriation is accomplished not so much by attention as by habit. As regards architecture, habit determines to a large extent even optical reception. The latter, too, occurs much less through rapt attention than by noticing the object in incidental fashion. This mode of appropriation, developed with reference to architecture, in certain circumstances acquires canonical value. For the tasks which face the human apparatus of perception at the turning points of history cannot be solved by optical means, that is, by contemplation, alone. They are mastered gradually by habit, under the guidance of tactile appropriation.

The distracted person, too, can form habits. More, the ability to master certain tasks in a state of distraction proves that their solution has become a matter of habit. Distraction as provided by art presents a covert control of the extent to which new tasks have become soluble by apperception. Since, moreover, individuals are tempted to avoid such tasks, art will tackle the most difficult and most important ones where it is able to mobilize the masses. Today it does so in the film. Reception in a state of distraction, which is increasing noticeably in all fields of art and is symptomatic of profound changes in apperception, finds in the film its true means of exercise. The film with its shock effect meets this mode of reception halfway. The film makes the cult value recede into the background not only by putting the public in the position of the critic, but also by the fact that at the movies this position requires no attention. The public is an examiner, but an absent-minded one.

Epilogue

The growing proletarianization of modern man and the increasing formation of masses are two aspects of the same process. Fascism attempts to organize the newly created proletarian masses without affecting the property structure which the masses strive to eliminate. Fascism sees its salvation in giving these masses not their right, but instead a chance to express themselves.[32] The masses have a right to change property relations; Fascism seeks to give them an expression while preserving property. The logical result of Fascism is the introduction of aesthetics into political life. The violation of the masses, whom Fascism, with its *Führer* cult, forces to their knees, has its counterpart in the violation of an apparatus which is pressed into the production of ritual values.

All efforts to render politics aesthetic culminate in one thing: war. War and war only can set a goal for mass movements on the largest scale while respecting the traditional property system. This is the political formula for the situation. The technological formula may be stated as follows: only war makes it possible to mobilize all of today's technical resources while maintaining the property system. It goes without saying that the Fascist apotheosis of war does not employ such arguments. Still, Marinetti says in his manifesto on the Ethiopian colonial war:

> For twenty-seven years we Futurists have rebelled against the branding of war as antiaesthetic. . . . Accordingly we state: . . . War is beautiful because it establishes man's dominion over the subjugated machinery by means of gas masks, terrifying megaphones, flame throwers, and small tanks. War is beautiful because it initiates the dreamt-of metalization of the human body. War is beautiful because it enriches a flowering meadow with the fiery orchids of machine guns. War is beautiful because it combines the gun-fire, the cannonades, the cease-fire, the scents, and the stench of putrefaction into a

symphony. War is beautiful because it creates new architecture, like that of the big tanks, the geometrical formation flights, the smoke spirals from burning villages, and many others. . . . Poets and artists of Futurism! . . . remember these principles of an aesthetics of war so that your struggle for a new literature and a new graphic art . . . may be illumined by them!

This manifesto has the virtue of clarity. Its formulations deserve to be accepted by dialecticians. To the latter, the aesthetics of today's war appears as follows: if the natural utilization of productive forces is impeded by the property system, the increase in technical devices, in speed, and in the sources of energy will press for an unnatural utilization, and this is found in war. The destructiveness of war furnishes proof that society has not been mature enough to incorporate technology as its organ, that technology has not been sufficiently developed to cope with the elemental forces of society. The horrible features of imperialistic warfare are attributable to the discrepancy between the tremendous means of production and their inadequate utilization in the process of production – in other words, to unemployment and the lack of markets. Imperialistic war is a rebellion of technology which collects, in the form of "human material", the claims to which society has denied its natural material. Instead of draining rivers, society directs a human stream into a bed of trenches; instead of dropping seeds from airplanes, it drops incendiary bombs over cities; and through gas warfare the aura is abolished in a new way.

"Fiat ars – pereat mundus", says Fascism, and, as Marinetti admits, expects war to supply the artistic gratification of a sense perception that has been changed by technology. This is evidently the consummation of "l'art pour l'art". Mankind, which in Homer's time was an object of contemplation for the Olympian gods, now is one for itself. Its self-alienation has reached such a degree that it can experience its own destruction as an aesthetic pleasure of the first order. This is the situation of politics which Fascism is rendering aesthetic. Communism responds by politicizing art.

Notes

1 Quoted from Paul Valéry, Aesthetics, "The Conquest of Ubiquity", translated by Ralph Manheim, 225. Pantheon Books, Bollingen Series, New York, 1964.
2 Ibid., 226.
3 Of course, the history of a work of art encompasses more than this. The history of the "Mona Lisa", for instance, encompasses the kind and number of its copies made in the seventeenth, eighteenth and nineteenth centuries.
4 Precisely because authenticity is not reproducible, the intensive penetration of certain (mechanical) processes of reproduction was instrumental in differentiating and grading authenticity. To develop such differentiations was an important function of the trade in works of art. The invention of the woodcut may be said to have struck at the root of the quality of authenticity even before its late flowering. To be sure, at the time of its origin a medieval picture of the Madonna could not yet be said to be "authentic". It became "authentic" only during the succeeding centuries and perhaps most strikingly so during the last one.
5 The poorest provincial staging of Faust is superior to a Faust film in that, ideally, it

competes with the first performance at Weimar. Before the screen it is unprofitable to remember traditional contents which might come to mind before the stage – for instance, that Goethe's friend Johann Heinrich Merck is hidden in Mephisto, and the like.

6 Abel Gance, "Le Temps de l'image est venu", L'Art cinématographique, Vol. 2, 94 f, Paris, 1927.

7 To satisfy the human interest of the masses may mean to have one's social function removed from the field of vision. Nothing guarantees that a portraitist of today, when painting a famous surgeon at the breakfast table in the midst of his family, depicts his social function more precisely than a painter of the seventeenth century who portrayed his medical doctors as representing this profession, like Rembrandt in his "Anatomy Lesson".

8 The definition of the aura as a "unique phenomenon of a distance however close it may be" represents nothing but the formulation of the cult value of the work of art in categories of space and time perception. Distance is the opposite of closeness. The essentially distant object is the unapproachable one. Unapproachability is indeed a major quality of the cult image. True to its nature, it remains "distant, however close it may be". The closeness which one may gain from its subject matter does not impair the distance which it retains in its appearance.

9 To the extent to which the cult value of the painting is secularized, the ideas of its fundamental uniqueness lose distinctness. In the imagination of the beholder the uniqueness of the phenomena which hold sway in the cult image is more and more displaced by the empirical uniqueness of the creator or of his creative achievement. To be sure, never completely so; the concept of authenticity always transcends mere genuineness. (This is particularly apparent in the collector who always retains some traces of the fetishist and who, by owning the work of art, shares in its ritual power.) Nevertheless, the function of the concept of authenticity remains determinate in the evaluation of art; with the secularization of art, authenticity displaces the cult value of the work.

10 In the case of films, mechanical reproduction is not, as with literature and painting, an external condition for mass distribution. Mechanical reproduction is inherent in the very technique of film production. This technique not only permits in the most direct way but virtually causes mass distribution. It enforces distribution because the production of a film is so expensive that an individual who, for instance, might afford to buy a painting no longer can afford to buy a film. In 1927 it was calculated that a major film, in order to pay its way, had to reach an audience of nine million. With the sound film, to be sure, a setback in its international distribution occurred at first: audiences became limited by language barriers. This coincided with the Fascist emphasis on national interests. It is more important to focus on this connection with Fascism than on this set-back, which was soon minimized by synchronization. The simultaneity of both phenomena is attributable to the depression. The same disturbances which, on a larger scale, led to an attempt to maintain the existing property structure by sheer force led the endangered film capital to speed up the development of the sound film. The introduction of the sound film brought about a temporary relief, not only because it again brought the masses into the theaters but also because it merged new capital from the electrical industry with that of the film industry. Thus, viewed from the outside, the sound film promoted national interests, but seen from the inside it helped to internationalize film production even more than previously.

11 This polarity cannot come into its own in the aesthetics of Idealism. Its idea of beauty comprises these polar opposites without differentiating between them and consequently

excludes their polarity. Yet in Hegel this polarity announces itself as clearly as possible within the limits of Idealism. We quote from his *Philosophy of History*:

> Images were known of old. Piety at an early time required them for worship, but it could do without *beautiful* images. These might even be disturbing. In every beautiful painting there is also something nonspiritual, merely external, but its spirit speaks to man through its beauty. Worshipping, conversely, is concerned with the work as an object, for it is but a spiritless stupor of the soul. . . . Fine art has arisen . . . in the church . . . although it has already gone beyond its principle as art.

Likewise, the following passage from *The Philosophy of Fine Art* indicates that Hegel sensed a problem here. "We are beyond the stage of reverence for works of art as divine and objects deserving our worship. The impression they produce is one of a more reflective kind, and the emotions they arouse require a higher test . . ." (G. W. F. Hegel, *The Philosophy of Fine Art*, trans., with notes, by F. P. B. Osmaston, Vol. 1, 12, London, 1920).

The transition from the first kind of artistic reception to the second characterizes the history of artistic reception in general. Apart from that, a certain oscillation between these two polar modes of reception can be demonstrated for each work of art. Take the Sistine Madonna. Since Hubert Grimme's research it has been known that the Madonna originally was painted for the purpose of exhibition. Grimme's research was inspired by the question: what is the purpose of the molding in the foreground of the painting which the two cupids lean upon? How, Grimme asked further, did Raphael come to furnish the sky with two draperies? Research proved that the Madonna had been commissioned for the public lying-in-state of Pope Sixtus. The Popes lay in state in a certain side chapel of St Peter's. On that occasion Raphael's picture had been fastened in a nichelike background of the chapel, supported by the coffin. In this picture Raphael portrays the Madonna approaching the papal coffin in clouds from the background of the niche, which was demarcated by green drapes. At the obsequies of Sixtus a pre-eminent exhibition value of Raphael's picture was taken advantage of. Some time later it was placed on the high altar in the church of the Black Friars at Piacenza. The reason for this exile is to be found in the Roman rites which forbid the use of paintings exhibited at obsequies as cult objects on the high altar. This regulation devalued Raphael's picture to some degree. In order to obtain an adequate price nevertheless, the Papal See resolved to add to the bargain the tacit toleration of the picture above the high altar. To avoid attention the picture was given to the monks of the far-off provincial town.

12 Bertolt Brecht, on a different level, engaged in analogous reflections:

> If the concept of "work of art" can no longer be applied to the thing that emerges once the work is transformed into a commodity, we have to eliminate this concept with cautious care but without fear, lest we liquidate the function of the very thing as well. For it has to go through this phase without mental reservation, and not as noncommittal deviation from the straight path; rather, what happens here with the work of art will change it fundamentally and erase its past to such an extent that should the old concept be taken up again – and it will, why not? – it will no longer stir any memory of the thing it once designated.

13 Abel Gance, op. cit., 100–1.

14 Séverin-Mars, quoted by Abel Gance, op. cit., 100.

15 Alexandre Arnoux, *Cinéma pris*, 1929, 28.

16 Franz Werfel, "Ein Sommernachtstraum, Ein Film von Shakespeare und Reinhardt", *Neues Wiener Journal*, cited in *Lu* 15, November, 1935.

17

> The film . . . provides – or could provide – useful insight into the details of human actions. . . . Character is never used as a source of motivation; the inner life of the persons never supplies the principal cause of the plot and seldom is its main result.
>
> (Bertolt Brecht, *Versuche*, "Der Dreigroschenprozess", 268.)

The expansion of the field of the testable which mechanical equipment brings about for the actor corresponds to the extraordinary expansion of the field of the testable brought about for the individual through economic conditions. Thus, vocational aptitude tests become constantly more important. What matters in these tests are segmental performances of the individual. The film shot and the vocational aptitude test are taken before a committee of experts. The camera director in the studio occupies a place identical with that of the examiner during aptitude tests.

18 Luigi Pirandello, *Si Gira*, quoted by Léon Pierre-Quint, "Signification du cinéma", *L'Art cinématographique*, op. cit., 14–15.

19 Rudolf Arnheim, *Film als Kunst*, Berlin, 1932, 176 f. In this context certain seemingly unimportant details in which the film director deviates from stage practices gain in interest. Such is the attempt to let the actor play without make-up, as made among others by Dreyer in his *Jeanne d'Arc*. Dreyer spent months seeking the forty actors who constitute the Inquisitors' tribunal. The search for these actors resembled that for stage properties that are hard to come by. Dreyer made every effort to avoid resemblances of age, build, and physiognomy. If the actor thus becomes a stage property, this latter, on the other hand, frequently functions as actor. At least it is not unusual for the film to assign a role to the stage property. Instead of choosing at random from a great wealth of examples, let us concentrate on a particularly convincing one. A clock that is working will always be a disturbance on the stage. There it cannot be permitted its function of measuring time. Even in a naturalistic play, astronomical time would clash with theatrical time. Under these circumstances it is highly revealing that the film can, whenever appropriate, use time as measured by a clock. From this more than from many other touches it may clearly be recognized that under certain circumstances each and every prop in a film may assume important functions. From here it is but one step to Pudovkin's statement that "the playing of an actor which is connected with an object and is built around it . . . is always one of the strongest methods of cinematic construction" (W. Pudovkin, *Filmregie und Filmmanuskript*, Berlin, 1928, 126.). The film is the first art form capable of demonstrating how matter plays tricks on man. Hence, films can be an excellent means of materialistic representation.

20 The change noted here in the method of exhibition caused by mechanical reproduction applies to politics as well. The present crisis of the bourgeois democracies comprises a crisis of the conditions which determine the public presentation of the rulers. Democracies exhibit a member of government directly and personally before the nation's represen-

tatives. Parliament is his public. Since the innovations of camera and recording equipment make it possible for the orator to become audible and visible to an unlimited number of persons, the presentation of the man of politics before camera and recording equipment becomes paramount. Parliaments, as much as theaters, are deserted. Radio and film not only affect the function of the professional actor but likewise the function of those who also exhibit themselves before this mechanical equipment, those who govern. Though their tasks may be different, the change affects equally the actor and the ruler. The trend is toward establishing controllable and transferrable skills under certain social conditions. This results in a new selection, a selection before the equipment from which the star and the dictator emerge victorious.

21 The privileged character of the respective techniques is lost. Aldous Huxley writes:

> Advances in technology have led . . . to vulgarity. . . . Process reproduction and the rotary press have made possible the indefinite multiplication of writing and pictures. Universal education and relatively high wages have created an enormous public who know how to read and can afford to buy reading and pictorial matter. A great industry has been called into existence in order to supply these commodities. Now, artistic talent is a very rare phenomenon; whence it follows . . . that, at every epoch and in all countries, most art has been bad. But the proportion of trash in the total artistic output is greater now than at any other period. That it must be so is a matter of simple arithmetic. The population of Western Europe has a little more than doubled during the last century. But the amount of reading- and seeing-matter has increased, I should imagine, at least twenty and possibly fifty or even a hundred times. If there were n men of talent in a population of x millions, there will presumably be 2n men of talent among 2x millions. The situation may be summed up thus. For every page of print and pictures published a century ago, twenty or perhaps even a hundred pages are published today. But for every man of talent then living, there are now only two men of talent. It may be of course that, thanks to universal education, many potential talents which in the past would have been stillborn are now enabled to realize themselves. Let us assume, then, that there are now three or even four men of talent to every one of earlier times. It still remains true to say that the consumption of reading- and seeing-matter has far outstripped the natural production of gifted writers and draughtsmen. It is the same with hearing-matter. Prosperity, the gramophone and the radio have created an audience of hearers who consume an amount of hearing-matter that has increased out of all proportion to the increase of population and the consequent natural increase of talented musicians. It follows from all this that in all the arts the output of trash is both absolutely and relatively greater than it was in the past; and that it must remain greater for just so long as the world continues to consume the present inordinate quantities of reading-matter, seeing-matter, and hearing-matter.
>
> (Aldous Huxley, *Beyond the Mexique Bay. A Traveller's Journal*, London, 1949, 274 ff. First published in 1934.)

This mode of observation is obviously not progressive.

22 The boldness of the cameraman is indeed comparable to that of the surgeon. Luc Durtain lists among specific technical sleights of hand those

which are required in surgery in the case of certain difficult operations. I choose as an example a case from oto-rhinolaryngology; . . . the so-called endonasal perspective procedure; or I refer to the acrobatic tricks of larynx surgery which have to be performed following the reversed picture in the laryngoscope. I might also speak of ear surgery which suggests the precision work of watchmakers. What range of the most subtle muscular acrobatics is required from the man who wants to repair or save the human body! We have only to think of the couching of a cataract where there is virtually a debate of steel with nearly fluid tissue, or of the major abdominal operations (laparotomy).

(Luc Durtain)

23 This mode of observation may seem crude, but as the great theoretician Leonardo has shown, crude modes of observation may at times be usefully adduced. Leonardo compares painting and music as follows:

Painting is superior to music because, unlike unfortunate music, it does not have to die as soon as it is born. . . . Music which is consumed in the very act of its birth is inferior to painting which the use of varnish has rendered eternal.

(Trattato I, 29.)

24 Renaissance painting offers a revealing analogy to this situation. The incomparable development of this art and its significance rested not least on the integration of a number of new sciences, or at least of new scientific data. Renaissance painting made use of anatomy and perspective, of mathematics, meteorology, and chromatology. Valéry writes:

What could be further from us than the strange claim of a Leonardo to whom painting was a supreme goal and the ultimate demonstration of knowledge? Leonardo was convinced that painting demanded universal knowledge, and he did not even shrink from a theoretical analysis which to us is stunning because of its very depth and precision.

(Paul Valéry, Pièces sur l'art, "Autour de Corot", Paris, 191)

25 Rudolf Arnheim, loc. cit., 138.

26 "The work of art", says André Breton, "is valuable only in so far as it is vibrated by the reflexes of the future." Indeed, every developed art form intersects three lines of development. Technology works toward a certain form of art. Before the advent of the film there were photo booklets with pictures which flitted by the onlooker upon pressure of the thumb, thus portraying a boxing bout or a tennis match. Then there were the slot machines in bazaars; their picture sequences were produced by the turning of a crank.

Second, the traditional art forms in certain phases of their development strenuously work toward effects which later are effortlessly attained by the new ones. Before the rise of the movie the Dadaists' performances tried to create an audience reaction which Chaplin later evoked in a more natural way.

Third, unspectacular social changes often promote a change in receptivity which will benefit the new art form. Before the movie had begun to create its public, pictures that were no longer immobile captivated an assembled audience in the so-called

Kaiserpanorama. Here the public assembled before a screen into which stereoscopes were mounted, one to each beholder. By a mechanical process individual pictures appeared briefly before the stereoscopes, then made way for others. Edison still had to use similar devices in presenting the first movie strip before the film screen and projection were known. This strip was presented to a small public which stared into the apparatus in which the succession of pictures was reeling off. Incidentally, the institution of the *Kaiserpanorama* shows very clearly a dialectic of the development. Shortly before the movie turned the reception of pictures into a collective one, the individual viewing of pictures in these swiftly outmoded establishments came into play once more with an intensity comparable to that of the ancient priest beholding the statue of a divinity in the cella.

27 The theological archetype of this contemplation is the awareness of being alone with one's God. Such awareness, in the heyday of the bourgeoisie, went to strengthen the freedom to shake off clerical tutelage. During the decline of the bourgeoisie this awareness had to take into account the hidden tendency to withdraw from public affairs those forces which the individual draws upon in his communion with God.

28 Georges Duhamel, *Scènes de la vie future*, Paris, 1930, 52.

29 The film is the art form that is in keeping with the increased threat to his life which modern man has to face. Man's need to expose himself to shock effects is his adjustment to the dangers threatening him. The film corresponds to profound changes in the apperceptive apparatus – changes that are experienced on an individual scale by the man in the street in big-city traffic, on a historical scale by every present-day citizen.

30 As for Dadaism, insights important for Cubism and Futurism are to be gained from the movie. Both appear as deficient attempts of art to accommodate the pervasion of reality by the apparatus. In contrast to the film, these schools did not try to use the apparatus as such for the artistic presentation of reality, but aimed at some sort of alloy in the joint presentation of reality and apparatus. In Cubism, the premonition that this apparatus will be structurally based on optics plays a dominant part; in Futurism, it is the premonition of the effects of this apparatus which are brought out by the rapid sequence of the film strip.

31 Duhamel, op. cit., 58.

32 One technical feature is significant here, especially with regard to newsreels, the propagandist importance of which can hardly be overestimated. Mass reproduction is aided especially by the reproduction of masses. In big parades and monster rallies, in sports events, and in war, all of which nowadays are captured by camera and sound recording, the masses are brought face to face with themselves. This process, whose significance need not be stressed, is intimately connected with the development of the techniques of reproduction and photography. Mass movements are usually discerned more clearly by a camera than by the naked eye. A bird's-eye view best captures gatherings of hundreds of thousands. And even though such a view may be as accessible to the human eye as it is to the camera, the image received by the eye cannot be enlarged the way a negative is enlarged. This means that mass movements, including war, constitute a form of human behavior which particularly favors mechanical equipment.

The Scene of the Screen

12

Envisioning Cinematic and Electronic "Presence"

VIVIAN SOBCHACK

It is obvious that cinematic and electronic technologies of representation have had enormous impact upon our means of signification during the past century. Less obvious, however, is the similar impact these technologies have had upon the historically particular significance or "sense" we have and make of those temporal and spatial coordinates that radically inform and orient our social, individual, and bodily existences. At this point in time in the United States, whether or not we go to the movies, watch television or music videos, own a video tape recorder/player, allow our children to play video and computer games, or write our academic papers on personal computers, we are all part of a moving-image culture and we live cinematic and electronic lives. Indeed, it is not an exaggeration to claim that none of us can escape daily encounters – both direct and indirect – with the *objective* phenomena of motion picture, televisual, and computer technologies and the networks of communication and texts they produce. Nor is it an extravagance to suggest that, in the most profound, socially pervasive, and yet personal way, these objective encounters transform us as *subjects*. That is, although relatively novel as "materialities" of human communication, cinematic and electronic media have not only historically *symbolized* but also historically *constituted* a radical alteration of the forms of our culture's previous temporal and spatial consciousness and of our bodily sense of existential "presence" to the world, to ourselves, and to others.

This different sense of *subjective* and *material* "presence" both signified and supported by cinematic and electronic media emerges within and co-constitutes *objective* and *material* practices of representation and social existence. Thus, while cooperative in creating the moving-image culture or "life-world" we now inhabit, cinematic and electronic technologies are quite different from each other in their concrete "materiality" and particular existential significance. Each offers our lived-bodies radically different ways of "being-in-the world". Each implicates us in different structures of material investment, and – because each has a particular affinity with different cultural functions, forms, and contents – each stimulates us through differing modes of representation to different aesthetic responses and ethical responsibilities. In sum, just as the photograph did in the last century, so in this one, cinematic and electronic screens differently demand and shape our "presence" to the world and our representation in it. Each differently and objectively alters our subjectivity while each invites our complicity in formulating space, time, and bodily investment as significant personal and social experience.

These preliminary remarks are grounded in the belief that, during the last century, historical changes in our contemporary "sense" of temporality, spatiality, and existential and embodied presence cannot be considered less than a consequence of correspondent changes in our technologies of representation. However, they also must be considered something more, for as Martin Heidegger reminds us, "The essence of technology is nothing technological".[1] That is, technology never comes to its particular material specificity and function in a neutral context for neutral effect. Rather, it is always historically informed not only by its materiality but also by its political, economic, and social context, and thus always both co-constitutes and expresses cultural values. Correlatively, technology is never merely "used", never merely instrumental. It is always also "incorporated" and "lived" by the human beings who engage it within a structure of meanings and metaphors in which subject–object relations are cooperative, co-constitutive, dynamic, and reversible. It is no accident, for example, that in our now dominantly electronic (and only secondarily cinematic) culture, many human beings describe and understand their minds and bodies in terms of computer systems and programs (even as they still describe and understand their lives as movies). Nor is it trivial that computers are often described and understood in terms of human minds and/or bodies (for example, as intelligent, or as susceptible to viral infection) – and that these new "life forms" have become the cybernetic heroes of our most popular moving image fictions (for example, *Robocop* or *Terminator* II).[2] In this sense, a qualitatively new techno-logic can begin to alter our perceptual orientation in and toward the world, ourselves, and others. And as it becomes culturally pervasive, it can come to profoundly inform and affect the socio-logic, psycho-logic, and even the bio-logic by which we daily live our lives.

This power to alter our perceptions is doubly true of technologies of representation. A technological artifact like the automobile (whose technological function is not representation but transportation) has profoundly changed the temporal and spatial shape and meaning of our life-world and our own bodily and symbolic sense of ourselves.[3] However, representational technologies of photography, the motion picture, video, and computer inform us twice over: first, like the automobile, through the specific material conditions by which they latently engage our senses at the bodily level of what might be called our *microperception*, and then again through their explicit representational function by which they engage our senses textually at the hermeneutic level of what might be called our *macroperception*.[4] Most theorists and critics of the cinematic and electronic have been drawn to macroperceptual analysis, to descriptions and interpretations of the hermeneutic-cultural contexts that inform and shape both the materiality of the technologies and their textual representations.[5] Nonetheless, "all such contexts find their fulfillment *only* within the range of microperceptual possibility".[6] We cannot reflect upon and analyze either technologies or texts without having, at some point, engaged them *immediately* – that is, through our perceptive sensorium, through the materiality (or *immanent mediation*) of our own bodies. Thus, as philosopher of technology Don Ihde puts it, while "there is no microperception (sensory-bodily) without its location within a field of macroperception", there can be "no macroperception without its micro-perceptual foci".[7] It is important to note, however, that since perception is constituted and organized as a bodily and sensory *gestalt* that is always already meaningful, a microperceptual focus is not the same as a physiological or anatomical focus. The perceiving and sensing body is always also a *lived-body* – immersed in and making social meaning as well as physical sense.

The aim of this essay, then, is to figure certain microperceptual aspects of our engagement with the technologies of cinematic and electronic representation and to suggest some ways in which our microperceptual experience of their respective material conditions informs and transforms our temporal and spatial sense of ourselves and our cultural contexts of meaning. Insofar as the cinematic and the electronic have each been *objectively constituted* as a new and discrete techno-logic, each also has been *subjectively incorporated*, enabling a new perceptual mode of existential and embodied "presence". In sum, as they have mediated our engagement with the world, with others, and with ourselves, cinematic and electronic technologies have transformed us so that we currently see, sense, and make sense of ourselves as quite other than we were before them.

It should be evident at this point that the co-constitutive, reversible, and dynamic relations between objective material technologies and embodied human subjects invite a phenomenological investigation. Existential phenomenology, to use Ihde's characterization, is a "philosophical style that emphasizes a certain interpretation of human *experience* and that, in particular, concerns *perception* and *bodily* activity".[8] Often misunderstood as ungrounded "subjective" analysis, existential phenomenology is instead concerned with describing, thematizing, and interpreting the structures of lived spatiality, temporality, and meaning that are co-constituted dynamically as embodied human subjects perceptually engage an objective material world. It is focused, therefore, on the *relations between* the subjective and objective aspects of material, social, and personal existence and sees these relations as constitutive of the meaning and value of the phenomena under investigation.[9]

Existential phenomenology, then, attempts to describe, thematize, and interpret the *experiential* and *perceptual field* in which human beings play out a particular and meaningful structure of spatial, temporal, and bodily existence. Unlike the foundational, Husserlian transcendental phenomenology from which it emerged, existential phenomenology rejects the goal of arriving at universal and "essential" description, and "settles" for a historicized and "qualified" description as the only kind of description that is existentially possible or, indeed, desirable. It is precisely *because* rather than *in spite of* its qualifications that such a description is existentially meaningful – meaningful, that is, to human beings who are themselves particular, finite, and partial, and thus always in culture and history, always open to the world and further elaboration. Specifically, Maurice Merleau-Ponty's existential phenomenology departs from the transcendental phenomenology most associated with Edmund Husserl in that it stresses the *embodied* nature of human consciousness and views bodily existence as the original and originating *material premise* of sense and signification. We sit in a movie theater, before a television set, or in front of a computer terminal not only as *conscious* beings but also as *carnal* beings. Our vision is not abstracted from our bodies or from our other modes of perceptual access to the world. Nor does what we see merely touch the surface of our eyes. Seeing images mediated and made visible by technological vision enables us not only to see technological images but also to see technologically. As Ihde emphasizes, "the concreteness of [technological] 'hardware' in the broadest sense connects with the equal concreteness of our bodily existence", and, in this regard, "the term 'existential' in context refers to perceptual and bodily experience, to a kind of 'phenomenological materiality'".[10]

This correspondent and objective materiality of both human subjects and worldly objects not only suggests some commensurability and possibilities of exchange between them, but also suggests that any phenomenological analysis of the existential relation between human subjects and technologies of representation must be semiological and historical even at the microperceptual level. Description must attend both to the particular materiality and modalities through which meanings are signified and to the cultural and historical situations in which materiality and meaning come to cohere in the praxis of everyday life. Like human vision, the materiality and modalities of cinematic and electronic technologies of representation are not abstractions. They are concrete and situated and institutionalized. They inform and share in the spatiotemporal structures of a wide range of interrelated cultural phenomena. Thus, in its attention to the broadly defined "material conditions" and "relations" of production (specifically, the conditions for and production of existential meaning), existential phenomenology is not incompatible with certain aspects of Marxist analysis.

In this context, we might turn to Fredric Jameson's useful discussion of three crucial and expansive historical "moments" marked by "a technological revolution within capital itself" and the particular and dominant "cultural logic" that correspondingly emerges in each of them.[11] Historically situating these three "moments" in the 1840s, 1890s, and 1940s, Jameson correlates the three major technological changes that revolutionized the structure of capital – by changing market capitalism to monopoly capitalism and this to multinational capitalism – with the emergence and domination of three new "cultural logics": those axiological norms and forms of representation identified respectively as realism, modernism, and post-modernism. Extrapolating from Jameson, we can also locate within this conceptual and historical framework three correspondent technologies, forms, and institutions of visual (and aural) representation: respectively, the photographic, the cinematic, and the electronic. Each, we might argue, has been critically complicit not only in a specific *technological* revolution within capital", but also in a specific and radical *perceptual* revolution within the culture and the subject. That is, each has been co-constitutive of the very temporal and spatial structure of the "cultural logics" Jameson identifies as realism, modernism, and postmodernism. Writing about the nature of cultural transformation, phenomenological historian Stephen Kern suggests that some major cultural changes can be seen as *"directly* inspired by new technology", while others occur relatively independently of technology, and still others emerge from the new technological "metaphors and analogies" that *indirectly* alter the structures of perceptual life and thought.[12] Implicated in and informing each historically specific "technological revolution in capital" and transformation of "cultural logic", the technologically discrete nature and phenomenological impact of new "materialities" of representation co-constitute a complex cultural gestalt. In this regard, the technological "nature" of the photographic, the cinematic, and the electronic is graspable always and only in a qualified manner – that is, less as an "essence" than as a "theme".

Although I wish to emphasize the technologies of cinematic and electronic representation, those two "materialities" that constitute our current *moving*-image culture, something must first be said of that culture's grounding in the context and phenomenology of the *photographic*. The photographic is privileged in the "moment" of market capitalism – located by Jameson in the 1840s, and cooperatively informed and driven by the technological innovations of steam-powered mechanization that allowed for industrial expansion and the cultural logic of "realism". Not only did industrial expansion give rise to other forms of expansion, but expansion itself was historically unique in its unprecedented *visibility*. As Jean-Louis Comolli points out:

> The second half of the nineteenth century lives in a sort of frenzy of the visible. . . . [This is] the effect of the social multiplication of images. . . . [It is] the effect also, however, of

something of a geographical extension of the field of the visible and the representable: by journies, explorations, colonizations, the whole world becomes visible at the same time that it becomes appropriatable.[13]

Thus, while the cultural logic of "realism" has been seen as primarily represented by literature (most specifically, the bourgeois novel), it is, perhaps, even more intimately bound to the mechanically achieved, empirical, and representational "evidence" of the world constituted by photography.

Until very recently, the photographic has been popularly and phenomenologically perceived as existing in a state of testimonial verisimilitude – its film emulsions analogically marked with (and objectively "capturing") material traces of the world's concrete and "real" existence.[14] Photography produced images of the world with a perfection previously rivaled only by the human eye. Thus, as Comolli suggests, with the advent of photography, the human eye loses its "immemorial privilege" and is devalued in relation to "the mechanical eye of the photographic machine", which "now sees *in its place*".[15] This replacement of human with mechanical vision had its compensations however – among them, the material control, containment, and actual possession of time and experience.[16] Abstracting visual experience from a temporal flow, the photographic chemically and metaphorically "fixes" its ostensible subject as an *object* for vision, and concretely reproduces it in a *material* form that can be possessed, circulated, and saved, in a form that can over time accrue an increasing rate of interest, become more *valuable* in a variety of ways. Thus, identifying the photograph as a fetish object, Comolli links it with gold, and aptly calls it "the money of the 'real'" – of "life" – the photograph's materiality assuring the possibility of its "convenient circulation and appropriation".[17]

In his phenomenological description of human vision Merleau-Ponty tells us, "To see is *to have at a distance*".[18] This subjective activity of *visual* possession is objectified and literalized by the materiality of photography, which makes possible its *visible* possession. What you see is what you get. Indeed, this structure of objectification and empirical possession is doubled, even tripled. Not only does the photograph materially "capture" traces of the "real world", not only can the photograph itself be possessed concretely, but the photograph's culturally defined semiotic status as a mechanical reproduction (rather than a linguistic representation) also allows an unprecedentedly literal and material, and perhaps uniquely complacent, form – and ethics – of self-possession. Family albums serve as "memory banks" that authenticate self, other, and experience as empirically "real" by virtue of the photograph's material existence as an object and possession with special power.[19]

In regard to the materiality of the photograph's authenticating power, it is instructive to recall one of a number of particularly relevant ironies in *Blade Runner* (Ridley Scott 1982), a science fiction film focusing on the ambiguous ontological status of a group of genetically manufactured "replicants". At a certain moment, Rachel, the film's putative heroine and the latest replicant prototype, disavows the revelation of her own manufactured status by pointing to a series of keepsake photographs that give "proof" to her mother's existence, to her own existence as a little girl, to her subjective memory. Upon being told that both her memory and their material extroversion "belong to someone else", she is both distraught and ontologically re-signed as someone with no "real" life, no "real" history – although she still remembers what she remembers and the photographs still sit on her piano. Indeed, the photographs are suddenly foregrounded (for the human spectator as well as the narrative's replicant) as utterly suspect. That is, when interrogated, the photographs simultaneously both reveal and lose that great material and circulatory value they commonly hold for *all* of us as the "money of the 'real'".

The structures of objectification and material possession that constitute the photographic as both a "real" trace of personal experience and a concrete extroversion of experience that can "belong to someone else" give specific form to its temporal existence. In capturing aspects of "life itself" in a "real" object that can be possessed, copied, circulated, and saved as the "currency" of experience, the appropriable materiality and static form of photography accomplish a palpable intervention in what was popularly perceived in the mid-nineteenth century to be time's linear, orderly, and teleological flow from past to present to future. The photograph freezes and preserves the homogeneous and irreversible *momentum* of this temporal stream into the abstracted, atomized, and secured space of a *moment*. But at a cost. A moment cannot be inhabited. It cannot entertain in the abstraction of its visible space, its single and static *point* of view, the presence of a lived body – and so it does not really invite the spectator *into* the scene (although it may invite contemplation *of* the scene). In its conquest of time, the photographic constructs a space to hold and to look at, a "thin" insubstantial space that keeps the lived-body out even as it may imaginatively catalyze – in the parallel but temporalized space of memory or desire – an animated drama.

The radical difference between the transcendental, posited moment of the photograph and the existential momentum of the cinema, between the scene to be contemplated and the scene to be lived, is foregrounded in the remarkable short film La jetée (Chris Marker 1962).[20] A study of desire, memory, and time, La jetée is presented completely through the use of still photographs – except for one extraordinarily brief but utterly compelling sequence in which the woman who is the object of the hero's desire, lying in bed and looking toward the camera, blinks her eyes. The space between the camera's (and the spectator's) gaze and the woman becomes suddenly habitable, informed with the real possibility of bodily movement and engagement, informed with a lived temporality rather than an eternal timelessness. What, in the film, has previously been a mounting accumulation of nostalgic moments achieves substantial and present presence in its sudden accession to momentum and the consequent possibility of effective action.

As did André Bazin, we might think of photography, then, as primarily a form of mummi-fication (although, unlike Bazin, I shall argue that cinema is not).[21] While it testifies to and preserves a sense of the world and experience's real presence, it does not preserve their present. The photographic – unlike the cinematic and the electronic – functions neither as a coming-into-being (a presence always presently constituting itself) nor as being-in-itself (an absolute presence). Rather, it functions to fix a being-that-has-been (a presence in the present that is always past). Paradoxically, as it objectifies and preserves in its acts of possession, the photographic has something to do with loss, with pastness, and with death, its meanings and value intimately bound within the structure and investments of nostalgia.

Although dependent upon the photographic, the cinematic has something more to do with life, with the accumulation – not the loss – of experience. Cinematic technology *animates* the photographic and reconstitutes its visibility and verisimilitude in a difference not of degree but of kind. The *moving picture* is a visible representation not of activity finished or past, but of activity coming-into-being – and its materiality came to be in the 1890s, the second of Jameson's transformative moments of "technological revolution within capital itself". During this moment, the internal combustion engine and electric power literally reenergized market capitalism into the highly controlled yet expansive structure of monopoly capitalism. Correlatively, the new cultural logic of "modernism" emerged, restructuring and eventually dominating the logic of realism to represent more adequately the new perceptual experience of an age marked by the strange autonomy and energetic fluidity of, among other mechanical phenomena, the motion picture. The motion picture, while photographically verisimilar, fragments, reorders, and synthesizes time and space as animation in a completely new "cinematic" mode that finds no necessity in the objective teleo-logic of realism. Thus, although modernism has found its most remarked expression in the painting and photography of the futurists (who attempted to represent motion and speed in a static form) and the cubists (who privileged multiple perspectives and simultaneity), and in the novels of James Joyce, we can see in the cinema modernism's fullest representation.[22]

Philosopher Arthur Danto tells us, "With the movies, we do not just see *that* they move, we see them *moving*: and this is because the pictures themselves move".[23] While still objectifying the subjectivity of the visual into the visible, the cinematic qualitatively transforms the photographic through a materiality that not only claims the world and others as objects for vision but also signifies its own bodily agency, intentionality, and subjectivity. Neither abstract nor static, the cinematic brings the *existential activity* of vision into visibility in what is phenomenologically experienced as an *intentional stream* of moving images – its continuous and autonomous visual production and meaningful organization of these images testifying to the objective world and, further, to an anonymous, mobile, embodied, and ethically invested *subject* of worldly space. This subject (however physically anonymous) is able to inscribe visual and bodily changes of situation, to dream, hallucinate, imagine, and re-member its habitation and experience of the world. And, as is the case with human beings, this subject's potential mobility and experience are both open-ended and bound by the existential finitude and bodily limits of its particular vision and historical coherence (that is, its narrative).

Here, again, La jetée is exemplary. Despite the fact that the film is made up of what strike us as a series of discrete and still photographs rather than the "live" and animated action of human actors, even as it foregrounds the transcendental and atemporal non-becoming of the photograph, La jetée nonetheless phenomenologically *projects* as a temporal flow and an existential becoming. That is, *as a whole*, the film organizes, synthesizes, and enunciates the discrete photographic images into animated and intentional coherence and, indeed, makes this temporal synthesis and animation its explicit narrative theme. What La jetée allegorizes in its explicit narrative, however, is the transformation of the moment to momentum that constitutes the ontology of the cinematic, and the latent background of every film.

While the technology of the cinematic is grounded, in part, in the technology of the photographic, we need to remember that "the essence of technology is nothing technological". The fact that the technology of the cinematic *necessarily* depends upon the discrete and still photograph moving intermittently (rather than continuously) through the shutters of both camera and projector does not *sufficiently* account for the materiality of the cinematic as we experience it. Unlike the photograph, a film is semiotically engaged in experience not merely as a mechanical objectification – or material *reproduction* – that is, not merely as an object for vision. Rather, the moving picture, however mechanical and photographic its origin, is semiotically experienced as also subjective and intentional, as *presenting representation* of the objective world. Thus perceived as the subject of its own vision as well as an object for our vision, a moving picture is not precisely a *thing* that (like a photograph) can be easily controlled, contained, or materially possessed. Up until very recently in what has now become a dominantly electronic culture, the spectator could share in and thereby, to a degree, interpretively alter a film's presentation and representation of embodied and enworlded experience, but could not control or contain its autonomous and ephemeral flow and rhythm, or materially possess its animated experience. Now, of course, with the advent of videotape and VCRs, the spectator can alter the film's temporality and easily possess, at least, its inanimate "body". However, the ability to control the autonomy and flow of the cinematic experience through "fast forwarding", "replaying", and "freezing"[24] and the ability to possess the film's body and animate it at will at home are functions of the materiality and technological ontology of the electronic – a materiality that increasingly dominates, appropriates, and transforms the cinematic.

In its pre-electronic state and original materiality, however, the cinematic mechanically projected and made visible for the very first time not just the objective world but the very structure and process of subjective, embodied vision – hitherto only directly available to human beings as that invisible and private structure we each experience as "my own". That is, the materiality of the cinematic gives us concrete and empirical insight and makes objectively visible the reversible, dialectical, and social nature of our own subjective vision. Speaking of human vision, Merleau-Ponty tells us:

> As soon as we see other seers . . . henceforth, through other eyes we are for ourselves fully visible. . . . For the first time, the seeing that I am is for me really visible; for the first time I appear to myself completely turned inside out under my own eyes.[25]

The cinematic uniquely allows this philosophical turning, this objective insight into the subjective structure of vision, into oneself as both viewing subject and visible object, and, remarkably, into others as the same.

Again, the paradoxical status of the "more human than human" replicants in *Blade Runner* is instructive. Speaking to the biotechnologist who genetically produced and quite literally manufactured his eyes, replicant Roy Baty says with an ironic concreteness that resonates through the viewing audience even if its implications are not fully understood, "If you could only see what I've seen with your eyes." The perceptive and expressive materiality of the cinematic through which we engage this ironic articulation of the "impossible" desire for intersubjectivity is the very materiality through which this desire is visibly and objectively fulfilled.[26] Thus, rather than merely replacing human vision with mechanical vision, the cinematic mechanically functions to bring to visibility the reversible structure of human vision (the system visual/visible) – a lived-system that necessarily entails not only an enworlded object but always also an embodied and perceiving subject.

Indeed, through its motor and organizational agency (achieved by the spatial immediacy of the mobile camera and the reflective and temporalizing editorial re-membering of that primary spatial experience), the cinematic inscribes and provokes a sense of existential "presence" that is as synthetically centered as it is also mobile, split, and decentering. The cinematic subject (both film and spectator) is perceived as at once introverted and extroverted, as existing in the world as both subject and object. Thus, the cinematic does not evoke the same sense of self-possession as that generated by the photographic. The cinematic subject is sensed as never completely self-possessed, for it is always partially and visibly given over to the vision of others at the same time that it visually appropriates only part of what it sees and, indeed, also cannot entirely see itself. Further, the very mobility of its vision structures the cinematic subject as always in the act of displacing itself in time, space, and the world – and thus, despite its existence as embodied and centered, as always eluding its own (as well as our) containment.

The cinematic's visible inscription of the dual, reversible, and animated structure of embodied and mobile vision radically transforms the temporal and spatial structure of the photographic. Consonant with what Jameson calls the "high-modernist thematics of time and temporality", the cinematic thickens the photographic with "the elegaic mysteries of *durée* and of memory".[27] While its visible structure of "unfolding" does not challenge the dominant realist perception of objective time as an irreversibly directed stream (even flashbacks are contained by the film's vision in a forwardly directed momentum of experience), the cinematic makes time visibly *heterogeneous*. That is, we visibly perceive time as differently structured in its subjective and objective modes, and we understand that these two structures *simultaneously* exist in a demonstrable state of *discontinuity* as they are, nonetheless, actively and constantly *synthesized* in a specific lived-body experience (i.e. a personal, concrete, and spatialized history and a particularly temporalized narrative).

Cinema's animated presentation of representation constitutes its "presence" as always presently engaged in the experiential process of signifying and coming-into-being. Thus the significant value of the "streaming forward" that informs the cinematic with its specific form of temporality (and differentiates it from the atemporality of the photographic) is intimately bound to a structure not of possession, loss, pastness, and nostalgia, but of accumulation, ephemerality, and anticipation – to a "presence" in the present informed by its connection to a collective past and to a future. Visually (and aurally) presenting the subjective temporality of memory, desire, and mood through flashbacks, flash forwards, freeze framing, pixilation, reverse motion, slow motion, and fast motion, and the editorial expansion and contraction of experience, the cinema's visible (and audible) activity of *retension* and *protension* constructs a subjective temporality different from the irreversible direction and momentum of objective time, yet simultaneous with it. In so thickening the present, this temporal simultaneity also extends cinematic presence spatially – not only by embracing a multiplicity of situations in such visual/visible cinematic articulations as double exposure, superimposition, montage, parallel editing, but also primally, by expanding the space in every image between that Here where the enabling and embodied cinematic eye is situated and that There where its gaze locates itself in its object.

The cinema's existence as simultaneously presentational and representational, viewing subject and visible object, present presence informed by both past and future, continuous becoming that synthesizes temporal heterogeneity as the conscious coherence of embodied experience, transforms the thin abstracted space of the photographic into a thickened and concrete *world*. We might remember here the animated blinking of a woman's eyes in *La jetée* and how this visible motion transforms the photographic into the cinematic, the flat surface of a picture into the lived space of a lover's bedroom. In its capacity for movement, the cinema's embodied agency (the camera) thus constitutes visual/visible space as always also motor and tactile space – a space that is deep and textural, that can be materially inhabited, that provides not merely a ground for the visual/visible but also its particular *situation*. Indeed, although it is a favored term among film theorists, there is no such abstraction as *point of view* in the cinema. Rather, there are concrete *situations of viewing* – specific and mobile engagements of embodied, enworlded, and situated subjects/objects whose visual/ visible activity prospects and articulates a shifting field of vision from a world whose horizons always exceed it. The space of the cinematic, in-formed by cinematic time, is also experienced as heterogeneous – both discontiguous and contiguous, lived from within and without. Cinematic presence is multiply located – simultaneously displacing itself in the There of past and future situations yet orienting these displacements from the Here where the body at present is. That is, as the multiplicity and discontinuity of time are synthesized and centered and cohere as the *experience* of a specific lived-body, so are multiple and discontiguous spaces synopsized and located in the spatial *synthesis* of a particular *material* body. Articulated as separate shots and scenes, discontiguous spaces and discontinuous times are synthetically gathered together in a coherence that is the cinematic lived-body: the camera its perceptive organ, the projector its expressive organ, the screen its discrete and material center. In sum, the cinematic exists as a visible performance of the perceptive and expressive structure of lived-body experience.

Not so the electronic, whose materiality and various forms and contents engage its spectators and "users" in a phenomenological structure of sensual and psychological experience that seems to belong to *no-body*. Born in the USA with the nuclear age, the electronic emerged in the 1940s as the third "technological revolution within capital itself", and, according to Jameson, involved the unprecedented and "prodigious expansion of capital into hitherto uncommodified areas", including "a new and historically original penetration and colonization of Nature and the Unconscious".[28] Since that time, electronic technology has "saturated all forms of experience and become an inescapable environment, a 'technosphere'".[29] This expansive and totalizing incorporation of Nature by industrialized culture, and the specular production and commodification of the Unconscious (globally transmitted as visible and marketable "desire"), restructures capitalism as multinational. Correlatively, a new cultural logic identified as "postmodernism" begins to dominate modernism, and to alter our sense of existential presence.

A function of technological pervasion and dispersion, this new electronic sense of presence is intimately bound up in a centerless, network-like structure of instant stimulation and desire, rather than in a nostalgia for the past or anticipation of a future. Television, video cassettes, video tape recorder/players, video games, and personal computers all form an encompassing electronic representational system whose various forms "interface" to constitute an alternative and absolute world that uniquely incorporates the spectator/user in a spatially decentered, weakly temporalized, and quasi-disembodied state. Digital electronic technology atomizes and abstractly schematizes the analogic quality of the photographic and cinematic into discrete pixels and bits of information that are then transmitted serially, each bit discontinuous, discontiguous, and absolute – each bit being-in-itself even as it is part of a system.[30]

Once again we can turn to *Blade Runner* to provide illustration of how the electronic is neither photographic nor cinematic. Tracking Leon, one of the rebellious replicants, the human protagonist Deckard finds his empty rooms and discovers a photograph that seems, itself, to reveal nothing but an empty room. Using a science fictional device, Deckard directs its electronic eye to zoom in, close up, isolate, and enlarge to impossible detail various portions of the photograph. On the one hand, it might seem that Deckard is functioning like a photographer working in his darkroom to make, through optical discovery, past experience significantly visible. (Indeed, this sequence of the film recalls the photographic blow-ups of an ambiguously "revealed" murder in Michelangelo Antonioni's 1966 classic, B*low-up*.) On the other hand, Deckard can be and has been likened to a film director, using the electronic eye to probe photographic space intentionally and to animate a discovered narrative. Deckard's electronic eye, however, is neither photographic nor cinematic. While it constitutes a series of moving images from the static singularity of Leon's photograph and reveals to Deckard the stuff of which narrative can be made, it does so serially and in static, discrete "bits". The moving images do not move themselves, and they reveal no animated and intentional vision to us or to Deckard. Transmitted to what looks like a television screen, the moving images no longer quite retain the concrete and material "thingness" of the photograph, but they also do not achieve the subjective animation of the intentional and prospective vision objectively projected by the cinema. They exist less as Leon's experience than as Deckard's information.

Indeed, the electronic is phenomenologically experienced not as a discrete, intentional, and bodily centered projection in space but rather as simultaneous, dispersed, and insubstantial transmission across a network.[31] Thus, the "presence" of electronic representation is at one remove from previous representational connections between signification and referentiality. Electronic presence asserts neither an objective possession of the world and self (as does the photographic) nor a centered and subjective spatiotemporal engagement with the world and others accumulated and projected as conscious and embodied experience (as does the cinematic). Digital and schematic, abstracted both from *reproducing* the empirical objectivity of Nature that informs the photographic and from *presenting* a representation of individual subjectivity and the Unconscious that informs the cinematic, the electronic constructs a metaworld where ethical investment and value are located in *representation-in-itself*. That is, the electronic semiotically constitutes a system of *simulation* – a system that constitutes "copies" lacking an "original" origin. And, when there is no longer a phenomenologically perceived connection between signification and an "original" or "real", when, as Guy Debord tells us, "everything that was lived directly has moved away into a representation", referentiality becomes *intertextuality*.[32]

Living in a schematized and intertextual metaworld far removed from reference to a real world liberates the spectator/user from what might be termed the latter's moral and physical gravity. The materiality of the electronic digitizes *durée* and situation so that narrative, history, and a centered (and central) investment in the human lived-body become atomized and dispersed across a system that constitutes temporality not as the flow of conscious experience but as a transmission of random information. The primary value of electronic temporality is the bit or *instant* – which (thanks to television and videotape) can be selected, combined, and instantly replayed and rerun to such a degree that the previously irreversible direction and stream of objective time seems overcome in the creation of a recursive temporal network. On the one hand, the temporal cohesion of history and narrative gives way to the temporal discretion of chronicle and episode, to music videos, to the kinds of narratives that find both causality and intentional agency incomprehensible and comic. On the other hand, temporality is dispersed and finds resolution as part of a recursive, if chaotic, structure of coincidence. Indeed, objective time in postmodern electronic culture is perceived as phenomenologically discontinuous as was subjective time in modernist cinematic culture. Temporality is constituted paradoxically as a *homogeneous* experience of *discontinuity* in which the temporal distinctions between objective and subjective experience (marked by the cinematic) disappear and time seems to turn back in on itself recursively in a structure of equivalence and reversibility. The temporal move is from *Remembrance of Things Past*, a modernist re-membering of experience, to the recursive postmodernism of a *Back to the Future*.

Again "science fiction" film is illuminating.[33] While the *Back to the Future* films are certainly apposite, Alex Cox's postmodern, parodic, and deadpan *Repo Man* (1984) more clearly manifests the phenomenologically experienced homogeneity of postmodern discontinuity. The film is constructed as both a picaresque, episodic, loose, and irresolute tale about an affectless young man involved with car repossessors, aliens from outer space, Los Angeles punks, government agents, and others, and a tightly bound system of coincidences. Individual scenes are connected not through narrative causality but through the connection of literally material signifiers. A dangling dashboard ornament, for example, provides the acausal and material motivation between two of the film's otherwise disparate episodes. However, the film also re-solves its acausal structure through a narrative recursivity that links all the characters and events together in what one character calls both the "cosmic unconsciousness" and a "lattice of coincidence". Employment in *Repo Man* becomes diffused across a vast relational network. It is no accident that the car culture of Los Angeles figures in *Repo Man* to separate and segment experience into discrete and chaotic bits (as if it were metaphysically lived only through the window of an automobile) – while the "lattice of coincidence", the "network" of the Los Angeles freeway system, reconnects experience at another and less human order of magnitude.

The postmodern and electronic "instant", in its break from the temporal structures of retension and protension, constitutes a form of absolute presence (one abstracted from the continuity that gives meaning to the system past/present/future) and changes the nature of the space it occupies. Without the temporal emphases of historical consciousness and personal history, space becomes abstract, ungrounded, and flat – a site for play and display rather than an invested situation in which action "counts" rather than computes. Such a superficial space can no longer hold the spectator/user's interest, but has to stimulate it constantly in the same way a video game does. Its flatness – a function of its lack of temporal thickness and bodily investment – has to attract spectator interest at the surface. Thus, electronic space constructs objective and superficial equivalents to depth, texture, and invested bodily movement. Saturation of color and hyperbolic attention to detail replace depth and texture at the surface of the image, while constant action and "busyness" replace the gravity that grounds and orients the movement of the lived-body with a purely spectacular, kinetically exciting, often dizzying sense of bodily freedom (and freedom from the body). In an important sense, electronic space disembodies.

What I am suggesting is that, ungrounded and uninvested as it is, electronic presence has neither a point of view nor a visual situation, such as we experience, respectively, with the photograph and the cinema. Rather, electronic presence randomly disperses its being *across* a network, its kinetic gestures describing and lighting on the surface of the screen rather than inscribing it with bodily dimension (a function of centered and intentional projection). Images on television screens and computer terminals seem neither projected nor deep. Phenomenologically they seem, rather, somehow just there as they confront us.

The two-dimensional, binary superficiality of electronic space at once disorients and liberates the activity of consciousness from the gravitational pull and orientation of its hitherto embodied and grounded existence. All surface, electronic space cannot be inhabited. It denies or prosthetically transforms the spectator's physical body so that subjectivity and affect free-float or free-fall or free-flow across a horizontal/vertical grid. Subjectivity is at once decentered and completely extroverted – again erasing the modernist (and cinematic) dialectic between inside and outside and its synthesis of discontinuous time and discontiguous space as conscious and embodied experience. As Jameson explains:

> The liberation . . . from the older *anomie* of the centered subject may also mean, not merely a liberation from anxiety, but a liberation from every other kind of feeling as well, since there is no longer a self present to do the feeling. This is not to say that the cultural products of the postmodern era are utterly devoid of feeling, but rather that such feelings – which it might be better and more accurate to call "intensities" – are now free-floating and impersonal, and tend to be dominated by a peculiar kind of euphoria.[34]

Brought to visibility by the electronic, this kind of euphoric "presence" is not only peculiar. At the risk of sounding reactionary, I would like to suggest that it is also dangerous. Its lack of specific interest and grounded investment in the human body and enworlded action, its saturation with the present instant, could well cost us all a future.

Phenomenological analysis does not end with the "thick" description and thematization (or qualified reduction) of the phenomenon under investigation. It aims also for an interpretation of the phenomenon that discloses, however partially, the lived meaning, significance, and non-neutral value it has for those who engage it. In terms of contemporary moving-image culture, the material differences between cinematic and electronic representation emerge as significant differences in their meaning and value. Cinema is an objective phenomenon that comes – and becomes – before us in a structure that implicates both a sensible body and a sensual and sense-making subject. In its visual address and movement, it allows us to see what seems a visual impossibility: that we are at once intentional subjects and material objects in the world, the seer and the seen. It affirms both embodied being and the world. It also shows us that, sharing materiality and the world, we are intersubjective beings.

Now, however, it is the electronic and not the cinematic that dominates the form of our cultural representations. And, unlike cinematic representation, electronic representation by its very structure phenomenologically denies the human body its fleshly presence and the world its dimension. However significant and positive its values in some regards, the electronic trivializes the human body. Indeed, at this historical moment in our particular society and culture, the lived-body is in crisis. Its struggle to assert its gravity, its differential existence and situation, its vulnerability and mortality, its vital and social investment in a concrete life-world inhabited by others is now marked in hysterical and hyperbolic responses to the disembodying effects of electronic representation. On the one hand, contemporary moving images show us the human body relentlessly and fatally interrogated, "riddled with holes" and "blown away", unable to maintain its material integrity or gravity. If the Terminator doesn't finish it off, then electronic smart bombs will. On the other hand, the current popular obsession with physical fitness manifests the wish to transform the human body into something else – a lean, mean, and immortal "machine", a cyborg that can physically interface with the electronic network and maintain material presence in the current digitized life-world of the subject. (It is no accident that body builder Arnold Schwarzenegger played the cyborg Terminator.)

Within the context of this material and technological crisis of the flesh, one can only hope that the hysteria and hyperbole surrounding it is strategic – and that through it the lived-body has, in fact, managed to reclaim our attention to forcefully argue for its existence and against its simulation. For there are other subjects of electronic culture out there who prefer the simulated body and a virtual world. Indeed, they actually believe the body (contemptuously called "meat" or "wetware") is best lived only as an image or as information, and that the only hope for negotiating one's presence in our electronic life-world is to exist on a screen or to digitize and "download" one's consciousness into the neural nets of a solely electronic existence. Such an insubstantial electronic presence can ignore AIDS, homelessness, hunger, torture, and all the other ills the flesh is heir to outside the image and the datascape. Devaluing the physically lived-body and the concrete materiality of the world, electronic presence suggests that we are all in imminent danger of becoming merely ghosts in the machine.

Notes

1 Heidegger, M. (1977) *The Question Concerning Technology and Other Essays* (English translation by Lovitt, W.), New York: Harper & Row, 317.
2 *Robocop* (1987) was directed by Paul Verhoeven; *Terminator* II: *Judgment Day* (1991) by James Cameron.
3 Reference here is not only to the way in which automotive transportation has changed our lived sense of distance and space, the rhythms of our temporality, and the hard currency that creates and expresses our cultural values relative to such things as class and style, but also to the way in which it has changed the very sense we have of our bodies. The vernacular expression of regret at "being without wheels" is profound, and ontologically speaks to our very real incorporation of the automobile as well as its incorporation of us.
4 These terms are derived from Ihde, Don (1990) *Technology and the Lifeworld: From Garden to Earth*, Bloomington, Indiana: Indiana University Press, 29. Ihde distinguishes two senses of perception:

> What is usually taken as sensory perception (what is immediate and focused bodily in actual seeing, hearing, etc.), I shall call microperception. But there is also what might be called a cultural, or hermeneutic, perception, which I shall call macroperception. Both belong equally to the lifeworld. And both dimensions of perception are closely linked and intertwined.

5 Two types of theory that are, to some degree, attempts at microperceptual analysis are, first, psychoanalytic accounts of the processes of cinematic identification in which cinematic technology is deconstructed to reveal its inherent "illusionism" and its retrogressive duplication of infantile and/or dream states and, second, neo-Marxist accounts of both photography's and cinema's optical dependence upon a system of "perspective" based on an ideology of the individual subject and its appropriation of the "natural" world. One could argue, however, as I do here, that these types of theory are not microperceptual *enough*. Although both focus on the "technological" construction of subjectivity, they do so abstractly. That is, neither deals with the technologically constructed temporality and spatiality that *ground* subjectivity in a sensible and sense-making *body*.
6 Ihde, op. cit., 29; my emphasis.

7   Ibid.

8   Ibid., 21.

9   For the history, philosophy, and method of phenomenology, see Spiegelberg, H. (1965) *The Phenomenological Movement: A Historical Introduction*, 2nd edition, 2 volumes, The Hague: Martinus Nijhoff; Carr, D. (1967) "Maurice Merleau-Ponty: Incarnate Consciousness" in Schrader Jr, G. A. (ed.), *Existential Philosophers: Kierkegaard to Merleau-Ponty*, 369–429, New York: McGraw-Hill; Ihde, D. (1979) *Experimental Phenomenology: An Introduction*, New York: Paragon Books.

10 Ihde, op. cit., 26.

11 Jameson, F. (1984) "Postmodernism, or the Cultural Logic of Late Capitalism" in *New Left Review* 146 (July–August): 53–92.

12 Kern, S. (1983) *The Culture of Time and Space: 1880–1918*, Cambridge, Massachusetts: Harvard University Press, 6–7.

13 Comoli, J.-L. (1980) "Machines of the Visible" in de Lauretis, T. and Heath, S. (eds), *The Cinematic Apparatus* (*Published papers from a conference held 22–24 February 1978 by the Center for Twentieth Century Studies, University of Wisconsin-Milwaukee*), London: The Macmillan Press Ltd., 122–123.

14 The very recent erosion of "faith" in the photographic as "evidence" of the real in popular consciousness has been a result of the development of the *seamless electronic manipulation* of even the tiniest "bits" of the photographic image. While airbrushing and other forms of image manipulation have been around for a long while, they have left a discernible "trace" on the image; such is not the case with digital computer alterations of the photographic image. For an overview, see "Ask It No Questions: The Camera Can Lie", *New York Times*, 12 August 1990, sec. 2, 1, 29.

15 Comolli, op. cit., 123.

16 Most media theorists point out that photographic (and later cinematic) optics are structured according to a norm of perception based upon Renaissance perspective, which represented the visible as originating in and organized by an individual, centered subject. This form of representation is *naturalized* by photography and the cinema. Comolli says: "The mechanical eye, the photographic lens . . . functions . . . as a guarantor of the identity of the visible with the normality of vision . . . with the norm of visual perception", op. cit., 123–124.

17 Comolli, op. cit., 142.

18 Merleau-Ponty, M. (1964) "Eye and Mind" (English translation by Dallery, C. in Edie, J. (ed.) *The Primacy of Perception*, Evanston, Illinois, Northwestern University Press, 166.

19 It must be noted that the term "memory bank" is analogically derived in this context from electronic (not photographic) culture. It nonetheless serves us as a way of reading backward that recognizes a literal as well as metaphorical *economy* of representation and suggests that attempts to understand the photographic in its "originality" are pervasively informed by our contemporary electronic consciousness.

20 For readers unfamiliar with the film, *La jetée* is a narrative about time, memory, and desire articulated in a recursive structure. A survivor of the Third World War has a recurrent memory of a woman's face and a scene at Orly airport where, as a child, he has seen a man killed. Because of his vivid memory, his post-apocalyptic culture – underground, with minimal power and without hope – attempts experiments to send him back into his vivid past so that he can, perhaps, eventually time-travel to the future. This achieved, aware

he has no future in his own present, the protagonist, with the assistance of those in the future, ultimately returns to his past and the woman he loves. But his return to the scene of his original childhood memory at Orly reveals, first, that he (as an adult) has been pursued by people from his own present and, second, that his original memory was, in fact, the vision of his own adult death.

21 Bazin, A. (1967) "The Ontology of the Photographic Image" (English translation by Gray, H.) in Gray, H. (ed.), *What is Cinema?* Vol. 1, 9–16, Berkeley: University of California Press.

22 James Joyce, in 1909, was "instrumental in introducing the first motion picture theater in Dublin" (see Kern, op. cit., 76–77).

23 Danto, A. (1979) "Moving Pictures" in *Quarterly Review of Film Studies* 4: 1–21.

24 In the traditional cinema, an image can be "frozen" only by replicating it many times so that it can continue moving through the projector to appear frozen on the screen.

25 Merleau-Ponty, M. (1968) *The Visible and the Invisible* (English translation by Lingis, A.), Evanston, Illinois: Northwestern University Press, 143–144.

26 For a complete and lengthy argument supporting this assertion, see Sobchack, V. (1992) *The Address of the Eye: A Phenomenology of Film Experience*, Princeton, New Jersey: Princeton University Press.

27 Jameson, op. cit., 64.

28 Ibid., 78.

29 Landon, B. (1987) "Cyberpunk: Future So Bright They Gotta Wear Shades" in *Cinefantastique* 18.1 (December): 27–31.

30 It is important to point out that although all moving images follow each other serially, each cinematic image (or frame) is projected analogically rather than digitally. That is, the image is projected *as a whole*. Electronic images, however, are transmitted digitally, each bit of what appears as a single image sent and received as a discrete piece of information.

31 "Network" was a term that came into common parlance as it described the electronic transmission of television images. Now, we speak of our social relations as "networking". In spatial terms, however, a "network" suggests the most flimsy, the least substantial, of grounds. A "network" is constituted more as a lattice between nodal points than as grounded and physical presence.

32 Debord, G. (1983) *Society of the Spectacle*, Detroit: Black & Red, unpaginated.

33 It is no accident that all the films used illustratively here can be identified with the generic conventions and thematics of science fiction. Of all genres, science fiction has been most concerned with poetically mapping the new spatiality, temporality, and subjectivities informed and/or constituted by new technologies. As well, science-fiction cinema, in its particular materiality, has made these new poetic maps concretely visible. For elaboration of this mapping, see ch. 4, "Postfuturism", of Sobchack, V. (1987) *Screening Space*, New York: Ungar.

34 Jameson, op. cit., 64.

Select Bibliography

Altman, R. (1985) "The Evolution of Sound Technology" in Weis, E. and Belton, J. (eds), *Film Sound: Theory and Practice*, New York: Columbia University Press, 44–53.

Barr, C. (1963) "CinemaScope: Before and After" in *Film Quarterly* 16.4 (Summer): 4–24.

Baudry, J.-L. (1974) "Ideological Effects of the Basic Cinematographic Apparatus" (English translation by Williams, A.) in *Film Quarterly* 28.2 (Winter 1974–1975): 39–47. Originally (1970) "Cinéma: effets idéologiques produits par l'appareil de base" in *Cinéthique* 7–8: 1–8.

Bazin, A. (1967) "The Myth of Total Cinema" (English translation by Gray, H.) in Gray, H. (ed.), *What is Cinema? Vol. 1*, Berkeley: University of California Press, 17–22. Reprinted in this reader. Originally (1946) "Le mythe du cinéma total et les origines du cinématographe" in *Critique* 6 (November): 552–557.

Bazin, A. (1985) "Will CinemaScope Save the Cinema?" (English translation by Jones, C. and Neupert, R.) in *The Velvet Light Trap* 21 (Summer): 9–14. Originally (1953) "Le cinemascope sauvera-t-il le cinéma?" in *Esprit* 207–208 (October–November): 672–683.

Belton, J. (1985) "Technology and Aesthetics of Film Sound" in Weis, E. and Belton, J. (eds), *Film Sound: Theory and Practice*, New York: Columbia University Press, 63–72.

Belton, J. (1992) *Widescreen Cinema*, Cambridge, Massachusetts: Harvard University Press.

Benjamin, W. (1968) "The Work of Art in the Age of Mechanical Reproduction" (English translation by Zohn, H.) in Arendt, H. (ed.), *Illuminations: Essays and Reflections*, London: Harcourt Brace, 219–253. Reprinted in this reader. Originally (1936) "L'oeuvre d'art à l'époque de sa reproduction mécanisée" (French translation by Klossowski, P.) in *Zeitschrift für Sozialforschung* 5.1: 40–68.

Bolter, J. D. and Grusin, R. (1999) "Film," in *Remediation: Understanding New Media*, Cambridge, Massachusetts: The MIT Press, 147–158.

Bordwell, D., Staiger, J. and Thompson, K. (1985) *The Classical Hollywood Cinema: Film Style and Mode of Production to 1960*, London: Routledge & Kegan Paul.

Bordwell, D. and Thompson, K. (1993) "Technological Change and Classical Film Style" in Balio, T. (ed.), *Grand Design: Hollywood as a Modern Business Enterprise 1930–1939*, New York: Charles Scribner's Sons, 109–141.

Bukatman, S. (1993) *Terminal Identity: The Virtual Subject in Postmodern Science Fiction*, Durham, North Carolina: Duke University Press.

Buscombe, E. (1978) "Sound and Color" in *Jump Cut: A Review of Contemporary Cinema* 17 (April): 23–25.

Ceram, C. W. (1965) *Archaeology of the Cinema*, London: Thames & Hudson.

Comolli, J.-L. (1977) "Technique and Ideology: Camera, Perspective, Depth of Field" (English translation by Matias, D.) in *Film Reader* 2: 128–140. This is a revision of (1971–1972) "Technique et Idéologie: camera, perspective, profondeur de champ" in *Cahiers du Cinéma* 229 (May–June 1971): 4–21; 230 (July 1971): 51–57; 231 (August–September 1971): 42–49; 233 (November 1971): 39–45; 234–235 (December 1971–January 1972): 94–100; 241 (September–October 1972): 20–24.

Comolli, J.-L. (1980) "Machines of the Visible" in de Lauretis, T. and Heath, S. (eds), *The Cinematic Apparatus* (*Published papers from a conference held 22–24 February 1978 by the Center for Twentieth Century Studies, University of Wisconsin-Milwaukee*), London: The Macmillan Press Ltd., 121–142. Reprinted in this reader.

Creed, B. (2000) "The Cyberstar: Digital Pleasures and the End of the Unconscious" in *Screen* 41.1 (Spring): 79–86.

de Lauretis, T. and Heath, S. (eds) (1980) *The Cinematic Apparatus* (*Published papers from a conference held 22–24 February 1978 by the Center for Twentieth Century Studies, University of Wisconsin-Milwaukee*), London: The Macmillan Press Ltd.

Deslandes, J. (1966) *Histoire comparée du cinéma 1: de la cinématique au cinématographe 1826–1896*, Paris: Casterman.

Dickson, W. K. L. and Dickson, A. (1895) *History of the Kinetograph, Kinetoscope and Kinetophonograph*, New York: Albert Bunn.

Elsaesser, T. (2000) *Metropolis*, London: British Film Institute.

Elsaesser, T. and Hoffmann, K. (eds) (1998) *Cinema Futures: Cain, Abel or Cable? The Screen Arts in the Digital Age*, Amsterdam: Amsterdam University Press.

Feldman, S. (1998) "'Peace Between Man and Machine': Dziga Vertov's *The Man with a Movie Camera*" in Grant, B. K. and Sloniowski, J. (eds), *Documenting the Documentary: Close Readings of Documentary Film and Video*, Detroit: Wayne State University Press, 40–54.

Fulton, A. R. (1980) "The Machine" in *Motion Pictures: The Development of an Art* (revised edition), Norman, Oklahoma: University of Oklahoma Press, 3–13. This is a revision of (1960) "The Machine" in *Motion Pictures: The Development of an Art from Silent Films to the Age of Television*, Norman, Oklahoma: University of Oklahoma Press, 3–18.

Gomery, D. (1985a) "The Coming of Sound: Technological Change in the American Film Industry" in Balio, T. (ed.), *The American Film Industry* (revised edition), Madison, Wisconsin: The University of Wisconsin Press, 229–251. Reprinted in this reader. This is a revision of (1976) "The Coming of the Talkies: Invention, Innovation, and Diffusion" in Balio, T. (ed.), *The American Film Industry*, Madison, Wisconsin: The University of Wisconsin Press, 193–211.

Gomery, D. (1985b) "Technological Film History" in Allen, R. C. and Gomery, D., *Film History: Theory and Practice*, New York: Alfred A. Knopf, 109–130.

Gomery, D. (1992) *Shared Pleasures: A History of Movie Presentation in the United States*, London: British Film Institute.

Harries, D. (ed.) (2002) *The New Media Book*, London: British Film Institute.

Hayward, P. and Wollen, T. (eds) (1993) *Future Visions: New Technologies of the Screen*, London: British Film Institute.

Heilig, M. (1955) "The Cinema of the Future" in *Espacios: Review of Architecture, Town Planning and*

Arts 23–24 (January–April): unpaginated. Reprinted in this reader (extract). Published simultaneously in Spanish as "El Cine del Futuro".

Hendricks, G. (1961) *The Edison Motion Picture Myth*, Berkeley: University of California Press.

Hendricks, G. (1966) *The Kinetoscope*, New York: Theodore Gaus' Sons.

Hopwood, H. V. (1899) "Past, Present, and Future" in *Living Pictures: Their History, Photo-Production and Practical Working*, London: The Optician and Photographic Trades Review, 225–234. Reprinted in this reader (extract: 225–230, 232–234).

Huyssen, A. (1981–1982) "The Vamp and the Machine: Technology and Sexuality in Fritz Lang's *Metropolis*" in *New German Critique* 24–25: 221–237.

King, G. and Krzywinska, T. (eds) (2002) *ScreenPlay: Cinema/Videogames/Interfaces*, London: Wallflower Press.

Kuhn, A. (ed.) (1990) *Alien Zone: Cultural Theory and Contemporary Science Fiction Cinema*, London: Verso.

Kuhn, A. (ed.) (1999) *Alien Zone 2: The Spaces of Science Fiction Cinema*, London: Verso.

Le Grice, M. (2001) *Experimental Cinema in the Digital Age*, London: British Film Institute.

Leonardo (1990) *Digital Image–Digital Cinema Supplemental Issue*.

Makhmalbaf, S. (2000) "The Digital Revolution and the Future Cinema", transcription of a paper presented at the Cannes Film Festival, France (9 May).

Manovich, L. (1996a) "Cinema and Digital Media" in Schwarz, H. P. and Shaw, J. (eds), *Media Art Perspectives: The Digital Challenge – Museums and Art Sciences Respond*, Stuttgart: ZKM/Editions Cantz, 151–156. Reprinted in this reader. Published simultaneously in German as "Kino und Digitale Medien" (German translation by Haarkamp, A.).

Manovich, L. (1996b) "What is Digital Cinema? Cinema, the Art of the Index" in *Telepolis*: published online.

Manovich, L. (2001) *The Language of New Media*, Cambridge, Massachusetts: The MIT Press.

Marinetti, F. T. and Corra, B., Settimelli, E., Ginna, A., Balla, G., Chiti, R. (1972) "The Futurist Cinema" (English translation by Flint, R. W. and Coppotelli, A. A.) in Flint, R. W. (ed.), *Marinetti: Selected Writings*, New York: Farrar, Straus and Giroux, 130–134. Originally (1916) "La cinematografia futurista" in *L'Italia futurista* (15 November).

Metz, C. (1975) "The Imaginary Signifier" (English translation by Brewster, B.) in *Screen* 16.2 (Summer): 14–76. Originally (1975) "Le signifiant imaginaire" in *Communications* 23: 3–55.

Michelson, A. (ed.) (1984) *Kino-Eye: The Writings of Dziga Vertov* (English translation by O'Brien, K.), Berkeley: University of California Press.

Murray, J. H. (1997) *Hamlet on the Holodeck: The Future of Narrative in Cyberspace*, New York: The Free Press.

Neale, S. (1985) *Cinema and Technology: Image, Sound, Colour*, London: British Film Institute and Macmillan Education.

Nichols, B. (1988) "The Work of Culture in the Age of Cybernetic Systems" in *Screen* 29.1 (Winter): 22–46.

Ogle, P. L. (1972) "Technological and Aesthetic Influences Upon the Development of Deep Focus Cinematography in the United States" in *Screen* 13.1 (Spring): 45–72.

Penley, C., Lyon, E., Spigel, L. and Bergstrom, J. (eds) (1991) *Close Encounters: Film, Feminism, and Science Fiction*, Minneapolis: University of Minnesota Press.

Pierson, M. (2002) *Special Effects: Still in Search of Wonder*, New York: Columbia University Press.

Prince, S. (1996) "True Lies: Perceptual Realism, Digital Images, and Film Theory" in *Film Quarterly* 49.3 (Spring): 27–37.

Quigley Jr, M. (1948) *Magic Shadows: The Story of the Origin of Motion Pictures*, Washington, DC: Georgetown University Press.

Quigley Jr, M. (ed.) (1953) *New Screen Techniques*, New York: Quigley Publishing Company.

Ramsaye, T. (1926) *A Million and One Nights: A History of the Motion Picture*, New York: Simon & Schuster.

Rieser, M. and Zapp, A. (eds) (2002) *New Screen Media: Cinema/Art/Narrative*, London: British Film Institute.

Romney, J. (1997) "Million-Dollar Graffiti: Notes from the Digital Domain" in *Short Orders: Film Writing*, London: Serpent's Tail, 205–226.

Rossell, D. (1995) "A Chronology of Cinema 1889–1896" in *Film History* 7.2 (Summer): 115–236.

Rossell, D. (1998) *Living Pictures: The Origins of the Movies*, Albany: State University of New York Press.

Rushing, J. H. and Frentz, T. S. (1995) *Projecting the Shadow: The Cyborg Hero in American Film*, Chicago: The University of Chicago Press.

Rutsky, R. L. (1999) "The Spirit of Utopia and the Birth of the Cinematic Machine" in *High Techne: Art and Technology from the Machine Aesthetic to the Posthuman*, Minneapolis: University of Minnesota Press, 23–47.

Sadoul, G. (1946) *Histoire générale du cinéma 1: l'invention du cinéma 1832–1897*, Paris: Éditions Denöel.

Salt, B. (1983) *Film Style and Technology: History and Analysis*, London: Starword.

Schaub, J. C. (1998) "Presenting the Cyborg's Futurist Past: An Analysis of Dziga Vertov's Kino-Eye" in *Journal of Postmodern Culture* 8.2: published online.

Shaw, J. and Weibel, P. (eds) (2003) *Future Cinema: The Cinematic Imaginary After Film*, Cambridge, Massachusetts: ZKM/The MIT Press.

Sobchack, V. (1987) *Screening Space*, New York: Ungar. Originally (1980) *The Limits of Infinity: The American Science Fiction Film*, New York: Ungar.

Sobchack, V. (1994) "The Scene of the Screen: Envisioning Cinematic and Electronic 'Presence'" in Gumbrecht, H. U. and Pfeiffer, K. L. (eds), *Materialities of Communication*, Stanford, California: Stanford University Press, 83–106. Reprinted in this reader.

Spellerberg, J. (1985) "CinemaScope and Ideology" in *The Velvet Light Trap* 21 (Summer): 26–34.

Springer, C. (1991) "The Pleasure of the Interface" in *Screen* 32.3 (Autumn): 303–323. Reprinted in this reader.

Springer, C. (1996) *Electronic Eros: Bodies and Desire in the Postindustrial Age*, London: The Athlone Press.

Telotte, J. P. (1995) *Replications: A Robotic History of the Science Fiction Film*, Urbana and Chicago: University of Illinois Press.

Telotte, J. P. (1999) *A Distant Technology: Science Fiction Film and the Machine Age*, Hanover, New Hampshire: Wesleyan University Press/University Press of New England.

Telotte, J. P. (2001) *Science Fiction Film*, Cambridge: Cambridge University Press.

Vaughan, D. (1999) "From Today, Cinema is Dead" in *For Documentary: Twelve Essays*, Berkeley: University of California Press, 181–192.

Vertov, D. (1984) "Kinoks: A Revolution" (English translation by O'Brien, K.) in Michelson, A. (ed.), *Kino-Eye: The Writings of Dziga Vertov*, Berkeley: University of California Press, 11–21. Reprinted in this reader. Originally (1923) "Kinoki. Perevorot" in *Lef* 3 (June–July): 135–143.

Virilio, P. (1989) *War and Cinema: The Logistics of Perception* (English translation by Camiller, P.),

London: Verso. Originally (1984) *Guerre et cinema* 1: *Logistique de la perception*, Cahiers du Cinéma/ Éditions de l'Etoile.

Virilio, P. (1994) *The Vision Machine* (English translation by Rose, J.), London: British Film Institute. Originally (1988) *La machine de vision*, Paris: Éditions Galilée.

von Trier, L. and Vinterberg, T. (1995) "Dogme 95: The Vow of Chastity". Presented at the Odéon Théâtre de L'Europe, Paris (20 March). Reprinted in this reader.

Wasko, J. (1994) *Hollywood in the Information Age: Beyond the Silver Screen*, Austin: University of Texas Press.

Williams, C. (ed.) (1996) *Cinema: The Beginnings and the Future*, London: University of Westminster Press.

Winston, B. (1997) *Technologies of Seeing: Photography, Cinematography and Television*, London: British Film Institute.

Wood, A. (2002) *Technoscience in the Contemporary American Fiction Film: Beyond Science Fiction,* Manchester: Manchester University Press.

Youngblood, G. (1970) *Expanded Cinema*, New York: E. P. Dutton.

Youngblood, G. (1989) "Cinema and the Code" in *Leonardo: Computer Art in Context Supplemental Issue*: 27–30.

Zielinski, S. (1999) *Audiovisions: Cinema and Television as Entr'Actes in History* (English translation by Custance, G.), Amsterdam: Amsterdam University Press. Originally (1989) *Audiovisionen: Kino und Fernsehen als Zwischenspiele in der Geschichte*, Hamburg: Rowohlt Verlag.

Zimmermann, P. R. (2000) "Pirates of the New World Image Orders" in *States of Emergency: Documentaries, Wars, Democracies*, Minneapolis: University of Minnesota Press, 154–197. Reprinted in this reader (extract: 154–162).

Index

Weird Science (Hughes) 82
Welles, O. 45, 47
Wenham, F. 13, 14
Western Electric 56, 57, 58, 59, 61, 63, 64,
    65
widescreen 2, 5–6, 17, 20, 21, 24
Winston, B. 5

Wyler, W. 45, 46, 47

Youngblood, G. 7

Zapp, A. 7
Zimmermann, P. R. 70
Zuse, K. 12, 28

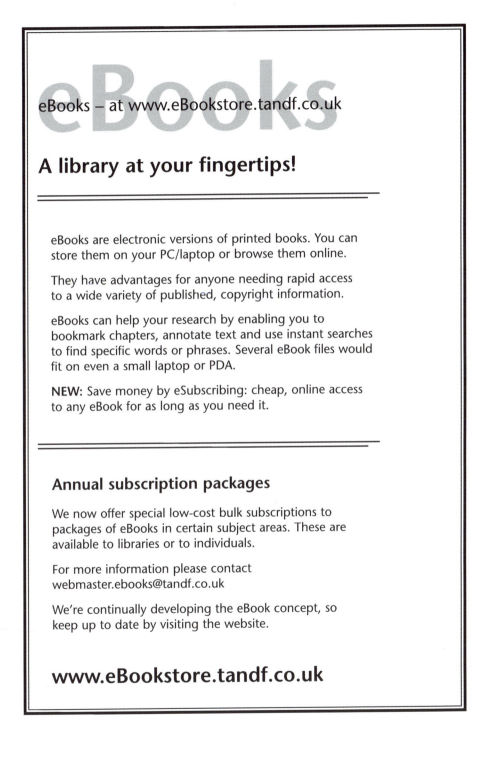

metropolis 2000 (26)
modern Times ('36)